Cultures of Internet

Cultures of Internet

*Virtual Spaces, Real Histories,
Living Bodies*

Edited by
ROB SHIELDS

SAGE Publications
London • Thousand Oaks • New Delhi

First published in 1996. Reprinted 1996

SAGE Publications Ltd
6 Bonhill Street
London EC2A 4PU

SAGE Publications Inc
2455 Teller Road
Thousand Oaks, California 91320

SAGE Publications India Pvt Ltd
32, M-Block Market
Greater Kailash – I
New Delhi 110 048

British Library Cataloguing in Publication data

A catalogue record for this book is available from the
British Library.

ISBN 0 8039 7518–X
ISBN 0 8039 7519–8 (pbk)

Library of Congress catalog record available

Typeset by Photoprint, Torquay, Devon
Printed in Great Britain by The Cromwell Press Ltd,
Broughton Gifford, Melksham, Wiltshire

Contents

List of Contributors

Jon Alexander is Professor of Political Science at Carleton University, Ottawa. His interests include social engineering and elite coalitions around science and technology development.

Katie Argyle is a long-time participant in online society and an independent craftsperson. She can be reached at aa992@freenet.carleton.ca. She is a student in the Medieval Studies programme of the Institute of Inter-disciplinary Studies at Carleton University.

Heather Bromberg is a graduate student in the Department of Sociology and Anthropology at Carleton University, Ottawa, Canada. Her current research focuses on the ways in which computer-mediated communication alters our perception of concepts such as: identity, reality and community as well as our relationships with machines and other humans.

Joerge Dyrkton is an Intellectual Historian who has taught at the University of Victoria and the University of the West Indies at Jamaica. He is currently teaching in British Columbia and is working on a History of the Middle.

Ken Hillis is a doctoral candidate in geography at the University of Wisconsin-Madison. His work examines virtual environments as cultural technologies informed by specific Western conceptions of space, and on to which are projected an alienated subjectivity's desire to transcend bodily limits.

Interrogate the Internet:
   Marco Campana was a member of Interrogate the Internet in 1994–95.
   Wade Deisman is an Epstien scholar and PhD candidate at the Department of Sociology and Social Anthropology at Carleton University. His dissertation focuses on regulative and public policy dimensions associated with the advent of the Internet.
   Reby Lee was a member of Interrogate the Internet in 1994–95. He is a student in the Department of Sociology and Anthropology at Carleton University.
   Robert E. Macleod is a doctoral candidate in anthropology at the University of British Columbia. His current research interest is ethnographic

approaches to the way individuals and cultures are affected by the change from a literate to a digital mode of communication.

Thomas Pardoe was a member of Interrogate the Internet in 1994–95.

Mark Tyrrel is a PhD candidate in the Department of Sociology and Anthropology at Carleton University. His research interests range from witchcraft (ancient and modern) to modern telecommunications issues and social responses to unemployment. He is currently involved in examining the culture of information and the informational construction of the self.

Mark Lajoie is a PhD candidate in the Humanities doctoral programme at Concordia University. He is currently researching cultural politics in Québec.

André Lemos is an engineer by training. He holds a Master of Science in the Politics of Science and Technology (COPPE/UFRJ) and a Doctorate in Sociology (Université de Paris V – Sorbonne). He is Professor in the Faculty of Communication, Federal University of Bahia, Brazil. He can be reached at alemos@ufba.br.

Sadie Plant is the author of *The Most Radical Gesture: The Situationist International in a Postmodern Age* (Routledge, 1992), and *Zeros and Ones* (forthcoming, Fourth Estate and Doubleday). She is a Research Fellow at the Cybernetic Culture Research Unit, University of Warwick.

Leslie Regan Shade is finishing a dissertation at McGill University's graduate programme in communications on 'Gender and Community in the Social Constitution of Computer Networks'. She has written extensively on social, policy and legal issues surrounding new information technologies. Her URL is http://www.facl.mcgill.ca/gpc/shade.html.

Rob Shields lectures in Culture and Communications at the University of Lancaster and maintains links with Carleton University where he is Associate Professor of Sociology and Anthropology. He is the author of *Places on the Margin* and *Henri Lefebvre: A Critical Introduction* (forthcoming), editor of *Lifestyle Shopping* and co-editor, with Adam Podgorecki and Jon Alexander, of *Social Engineering: The Technics of Change*.

Dan Thu Nguyen is a political theorist who has a special interest in the relationships between conception of time, mass media effects and politics.

Introduction: Virtual Spaces, Real Histories and Living Bodies

Rob Shields

Many issues surround the computer-mediated public sphere which currently exists through the Internet. Unlike commercial bulletin boards, Internet evolved as a network of computers in public institutions allowing cooperative research between universities, hospitals and government research establishments. The computers of many corporations are now also connected to Internet. Given its decentralized character and ever-growing expansion, attempts to list or 'map' its interconnected computer sites are difficult. The Internet has been the model for still-fictional and idealized notions of cyberspace – described as a new and unregulated 'frontier'. A new network of virtual 'sites' is being superimposed on the world of places. Internet has been viewed as a 'free-space' unfettered by moral codes. Whether for or against this freedom, both the vanguard and critics have tended to ignore the complexity of the issues involved. Over-hyped and over-sensationalized – whether for its promise or scandal – Internet and all existing versions of cyberspace have been under-examined.

Policy problems and cultural challenges

The Internet raises challenging policy issues of access, privacy, copyright and regulation. It poses cultural problems as information is made available regardless of social and cultural boundaries and the policies of nation-states. Likened to a world of data and computerized interaction, Internet has been called the first true 'cyberspace'. With this, it has raised questions concerning the nature of social interaction. The neglect of face-to-face communities and has also raised fears about the decline of the public sphere into a virtual world controlled by telecommunications corporations where only the privileged have access and the body is disdained as an embarrassing and imperfect support for minds infatuated with virtual, representational bodies.

Leap-frogging ahead of policy frameworks, cyberspaces such as Internet offer temporary autonomous zones (cf. Hakim Bey 1991) where illegitimate contents and forms of communication may flow unrestricted (for example the widespread dissemination of child pornography via downloaded computer-image files). In North America, universities are the centres of a growing student-oriented 'Net culture'. The development of such broadband telecommunications networks has been experienced most widely there. However, the Internet and its communications standards and protocols now connect millions of users around the world through terminals, networks and home computers (PCs) logged-on over telephone lines to hundreds of thousands of commercial and institutional computers. The Internet began amongst an elite of engineers and researchers, but the required equipment is now available in North America at under $100 on the second-hand market. While much interest has been generated in graphical versions such as the home pages used in the World Wide Web system, the bulk of computer-mediated communications remains simple, brief notes written in romanized versions of local languages or, more often than not, in English. The very simplest PC equipped with the slowest of modems can perform adequately for the average typist. Other requirements are a computer account giving access to the Internet (increasingly available through local 'Freenets' at minimal charge), and either access to a computer terminal (at work or at school) or a telephone. This last is already a basic requirement for full participation in most North American lifestyles.

Free local-area telephone calling has been the key to the acceptance of Internet as a practical service, a leisure activity, and a medium of sociability used by people at home. All sorts of services are available and any sort of social contact can be made. Allowing widespread access by students and by the public through dial-up 'Freenets' to Internet e-mail and newsgroups, universities have found themselves charged for purveying pornography. While Chinese foreign students managed to exploit computer-mediated communications at the time of the Tienanmen Square protests, Internet is still the territory of 'Westerners' or those 'Western'-educated elites in close contact with the 'West'. The potential for a progressive cyberspace is thus still largely unrealized.

Meanwhile, the Internet has become one aspect of state development of national information infrastructures. Accepted on faith, broadband tele-communications systems allowing the rapid transfer of information, video images, text and voice are being proposed as 'information superhighways' essential to economic development. In effect, 'super-telephones' with voice, text and video images will integrate the services of cable television and automated banking machines drawing on sources which will likely be continent-wide in North America, and which could be global in the future.

For policy-makers in less secure cultures and their less powerful economies, however, easy global information access threatens both cultural identity and the regulatory sovereignty of the state – a loss of 'cultural sovereignty'. 'Disney' mass-entertainment, with its individualistic and capitalistic values spreads through Internet as much as through exported-television programming (from Saturday morning children's cartoons to talk shows and situation comedies). Given the number of American users, debates on US politics are most prominent and non-Americentric viewpoints are regarded as abnormal. Moralists and conservatives have attacked the online provision of uncontrolled debate and unbridled fantasies as a threat to religious control. Technologies oriented to maximum speed and unchecked flow make it difficult to control the content of that flow. Who will censor questionable messages or sadistic fantasies? Can fraudulent advertisements be discouraged? How would it be done, other than unplugging specific users and blocking access to entire areas of debate (entire special interest groups or 'Usegroups')? Even as laws begin to catch up with these dilemmas, questions remain. Is there freedom of speech and are there meaningful civil liberties in this new privately owned cyberspace?

Internet has become the preferred venue for pre-publication of articles, the airing of views and testing of ideas. Without doubt e-mail conventions and the sophistication of hypertext documents will leak over on to the printed page. New discursive norms are being invented and disseminated on the Internet and from there 'infect' the design, layout and textual strategies of advertising, literary works and research reports. In this work we have made full use of textual conventions to interweave different voices and narratives. Footnotes form a counter-text and should be given the same status and weight as the main text. Endnotes to each chapter carry the burden of the usual social science marginalia and sources. We have also attempted to indicate through variations in type the interplay of voices from the 'Net' within our own chapters.

Histories and localities

To understand these problems the different histories of the development of Internet in different contexts need to be untangled. Internet, while an overarching computer communications network, came to be available in different locales through very different processes. An outgrowth of ARPANET, a military computer network in the United States, Internet in other countries was most often installed to allow the interconnection of university campuses or the integration of regional government offices. Internet itself exists in multiple, different conditions. In many North American cities it is freely accessible to those with the inclination – even children. In other countries, Internet coexists alongside non-functioning telephones and is accessed only by a small elite. We contrast the development of this new medium in France (in the form of Minitel), in North America and in Jamaica. We compare the emergent social issues surrounding Internet in these different contexts – cultural and legal sovereignty in Canada, the strategies of an information superpower in the United States, over-centralized planning in France, and local uses versus expatriate/elite uses of e-mail in Jamaica.

It is essential to treat telecommunications and computer-mediated communications networks as *local* phenomena, as well as global networks. Embedded within locally specific routines of daily schedules and the 'place-ballets' of individuals, Internet has been shaped by its users. It has defied the imposition of communications protocols preferred by governments and encryption standards limited by legal and censorious agencies. Thus, in the case of Minitel, the network of *messageries* or bulletin boards grew out of the pirating of the Minitel communications software by computer hackers. Similarly, the Japanese government has found it impossible to displace the popular TC/IP protocol used by systems operators.

It is essential to treat computer-mediated communication as a process involving differentiated *bodies*. The tendency has been to treat all users as alike according to a stereotype of young, socially inept and thus culturally marginalized male 'computer addicts'. Nor has this been examined as a social commentary on unapproved forms of masculinity. Instead, we insist on the diversity of users and the diverse character of the uses made of Internet, the durations of use, and the forms of engagement or participation. That the majority of users who 'post' to the lists and fora of Usenet groups are male is a preliminary and inadequate observation which has been used to discredit and discourage sociological investigations of the social status of computer-mediated communications. It is from amongst women that many contributors have drawn the most creative and striking examples of the growing cultural importance of Internet and its social value within everyday life.

Spatially, messages originated in one place are disseminated immediately and have impacts far beyond the limits of a traditional face-to-face community and beyond the borders of state-sanctioned public spheres, without the limiting quality of context, community sanctions and the ability of moral arbiters to limit debates and censor topics in a locality through the threat of local sanctions. In the case of Usenet postings, messages can be sent to automated, anonymous posting services overseas and then disseminated back into the originator's locality. The case of the Canadian court ban on publicly disseminating the gory details in the trials of Karla Homolka and Paul Teale is examined in Chapter 1 by Leslie Regan Shade to illustrate the difficulties facing regulators and those attempting to create a policy framework to ensure the development of an equitable public sphere. A comment 'posted' in a discussion group can receive a reply immediately or in real time. At the same time, that comment is archived and persists in the list of 'postings' which appears to anyone 'browsing' through the 'Usenet group', allowing others to take up the original comment, edit it and attach their own words in a follow-up posting to form a 'thread' of postings which may not keep to the original theme but changes over time.

In Chapter 2, André Lemos shows how the history of France's Minitel demonstrates the importance of users' informal computer-mediated sociability in over-running the system priorities of the communications providers.

The problems of the local and extra-local are highlighted in Joerge Dyrkton's history of the case of Jamaica in Chapter 3. In tropical countries beset by the problems of underdevelopment, political violence and poverty, where regular mail is slow and where foreigners typically eschew the local telephone networks in favour of cellular technologies installed and maintained by extra-local multinational telephone companies such as AT&T, e-mail is an anomaly. Dyrkton argues that e-mail and the Internet are too 'cool' to bring about improvements in unemployment or other immediate social gains in Jamaica. Internet is inaccessible to most Jamaicans and is used by few locals when it is available. The cost of computers, let alone telephone charges, towers above the local daily wage of US $8.00 (about £4, or $10.00 Canadian). It represents stronger links to the 'First World' rather than the 'Third World' or the local: 'In Jamaica the breeze of the computer fan empties itself into an abyss of unrelenting everyday life', complicated by a crumbling built environment and collective impoverishment. E-mail itself not only challenges the Jamaican state custom's regulatory control over foreign material, but is an assault on the local cultural notion of an isolated island paradise where everything must conform to a slower, tropical tempo.

In such a situation it is hard to doubt the corrosive cultural impact and widened social divisions between the local computer 'haves' and 'have-nots' that Internet is creating. Perhaps this is all the more poignant for Hakim Bey's argument that within the interstices of such global frameworks it is still possible to find local moments of freedom outside of the purchase of regulatory powers and the governing gaze of 'the system'. Jamaica is no such 'island in the Net' (Bey 1991).

Technology is often viewed as source of *separation*. In allowing interaction at a distance, first the telegraph, then the telephone and now the computer have negated the limitations of physical presence. Conversations are held with distant and absent others. Nonetheless, the local and the co-present remain privileged. There is an all too easy tendency to contrast the here and now with the distant. Instead, Argyle and Shields argue in Chapter 4 that technology mediates presence. Like language, which allows us to envision within our mind's eye abstract and invisible concepts, technology makes the distant and foreign, present and tangible. The simple technology of text on a computer screen has allowed Internet to become a medium in which users may develop a palpable sense of others' bodies, even engaging in forms of public sex over the computer wires, elaborating sensual fantasies and sexual dialogues in 'hotchats' and 'cybersex'.

In this work, we distinguish 'cyberspace' as a generic concept for the imagined 'world within' the computer or the social landscape portrayed in the lists of Usenet groups and postings. In this sense, Internet is a cyberspace. However, the concept of virtual reality (VR) denotes a simulated world within which a computer user can have a sense of 'entering' either through 180-degree surround goggles and an interface fitted to the body, or through simple animated representations of a three-dimensional world – such as architects' commonly create to illustrate proposed buildings to clients. In Chapter 5 Ken Hillis reminds us that,

> To date, no single technology or machine circumscribes this emerging technology/ medium of virtual reality (VR) – a term confusingly interchanged with cyberspace but here understood as the technical means of access to the 'parallel', disembodied and increasingly networked visual 'world' named cyberspace. An increasing variety of virtual technologies offer windows onto this cyberspatial environment that also has been defined as one in which the user feels *present*

. . . , yet where things have no physical form and are composed of electronic data bits and particles of light.

Still, one can talk of a virtual social world, or virtual interaction and a sense of a virtual self even within the context of what exists now: mostly text-based electronic mail and bulletin-board postings. Thus, in North America, even without the aid of VR technology, Internet is conceived of as a cyberspace, a tropospheric 'world in the wires' which links myriad computers and databases. The mid-1990s has seen this cognitive mapping of Internet disseminated to the population via widespread media coverage, moral panics and sensational coverage of the economic potential of VR as a vector of service sector development and a new 'consumption space'.

Cyberspaces such as Internet are closely linked to the spaces and activities of everyday life. The technology and agency of corporate product development labs is often neglected in superficial analyses of the Internet as a new medium or a new public sphere disconnected from 'real' life. We require a full command of the registers of the complex, multiple histories of Internet as a basis for the critical assessment of the social and political relevance of computer-mediated communication.

Furthermore, electronic communication, and the culture of Internet in particular, has provided an audience interested in the development of better modes of interface, up to the extent of simulations of everyday life through graphics and sensory interfaces which present a 'virtual reality'. Virtual reality, of course, is still a glint in entrepreneurs' eyes. At present, virtual realities are easily generated (for example in flight simulation games) but interfaces such as goggles which free a user from the 'frame' of a CRT screen; gloves which interpret hand signals and relay back tactile sensations; and eventually whole body suits are not available, although it appears they would be commercially successful at almost any price. The current status of Internet and its technologies represents a critical juncture in the development of 'virtual reality'. This is more than simply a stage in technical development or a marketing test: it is a *conjuncture* in the most profound sense of social arrangements and technological capabilities which stretches the 'lifeworld' and spills out of the computer world to refigure the conventions and routines of daily life. We have attempted to ground our critical analysis in the 'real history' and 'living bodies' of Internet and its users.

Crisis of boundaries

Keeping a division between online and life outside of the Net requires that one maintain a distinction between social interaction in Net groups and face-to-face social interaction. There are differences in proximity, communication medium and the redundancy of information – in face-to-face talk one also sees one's interlocutor whereas in computer-mediated communication one usually types a message to an absent recipient, like writing a letter. These divisions are clear, but to label one activity antisocial, as some journalists have done, is an over-hasty and stereotyped conclusion. Both forms of communication are types of social interaction.

The Internet creates a *crisis of boundaries* between the real and the virtual, between time zones and between spaces, near and distant. Above all, boundaries between bodies and technologies, between our sense of self and our sense of our changing roles: the personae we may play or the 'hats we wear' in different situations are altered.

In Chapter 6 Dan Thu Nguyen and Jon Alexander question the adequacy of current analytic frameworks for understanding the politics of an emergent cyberspace. In a quest for wisdom and meaningful interaction, we throw ourselves into the disembodied flows of data. Machine-readable information is technical and abstracted from bodily existence. By maintaining the distinctions between the body and the machine, a loss of the body occurs – which ends up being referred to as merely 'the meat' or 'data trash' (Kroker and Weinstein 1994). The old seat of knowledge and wisdom, grounded in bodily experience, is lost. The equation linking knowledge to power – key to the consolidation of modernity as Foucault argued (1980) – is altered, fundamentally changing notions of agency, action and norms.

Nguyen and Alexander sound a warning that the loss of dichotomies leads to a loss of traditional political directions and divisions amidst a *political space* of burgeoning difference. In such a situation, traditional concepts of 'progress' become meaningless because no one option or project dominates. In this postmodern situation, as Lemos points out in Chapter 2, new consensuses must be established through dialogical processes rather than the overcoming of one option by another. In this situation of dialogism, or perpetual dialogue, no single force dominates in a confrontation of opposed logics which persist and do not meld or lead to a synthesis despite their engagement and development over time.

The critical theme is taken up in Chapter 7 by 'Interrogate the Internet', a collective of Internet users. The possibilities for emancipation as well as oppression have been poorly understood in this new medium and its supporting technologies and institutional arrangements. Information is not knowledge.

The final chapters examine the experience of users. In Chapter 8 Katie Argyle traces the experience of grief and pain upon learning of the death of a well-known user. Heather Bromberg, in Chapter 9, examines identity-play amongst participants in an online multi-user role-playing environment. The erotic potential and promise of mastery of a virtual environment are important parts of the seductive lure Internet users have encountered. But rather than a temporary transcendence, or an indulgence in simulated mastery, Argyle documents the cross-over of physically felt anguish from the Net to her own grief. While online encounters are abstract and intellectualized, bodies remain an essential component and reference. This experience of loss, and thus of rupture and transformation, highlights the carnivalesque qualities of computer-mediated communication. Irreverent parody, wit and corrosive criticism, and experiments with text layout, upend the oppressive domination of content by the medium and technology. On the screen, the textual narratives appeal to bodily emotions and desires and to the off-line agency of actors (compare Bakhtin 1986). In so doing, they subvert the apparent suppression of agency, dependence on the terms of computer technology, and the users' unacknowledged dependence on corporate telecommunications giants (DeCerteau 1984). The tactical manoeuvres of individual users include separated lovers exchanging e-hugs, students seeking answers to assignments, activists garnering support for a petition, and music fans trading trivia. They dart under the giant pedestals of corporate and national information infrastructure strategies, appropriating work time, stealing computer resources to self-publish and to reach out to into the collectivity. Such tactics, however picknoleptic and short-lived, ensure the vitality and change of societies.

On Internet, the individual is not alone. As Argyle comments in Chapter 4, 'The individual is part of a larger group that spreads further than the single user can imagine. Everywhere we rub shoulders with each other. Everywhere users present themselves to each other, freely saying and doing what they choose. This freedom is the cornerstone of the carnivalesque, and where there is carnivalesque, there is transformation.' This community extends beyond Internet into face-to-face communities, inextricably linking the Net into local communities and struggles. Conversely, such struggles and perceptions are bound into a network which is mediated through the Internet, through other mass media such as television, and through individual social dialogue. The Net itself is mediated by everyday life.

While we insist upon the multiple histories of Internet, it is also imperative to recognize the multiple agencies exercised through it. Internet is a network, linking interactants across space and time, not a 'thing' or a set of computers communicating autonomously without human actors. It is essential to foreground the human in the Net. This resets the Internet as a phenomenon of social and political interest, not just a bright technical toy for engineers.

Re-enchantment and cool media

Despite the image of the socially inept Net-addict, this image has not been understood as a warning signal to contemporary society regarding its banality and lack of opportunities for meaningful interaction. Users reach out via an alternative medium for social interaction. Their disenchantment can be read as evidence of the sterility and suppression of the vitality of many local communities. By contrast, 'Interrogate the Internet' argue in Chapter 7 that the Internet indicates a *re-enchantment* in Western societies. While the Net functions in a classically modernist mode by promising transcendence, it induces a postmodern cultural gloss or 'moment' (Jameson 1984) of re-enchantment rather than disenchantment through rational-technical means. While one observes a continuation of the modern dialectic of enlightenment and alienation, Max Weber's observation of the disenchantment of modernity is thereby inverted.

As both the producers and consumers of content, Net users can be located as part of a technoclass hierarchy that lives both sides of this dialectic, both benefiting from and subjecting themselves to the limits of the medium. These are situations of 'ironic complicity'. Here, the Net serves as a truly *social medium* which connects and integrates its users. Like language – another medium – it 'speaks' its speaker, even while the speaker speaks the language. The medium restricts the speaker to the conventions of that language or medium. Thus the conventional class distinctions based most notably on relationships to the mode of production are displaced into a dual structure of 'virtualized' production *and* consumption classes articulated through the medium of cyberspace and VR even while disrupted through the carnivalesque and ecstatic *excess* of the vital activities of those same users (Bakhtin 1984; Baudrillard 1983).

As Mark Lajoie notes in Chapter 10, cyberspace and its users form a public sphere: 'Publics, and more importantly public space, allow for lateral communication, communication with others who share similar economic, political, or material conditions . . . Individuating technologies eliminate the ability to speak laterally, to trust others, or to occupy public spaces with others' who are different. The risk of computer mediation is that traditional public spaces – not only modernist public spheres but pre-modernist public sites – will be replaced or weakened by the promise of the fulfilment of users' desires and the transcendence of their own particularity through a simulacrum where the virtual comes to be seen as more real than the real (Baudrillard 1983). After Deleuze and Guattari (1976), the Internet appears as a rhizomatic desiring-machine which frees up and allows desire to be set in motion. Its rhizomatic quality stems from the acentred web of interconnections in which any point of control can be so easily bypassed that such concepts of control are displaced and outmoded.

Still, for others, cyberspaces remain the open frontier for those oppressed by social norms – patriarchy, capitalism, sexual ideologies. In Chapter 11 Sadie Plant celebrates what Nguyen and Alexander fear: the opportunity for the expression and elaboration of difference in opposition to any tyranny of the status quo and the world-view and institutionalized structures of patriarchal control. 'There is more to cyberspace than meets the male gaze.'

Computer viruses and cyberpunk lifestyles developed in literary fiction and depicted in mass media provide models of resistance which are unusually visible and widely known, even if they are de-fanged by their incorporation within television entertainment formats. 'Cyberfeminism' takes advantage of the ambiguous status of users and the crisis of boundaries and moral categories on the Net to spread this into social life in general. Rather than new relations between women and men, the amoral quality of Net ethics throws into question essentialized identities and dualistic sexual categories in which male and female are the unquestioned alpha and omega of sexuality: where every body is one or the other. Instead, notions of authenticity, of essential femininity and of the self are displaced in favour of multiple roles, alternative personae and a matrix of potentialities which allows people to recode themselves ahead of disciplinary technologies. This, last, history of cyberspace is the history of hackers, as Plant argues, 'perverting the codes, corrupting the transmissions, multiplying zeros, and teasing open new holes in the world ... unashamedly opportunist, entirely irresponsible, and committed only to the infiltration and corruption of a world which already rues the day they left home'.

Rob Shields
Spencerville, May 1995

References

Bakhtin, M.M. 1984. *Rabelais and His World*, London: Midland.

Bakhtin, M.M. 1986. *Speech Genres and Other Late Essays*, trans. Vern W. McGee; ed. Caryl Emerson and Michael Holquist, Austin: University of Texas Press.

Baudrillard, J. 1983. *The Precession of Simulacra*, New York: Semiotexte.

Bey, Hakim 1991. *TAZ: The Temporary Autonomous Zone*, New York: Autonomedia.

DeCerteau, Michel 1984. *The Practice of Everyday Life*, Berkeley: University of California Press.

Deleuze, G. and Guattari, F. 1976. *The Anti-Oedipus*, Paris: Minuit.

Foucault, M. 1980. *Power-Knowledge*, ed. Colin Gordon, New York: Pantheon.

Jameson, F. 1984. 'Postmodernism or the cultural logic of late capitalism', *New Left Review*, 146 (July–Aug.): 53–93.

Kroker, A. and Weinstein, M. 1994. *Data Trash*, Montreal: New World Perspectives.

1

Is there Free Speech on the Net? Censorship in the Global Information Infrastructure

Leslie Regan Shade

The Internet has raised a plethora of challenging policy issues, which presage the future of broadband telecommunications networks. These policy issues are now being debated in the international realm, but most particularly in North America.

In the US, the Clinton Administration unveiled their National Information Infrastructure Agenda for Action in the fall of 1993, rallying private industry, labour, academics, public interest groups, state and local governments, and Congress to 'ensure the development of a National Information Infrastructure (NII) that enables all Americans to access information and communicate with each other using voice, data, image, or video at anytime, anywhere'. Likewise, in Canada, the Information Highway Advisory Council published a discussion paper in the winter of 1994 on issues including regulation and economics, copyright and intellectual property, privacy, universal access, and issues of cultural sovereignty.[1]

Until recently, these debates have been couched within the domestic purview of national policies, while giving scant attention to the global issues created by networked communications – deregulation, intellectual property rights and privacy protection. Such parochialism seems short-sighted, given the rapidity and ease of globalized communication (Drake 1995). However, at the G7 Information Society Conference, held in February 1995 in Brussels, G7 representatives from the United States, the United Kingdom, Germany, France, Italy, Japan and Canada addressed the economic, social and technical issues relating to the growth of new technologies and endorsed the initiation of eleven pilot projects to accelerate the implementation of the global information society (Industry Canada 1995). The slippery nature of transborder flows promulgated by the seeming irresolution of global laws is most evident in recent debates surrounding free speech and censorship on the Internet and on Usenet, a huge collection of newsgroups whose scope is international.*[2] For

---

* Usenet is not the Internet, and actually predates the Internet of today; but the Internet is used to transfer much of Usenet's traffic. So, often when people talk about 'the Internet' what they are referring to is Usenet.

instance, Singapore, realizing the futility of controlling the flow of information crossing its data highway, has limited access to Internet to all but a very few approved users, such as certain university departments and a few commercial sites (Sandfort 1993: 54–5).

This chapter will explore these issues as they have primarily affected the academic community, through two case studies: (1) the removal of certain Usenet newsgroups from university computing facilities due to their sexually explicit and potentially offensive content; and (2) a recent case concerning censorship of a Usenet newsgroup, alt.fan.karla-homolka, whose purpose was to discuss the court-imposed media ban of the controversial Canadian case surrounding Karla Homolka, convicted of manslaughter in the sex-slayings of two teenage girls.[3]

The questions to be broached here include: What is free speech in the electronic environment? How can one regulate censorship on global computer networks, and how are new legal remedies for computer net-working being framed in light of current legal and regulatory mechanisms for other communication technologies?

Usenet, the 'user's network', or the 'poor man's ARPANET', is a worldwide distributed bulletin-board system supported mainly by Unix machines. (Unix is one of the most widely used and reviled multi-user general-purpose operating systems in the world.) Typically institutionally based, Usenet's user base has been expanding from academic and commer-cial sites to include the many community networks, or 'free-nets', and commercial bulletin boards sprouting up in North America that provide a gateway to Usenet newsgroups.

At most universities, Usenet is essentially free and available to all qualified students, staff and faculty. Usually Usenet piggybacks on top of the existing network infrastructure, and university computing facilities receive Usenet postings and store them for several days; they are then distributed to other campus centres, or individual articles can be read one by one. Usenet easily allows for a person to post a message, or comment directly on a previous post or posts, reproducing pieces of them within a new posting. Thus, one can build up a self-referential conversational thread almost *ad infinitum*. One of the advantages of Usenet is that it is easily browsable; users can dip in and out of various newsgroups on their own accord.

Usenet consists of newsgroups grouped into 'hierarchies' where users post and reply to 'articles' or postings. Thousands of newsgroups are organized around a multifarious array of topics. The 'Seven Sisters' hierarchy includes the main newsgroups: comp (topics of interest to computer professionals and hobbyists); misc (addressing themes not easily integrated into other categories, i.e. job-hunting, fitness, law, invest-ments); news (concerned with the news network, group maintenance, software); rec (groups oriented towards hobbies and recreational activities, i.e. cars, games, food, TV shows, movies); sci (topics particularly related to research or application of established sciences); soc (groups addressing social issues and socializing – world cultures, politics, gender issues); and talk (debate-oriented groups).

The alternative hierarchy includes the alt, or alternative, newsgroups. The alt. hierarchy consists of newsgroups whose purpose and content range from the recreational (i.e the alt.sports and alt.music hierarchy); to popular culture (the TV and film hierarchy, including alt.tv.dinosaur. barney.die.die.die); to the theoretical (alt.postmodern); the gossipy (the alt.fan groups and alt.showbiz.gossip); to the wacky (alt.fan.lemurs-cooked, alt.fax.bondage, alt.prophecies.nostradamus) to the tasteless (alt.mcdonalds.ketchup) and the questionable (alt.flame.fucking.faggots), to the sex hierarchy, including alt.sex, alt.sex.bondage, and so on. Usenet readership figures show how popular the alt.sex newsgroup is: for the month of October 1993, there were an estimated 3.3 million readers world-wide; with 67 per cent of sites receiving the newsgroup and approximately 2,300 messages per month, for a total share of 8 per cent of Usenet readers (Reid 1993).

Usenet's size is also impressive: it consists of over 3,000 newsgroups and over 7 million users worldwide. For instance, in a two-week period in May 1992 there were an estimated 240,000 articles posted, totalling over 445 million bytes, submitted by over 20,000 different users to 4,500 newsgroups for an average of 32 million bytes per day. There are further estimated to be 2 million people at 40,000 sites in the US, Canada, Europe, Japan, Korea and Australia who read news (Greenberg and Hall 1992: 2).

Rules have been devised for creating Usenet newsgroups, including dis-seminating a Request for Discussion (RFD) to news.announce.newgroup and other newsgroups similar in topic, discussion of the RFD in newsgroups, a call for votes (CFV) announcement in news.announce.newsgroups, and a period of voting. Alternative newsgroups, however, do not have to adhere to these rules. Creation of an alt. newsgroup does not necessitate formal votes, and involves merely choosing a name for the group and posting a proposal and charter in alt.config. If the proposal is received in favourable terms, then a 'newsgroup' control message can be posted, and newsgroup administrators can choose whether or not to carry the news-group (Aboba 1993: 240–1).

The equivalent to Miss Manners on the net are informal guidelines called 'netiquette', slang for network etiquette. Throughout the years, Usenet denizens have formulated particular rules of conduct (Horton and Spafford 1993). McLaughlin and her colleagues designed a 'Taxonomy of Reproach-able Conduct on Usenet', as a preliminary approach to the question of Usenet standards. Conduct ranged from incorrect/novice use of technology, bandwidth waste, violation of networkwide and newsgroup-specific con-ventions, ethical violations, inappropriate language, and factual errors. 'The rules of conduct on Usenet as currently constituted can be understood as a complex set of guidelines driven by economic, cultural, social-psychological and discursive factors both within and outside the network' (McLaughlin *et al.* 1995: 107). For instance, 'proper' netiquette dictates that postings should be distributed in as limited a manner as possible; that the same article should not be posted twice to different groups; that postings should not be repeated; that posting other people's work without permission is not allowed; that postings should be appropriate to Usenet and the newsgroup; that postings should not be used for blatantly commercial purposes; and that postings should not be made when anyone is, 'upset, angry, or intoxicated' (Horton and Spafford 1993). ' "Flaming" refers to posting messages with emotional and/or irrational outbursts, usually in response to someone or something; intentionally posting to insult or incite provocation; or especially high-noise, low-signal postings' (Raymond 1991: 158).

Usenet has, throughout the years, defined and refined its own culture. It is a raucous realm which respects no boundaries or borders, physical or mental. A diverse community of international users protects fiercely the notions of free and unfettered communication, and can hide anonymously behind a thick veneer of bandwidth. Stephenson's description of the 'Internet' is felicitous to Usenet:

> Nearly all academic computers are on the Internet, so access is open to anyone having an account on such a machine, which is to say, any student who bothers. The Internet is, therefore, still very much a college town and shares much the same ambience as Cambridge, Iowa City, or Berkeley: a dysfunctional blend of liquored-up freshmen and polymorphously perverse deconstructionists. The politically correct atmosphere may help to explain the generally frosty stance toward humor exhibited on Usenet, where people either use it badly – at the level of toilet-stall grafitti, or categorically reject it. (Stephenson 1993: 26)

From daguerreotypes to digitized images: sex and Usenet

Analysing the origins, social ramifications and moral imperatives of pornography has become an almost *de rigueur* academic quest now. The wildly popular metapornography market in academia has led one critic to dub it 'adventuring in the skin trade' (Wicke 1993: 62). As Lynn Hunt and others have shown, pornography was an invented notion, 'constituted by both the regulation of and the market for printed works. On the one hand, the efforts of religious and political authorities to regulate, censor, and prohibit works contributed to their definition. On the other, the desire of readers to buy certain books and of authors to produce them also contributed to the construction of a category of the pornographic' (Hunt 1993: 19). Walter Kendrick has described how, in the nineteenth century, pornography became something to regulate. Censoring led to the creation of 'secret museums' for the storage of pornographic writings and graphics, and such private enclaves were meant to exclude people of the lower classes and women (Kendrick 1987: 57).[4]

Historically, the introduction of electronic communications technologies has often been greeted with considerable moral consternation: it has been seen as a perceived threat to the sanctity of the home, and the encroachment of the public on to the private domain has been raised. In addition, the proliferation of electronic communications technologies is often accompanied by their adoption as a facilitator or carrier of material of a sexual nature.

This concern about the usage of electronic communications technologies can be traced back to the introduction of the telephone. Carolyn Marvin documents how parents were outraged at the telephone's use as a courting device: young men were able to call up young women – unaccompanied – so new codes of etiquette were quickly established (Marvin 1987: 73). Parents are now concerned that their children can call up 900 numbers and talk directly to sex hotlines. 'Dirty pictures' quickly became a lively pastime for early photographers, and now, of course, are a staple of modern newsstands and an often contested terrain on the pornography battleground: Dworkin versus Flynt.[5] Lynn Spigel documents the contra-dictory and often contentious debates that accompanied the introduction of television into the post-war home (Spigel 1992). Television was thought to be both a cementer of and a detractor from family ideals, and anxieties about parental control and the proper reflection of family values are still fought over: witness Dan Quayle vs. Murphy Brown, *c.* 1992. The rise of home VCR technology was encouraged by the availability of porn movies on video, and pornography became an item for private, rather than public, consumption.[*]

Computer pornography combines elements of the public and private spheres; in the privacy of one's home, one can participate in a diverse range of bulletin-board services and forums within commercial network providers, available to a relatively anonymous public. Surprisingly, the most popular use of France's Minitel system was within the *messageries roses*, 'sexual smorgasbords with something for every taste . . . Sextel, X-Tel, Desiropolic, Aphrodite . . . [which] advertise a selection of, "Rambos, machos, Latin Lovers, Romeos, and Big Bad Wolves" for women, and "mermaids, man-eaters, Little Red Riding Hoods, and femmes fatales" for men' (De Lacey 1987: 18). Likewise, one of the most popular chat-areas in Canada's ill-fated videotext system named 'Alex' was

---

* Ben Keen, in his brief history of the development of home video technology, reveals its double life: the shaping of video technology as foreseen by various corporations and their construction of an idealized consumption; versus the 'spaces and unintended possibilities' that allowed for the elaboration of new and unforeseen video practices by consumers. For instance video pirating, which came to dominate at least 70 per cent of the market in the mid-1980s, was an unintended consequence of its developmental trajectory. In 1976 Walt Disney Productions filed suit against Sony alleging that their 'time-shift' advertising campaign was an incitement to breach copyright regulations. By the time the suit was finally settled in favour of Sony, entrepreneurs had started a fledgling and very profitable video distribution business, having already bought up all the software rights they could find. The early video market was also dominated by products not readily available through television and film, such as pornography. As Keen mentions: 'as has happened so often in the past with the introduction of new communications technologies, the growth of video provided the ideal breeding ground for a moral panic of considerable proportions' (see Keen 1987).

the 'Eroticat' space (Pearson 1991: 19). IRC, or Internet Relay Chat, is an Internet service that allows groups of users to interact simultaneously in real time. Users create a channel and send messages to it, and each active participant of a given channel receives a copy of each message sent to the channel. As Elizabeth Reid found out in her study of IRC users:

> Much of the opportunity for uninhibited behaviour is invested by users of IRC in sexual experimentation. The usually culturally-enforced boundaries between sexual and platonic relationships are challenged in computer-mediated circumstances. Norms of etiquette are obscured by the lack of social context cues, and the safety given by anonymity and distance allows users to ignore otherwise strict codes regarding sexual behaviour. Conversations on IRC can be sexually explicit, in blatant disregard for social norms regarding the propositioning of strangers. . . . Such behaviour is often referred to as 'net.sleazing'. Perhaps because the majority of the users of IRC are in their late teens or early twenties, since the Internet primarily serves educational institutions and thus students, sexual experimentation is a popular Internet game. Adolescents, coming to terms with their sexuality in the 'real world', find that the freedom of 'virtual reality' allows them to safely engage in sexual experimentation. (Reid 1991)

And now the new era of 'cybersex' beckons: witness a flurry of 'general interest' net.sex books, magazines such as *Boing-Boing* and *Future Sex*, which extol the virtues of man-machine sex; and the hype over the Ted Nelson-dubbed 'teledildonics', or virtual sex (Rheingold 1991: 345).

Internationally, there have been isolated bannings of Usenet alt.sex newsgroups in various universities, from the United States to Europe and Australia, with Canadian universities seeming to have established more of a united front in censoring the newsgroups; for instance, the Computers and Academic Freedom (CAF) list of Banned Computer Materials for 1992 listed thirteen new US cases, several ongoing cases, and seven new Canadian cases for the year.

One of the first Usenet newsgroups to be banned in Canada was the alt.sex hierarchy. In 1992 the University of Manitoba banned it from its Usenet facility after complaints were received about its allegedly offensive nature. Two weeks previously, the *Winnipeg Free Press* had run a front-page story which claimed that students at the University of Manitoba were playing pornographic video games depicting bondage, and that these games were obtained from the Internet in the alt.sex.bondage file. The vice squad, the Attorney-General's office, and the university administration were solicited for their opinions, and the offending newsgroups (including alt.personals.bondage, alt.sex, alt.sex.bestiality, alt.sex.bondage, alt.binaries.pictures.erotica, alt.sex.pictures, even alt.sexual.abuse. recovery, and alt.sexy.bald.captains) were quickly shut down (Moon 1992: 6). Major media, including Canada's national newspaper, the *Globe and Mail*, reported that the material 'included descriptions of bondage and violence against women and children' (ibid.). Network users were outraged at the perceived violation of civil rights, and various debates within the newsgroups, campus computing facilities and the media were initiated as to the nature of censorship and the legal viability of cutting off newsgroups on the basis of their allegedly offensive content.

Other Canadian universities followed suit. A 'Memorandum to Executive Heads of all Colleges and Universities' sent out by Bernard Shapiro, then Deputy Minister of the Ontario Ministry of Colleges and Universities, explained the position:

> It is the Ministry's position that publicly-funded postsecondary institutions in Ontario should have appropriate policies and procedures in place to discourage the use of their computing systems for purposes of accessing or sending racist or pornographic materials. (Shapiro 1992)

Many of the institutions, such as the University of Toronto and University of Waterloo, reversed earlier decisions to ban the newsgroups, after input from the university community and *ad hoc* committee reports. The University of Waterloo recommended that the user be responsible for his or her decision to read an e-mail message, newsgroup or article posted to a newsgroup, as well as remaining personally responsible for the content of his or her messages or e-mail. However, the controversy was reopened later when the university, fearing that the contents of some of the newsgroups violated Canada's Criminal Code, removed five newsgroups (alt.sex-bondage, alt.sex.bestiality, alt.sex-stories, alt.sex-stories.d. and alt.tasteless) upon recommendation of a university ethics committee (Gooderham 1994: 1).

Alleged Usenet pornography comes in a variety of forms: stories, practical guides (in the form of FAQs – Frequently Asked Questions), jokes and limericks, digitized graphics, stories, and discussion groups. A childish and wickedly perverse sense of humour is exhibited in the alt.sex hierarchy. Newsgroups run the gamut from the ludicrously titled alt.sex.aluminum.baseball.bat to alt.sex.boredom. In alt.sex.bestiality, recent discussions included the topic of anonymity on the Internet; results of a survey on bestiality and 'furverts' – people who enjoy imagining sex with anthropomorphized animals; and a request for information on the reproductive activities of reptiles, particularly the morphological structure of the various reptilian genitalia. In alt.sex.bondage, participants have debated the merits of flogging – is it therapeutic?; attire for the ideal dom; and suggestions for the Bobbit Cookbook.[6]

Alt.sex.fetish.fashion features an FAQ with an extensive guide to products, magazines and shops, and suggestions on how to wear latex or PVC garments. In alt.sex.fetish.diapers, conversation is on the merits of Depends vs. Attends (commercial products for adult incontinence). In alt.sex.bestiality.hamster.duct-tape, an inquirer asks, 'how does one get duct-tape off furry critters?' Other newsgroups include alt.sex.enemas, alt.sex.exhibitionism, alt.sex.fetish.amputee, alt.sex.masturbation, alt.sex.movies, alt.sex.motss (members of the same sex), alt.sex.pictures, alt.sex.services, alt.sex.spanking, alt.sex.stories, alt.sex.wizards, and alt.sexy.bald.captains (should Sigourney Weaver be made a SBC

– Sexy Bald Captain? or Sean Connery?). On a more serious note, **alt.sexual.abuse.recovery** offers advice in a supportive environment.

The alt.sex hierarchy isn't always about sex or erotica. Thus, **alt.sex.bondage** frequently veers away from its original subject, to discuss the merits of various knotting techniques, including Boy Scout knots, which then leads into a digression on merit badges. A personal sexually-related post to an alt.sex group by a 13-year-old became sidetracked from its intent to a discussion of the privatization and commercialization of the Internet. Another poster said:

> This is funny! I've read alt.sex on occasion and I've NEVER found anything about SEX on that newsgroup. Anything but! No matter . . . What are the SEX POLICE going to do when alt.sex is closed down and ALT.SEX-like articles are suddenly found being posted to news.groups? Shutting down a 'newsgroup' is like trying to bail water with a sieve.

Many of the devoted alt.sex readers defend the newsgroups, saying that they deal only in consensual sex. One reader even suggested the creation of **alt.sex.nonconsensual**, so that

> the anti-censorshippers have a focus for their discontent (alt.sex.nonconsensual), and the rest of us (the vast majority that don't care jack about the supposed evils of censoring articles celebrating the joys of rape and sex with children) can correctly say that we're distributing nothing illegal.

Commenting on Canadian censorship of some of the newsgroups, one poster said:

> As before, there's a flap about the evil stuff in asb [alt.sex.bondage]. This time it's the Mounties. Ooooh, I'se [sic] scared. Been there, done that, got a system in my own house. I don't need the Canadian government's approval, any more than I need an NEA [National Endowment for the Arts] grant to fund my posting.[7]

Analysing the alt.sex hierarchy, Maureen Furniss concluded that 'sexually oriented boards act as a kind of support group for people who post notices to them, especially individuals whose sexual orientations are very marginalized (those who practice sadomasochism or bestiality, for example)' (Furniss 1993: 20). In addition, a large proportion of the Usenet audience is comprised of college-aged students, who might find the information posted in the newsgroups, and that collected in the 'Official alt.sex FAQ file with Answers', to be practical guides to sexuality and safe sex practices, a necessary component of the undergraduate curriculum, which students might not have recourse to otherwise. (See Appendix on p. 29.)

The debates about computerized pornography reflect the same sentiments as the unabated and impassioned pornography debates between feminists, with anti-pornography feminists contending that pornography is sex discrimination on one side; and 'anti-anti-porn' feminists, who distrust censorship and fear that freedom of speech rights will be abridged, on the other side.[8]

Supporters of the alt.sex newsgroups believe that open discussion of issues of sexuality is valuable, and should not be characterized as negative behaviour, or be confused with online harassment, such as sending personal and potentially offensive messages to an individual, or 'net-stalking'.

Some, however, believe that the availability of alleged pornography on university computer systems constitutes sexual harassment. The University of Waterloo investigated pornography on their network after a coordinator of the university's Women's Centre complained to university officials. Citing newsgroups which featured 'a picture of a boy engaged in oral sex with a donkey and a woman with a dog' and other examples of child pornography, the coordinator demanded the elimination of all sex-related files from Usenet, stating: 'this is an issue of harassment and human rights' (Aggerholm 1993).

Whether or not the alt.sex hierarchy newsgroups on Usenet can fit into legal definitions of obscenity is debatable, and so far no legal skirmishes have been waged to decide this. Many universities, erring on the side of safety and conservatism, have opted to discontinue some of the newsgroups. President James Downy of the University of Waterloo removed some of the newsgroups because of their 'certainly obscene' content. In a memo issued to the university community, he stated that advice from the university solicitor was, 'unequivocal: under the Criminal Code it is an offence for anyone to publish or distribute obscene material, and the University is running a risk of prosecution if it knowingly receives and distributes obscene material'. He recommended that complaints of newsgroup content be sent to the university's Ethics Committee, which in turn can make recommendations to senior levels of university administration for removal of the newsgroups.

Desperately seeking Karla: the case of alt.fan.karla-homolka

It would have been difficult for any Canadian in 1993 to miss the sensationalist coverage of the events leading up to the trial of Karla Homolka, convicted of manslaughter in the horrific sex-related slayings of two young women from St Catharine's, Ontario. In a surprise move, the court, under order of Judge Francis Kovacs, issued a time-limited ban on the publication of the details of Homolka's trial, stating that 'the considerations for a fair trial outweigh the right to freedom of the press in these exceptional circumstances'. The ban is enforceable until after the completion of the trial of Paul Teale, Homolka's husband, also implicated in the murders.*

---

* Kovacs stated that 'the considerations for a fair trial outweigh the right to freedom of the press in these exceptional circumstances', and also feared that the widespread publicity surrounding the case would both jeopardize the selection of an impartial jury for Teale's future trial, and act unfairly towards the families of the victims. Kovacs allowed in his courtroom Canadian media, the families of the victims and the accused, counsel for Paul Teale, and the court's law clerk. Foreign press were not allowed in the court, and the media were not allowed to publish details of the deaths of the victims, or reveal this information directly or indirectly to the foreign press (see R. v. Bernardo . . . 1993). Major media,

The media ban sparked controversial debate and a flurry of unanticipated activity on small bulletin board services (BBSs) and on Usenet. Debates raged over the issue of censorship versus free speech; electronic access to information surrounding the case and trial, prohibited for publication in Canadian mainstream media by the court-imposed ban, yet ferociously available through foreign media and computer bulletin boards; the legal differences between traditional print and broadcast media versus computerized media; and differing notions of free speech in the United States and Canada.

Ontario Attorney-General Marion Boyd accused the media of engaging in a 'feeding frenzy', seeking to profit from the lurid case (*Globe and Mail* 1993: A1). Amid a rapid proliferation of foreign news reports on the Homolka case, including coverage in the British *Sunday Mirror* and the *Guardian*, an article published by the *Washington Post* and reprinted in the *Buffalo News* and the *Detroit Free Press*, American television coverage on *A Current Affair*, and Detroit area radio reports, the Canadian public could procure the printed and broadcasted materials to glean details of the Homolka case.*

Judge Kovacs admitted in his ruling that it would be difficult to monitor American coverage of the charges, given the easy cross-border availability of American newspapers, television channels and radio stations, and the impossibility of enforcing an 'effective blackout of the cable television channels' (see R. v. Bernardo 1993). But Kovacs certainly did not anticipate how computer networks would subvert his ruling and spark intense debates amongst university administrators, librarians and the public.

---

including the Toronto Star Newspapers Ltd., Thomson Newspapers Co. Ltd., The *Toronto Sun*, and the Canadian Broadcasting Corporation opposed the ban, arguing that the public had a right to know certain details of Homolka's trial.

In November, 1994, Professor Frank Davey of the University of Western Ontario published a book by Penguin on the Homolka case, which reprinted parts of the Internet FAQ, but marked out passages which would violate the court-ordered ban. The book was packaged with a black paper band across it, which had to be ripped off to open the book, and book buyers are promised that they will be sent the withheld portions of the book by Penguin, once the ban is lifted (see Davey 1994) – see author's addendum.

* It was reported that residents of Southern Ontario streamed across the border to purchase or read copies of the *Buffalo News*. The Ottawa *Sun* reported that: 'US shopkeepers already stocked with double the normal number of papers called for more . . . Canadians waited outside B&B Cigar Store in Niagara Falls, New York, in the pre-dawn darkness and quickly bought up 120 copies . . . A few blocks away at the Wilson Farms store, more than 100 copies were cleared out by 10 a.m. More than half were purchased by Canadians. Fearing police would seize the papers at customs, Canadians read them in parking lots and parked cars.' Canadian border officials turned back trucks that carried copies of the *Detroit News* that contained a story about the blackout. Detroit television stations who reported that they would provide details of the trial had their signals blacked out by some cable companies. And, 'a Buffalo disc jockey standing on the American side of the Peace Bridge used a loudspeaker to bellow out details from a *Washington Post* story . . . "Hear ye, hear ye"' (see Burnside and Cairns 1993).

A number of BBSs, known as 'Bernardo Billboards', started appearing following the arrest of both Homolka and Teale (Paul Bernardo had changed his name to Paul Teale shortly after his arrest: see Duncanson and Pron 1993: A3). In July, a Usenet newsgroup, alt.fan.karla-homolka, was created and announced with the comment:

> Hey, has anyone noticed how cool Karla Homolka's eyes look? I like women who have a penchant for S&M, and who aren't afraid to take a video camera into the bedroom. This newsgroup is for people who share my tastes. My Canada includes Karla Homolka (and she's a babe).[9]

Alt.fan.karla-homolka, along with another Usenet newsgroup, ont.general, presented a mélange of rumours and innuendo, along with political commentary, surrounding the case, the trial and the media ban. The information was collected into an FAQ (Frequently Asked Question), an itemization of the alleged atrocities committed by Homolka and Teale. Much of the information was collected by Neal Parsons, self-named 'Neal the Trial Ban Breaker', and later corroborated by *Frank* magazine, the contemporary Canadian equivalent of the *libelles* of eighteenth-century Grub Street. It wasn't until several months later that universities shut down the newsgroup on their Usenet feeds, upon the advice of a memo distributed to CAnet management by a federal government network manager (CAnet is the Canadian backbone network that allows access to the Internet). McGill University was the first university to suspend the newsgroup (Jacqmotte and Broadhurst 1993: 8). Like other universities, McGill was concerned that by carrying alt.fan.karla-homolka, they could be viewed as potentially distributing information about the trial in violation of the Kovacs ban. Within a month, fifteen other universities in Canada (including eleven in Ontario), the National Capital FreeNet in Ottawa, and one American university had also discontinued the newsgroup.

Despite the shutting down of alt.fan.karla-homolka at many Canadian universities, there were still many ways for people to access the newsgroup and other information available on the trial. For instance, through anonymous cross-posting of the contents of alt.fan.karla-homolka to other non-censored newsgroups, personal requests, and accessing news-paper stories through commercial databases, a diligent citizen could amass a plethora of stories, 'facts' and rumours surrounding the case. As university sites discontinued the newsgroup, it became a fabulous Internet hunt to locate the sites where the banned material could be found.

Using an anonymous posting service located in Finland, a St Catharine's, Ontario gentleman (who chose to identify himself as Abdul), set up 'Teale Tales', a mailing list to provide information on the trial, including the FAQ, foreign press reports, such as those from the *Washington Post* and *Sunday Mirror*, and the transcript of *A Current Affair*. He was later asked by the operator to stop using the anonymous service for this purpose, and sent out an e-mail message with another e-mail address for procuring the articles.* Personal requests posted to various Usenet newsgroups was another way for people to find out about the case, as well as through individuals offering to e-mail information to interested parties. Cross-posting requests for information or direct posts from alt.fan.karla-homolka to other Usenet newsgroups, such as to soc.culture.canada, alt.censorship, alt.journalism, and tor.general; reading Usenet news at other sites which hadn't banned the newsgroup; and using the resource discovery tool, Gopher, to find out its location, was a common practice. The University of Toronto's student newspaper, the *Varsity*, published a detailed guide on how to access the newsgroup 'to show how easy it is to get information on Internet even in a case where the information is so tightly censored', according to editor Simona Choise (Micelli 1993: 3).

Several academic and public libraries, fearing they would be in violation of the publication ban, initially removed copies of newspaper articles that covered the case from their shelves, such as the one that appeared in the *Washington Post*. (Library patrons were able to retrieve the articles from the reference desk.) Later, on legal advice, McGill University, stating that, 'it is virtually impossible for the library to monitor the content of each and every periodical and newspaper it receives every day' (Mercille 1993: 3), restored the publications to their shelves. Other public libraries, including those in Halifax and Regina, also agreed to restore the US newspapers that carried coverage of the Homolka trial.

McGill's legal advice stated that foreign publications which printed information on the Homolka case and were available at libraries would be exempt from this ban, as 'the mere receipt and placing on shelves of a newspaper, which contains a large amount of other unrelated material, does not constitute an act of publication' (Mercille 1993: 3). McGill and public libraries relied on legal arguments that: (1) the libraries were outside of the province of Ontario, where the ban was, and Kovacs's ruling was unclear in terms of extra-provincial authority of provincial court orders; (2) Kovacs's order was directed at the representatives of news organizations who were present in the courtroom for the trial and sentencing of Homolka; and (3) Kovacs's ban was not on the publication of all evidence or legal argument – it was on the circumstances of deaths of persons referred to during the trial.

---

* An anonymous posting service, anon.penet.fi (residing in Finland) is specifically designed for anonymous postings to every Usenet newsgroup, and also provides capabilities for supporting anonymous e-mail. This service allows any mail messages sent to one's ID at anon.penet.fi to get redirected to one's original and real e-mail address. One doesn't know the true identity of any user, unless he or she chooses to reveal their identity explicitly. Anonymous posting services are widely used for posting to the alt. hierarchy within Usenet; as Johan Helsingius, a.k.a. 'Julf', the operator of the services writes:

  And remember this is a service that some people (in groups such as alt.sexual. abuse.recovery) need. Please don't do anything stupid that would force me to close down the service. As I am running my own company, there is very little political pressure anyone can put on me, but if somebody starts using the system for criminal activities, the authorities might be able to order me to shut down the service. I don't particulary want to find out, however (see help@anon.penet.fi: for information on the anonymous posting service).

Was the shutting down of alt.fan.karla-homolka at various universities constitutive of 'censorship', or was it a reasonable response to a fear of breaking the court-ordered ban? According to McGill University legal adviser Raynald Mercille, reading the newsgroup would not be contravening the ban, but distributing the material to third parties 'would constitute an act of publication which is prohibited' (Mercille 1993). Since McGill University is a hub for distribution of newsgroups throughout the province of Quebec, they felt that alt.fan.karla-homolka, which 'deliberately aims at breaking the ban', would leave the 'University open to an argument that in so doing, it was actively engaged in an act of publication as this term is understood under the Criminal Code, which could differ from other statutory definitions of publication such as copyright law and others' (Mercille 1993).*

Despite the politics of the media ban, the Homolka case was alluring to many Canadians – and Americans – because of its shocking and salacious qualities. As Wendy Lesser argues, there can be no 'discreet' inquiry into violent death: 'the enjoyment of murder . . . always consists of wallowing in gory details. The details are all we can grasp' (Lesser 1994). The court-ordered publication ban was unique in the way that technology was used to break the ban; and certainly Judge Kovacs could not apprehend how computer networks would so rapidly spread news and rumours of the Homolka–Teale escapades. The 'Bernardo Billboards' and alt.fan.karla-homolka were, in their own quirky fashion, tantamount to the proliferation of pamphlets, *libelles*, and *chroniques scandaleuses* during the Enlightenment (Darnton 1982).**

---

* The Canadian Library Association *Statement on Intellectual Freedom* (1985) evidently carried little weight. It states:

> All persons in Canada have the fundamental right, as embodied in the nation's Bill of Rights and the Canadian Charter of Rights and Freedoms, to have access to all expressions of knowledge, creativity and intellectual activity, and to express their thoughts publicly. This right to intellectual freedom, under the law, is essential to the health and development of Canadian society.
> Libraries have a basic responsibility for the development and maintenance of intellectual freedom. It is the responsibility of libraries to guarantee and facilitate access to all expressions of knowledge and intellectual activity, including those which some elements of society may consider to be unconventional, unpopular or unacceptable. To this end, libraries shall acquire and make available the widest variety of materials.
> It is the responsibility of libraries to guarantee the right of free expression by making available all the library's public facilities and services to all individuals and groups which need them. Libraries should resist all efforts to limit the exercise of these responsibilities while recognizing the right of criticism by individuals and groups. Both employees and employers in libraries have a duty, in addition to their institutional responsibilities, to uphold these principles.

** The Grub Street mentality that Darnton exposes so well reached its culmination in the politico-pornographic nature of the *libelles*: 'The grand monde was the real target of the libelles. They slandered the court, the church, the aristocracy, the academics, the salons, everything elevated and respectable, including the monarchy itself, with a scurrility that is difficult to imagine today' (Darnton 1982: 29). It is also interesting to compare the Internet 'underground' created by the alt.fan.karla-homolka newsgroup with the underground trajectory of the *libelles*, whose obscene or seditious contents were usually disguised by philosophical titles (the so called *livres philosophiques*).

Free speech and censorship in the era of global information

An often-quoted adage by net pioneer John Gilmore – 'The Net interprets censorship as damage and routes around it' certainly resounds with stark truth in the examples of alt.fan.karla-homolka and in regulation of the alt.sex newsgroups. Gilmore's statement refers to both the technical and the social realm. The distributed communication flow of the Internet – packet switching – divides messages into small packets of data before sending it out, thus encouraging easy dissemination of messages and infinite methods of propagating messages. Given that a message can be facilely forwarded and stored electronically in various permutations, and a cultural climate where 'information wants to be free', it becomes extremely difficult to 'kill' a message.[10]

The Homolka case and newsgroups such as as the alt.sex hierarchy challenge information professionals, university administrators, the media, and the public at large, to respond and formulate policies that deal with the growing complexity, in both social and legal terms, of new multi-media forms of communication. The resolution of these issues is at best precarious now, as the law has not kept up with technological currency. What is censorship in networked environments? Should electronic information stored on computer networks be accorded the same status as books and other materials housed in libraries? How can one police the contents of computer networks, if at all, given the peripatetic qualities of networked information?

The electronic environment raises many problems relative to controlling information and bypassing official channels. Is it even feasible to prevent access to offensive or potentially illegal newsgroups, given that networks such as Usenet are international in scope? Restricting access to such newsgroups will only create an underground network whereby different people outside the restricted zone simply copy the same files and propagate them locally. And since not all of the offensive or illegal material is centrally located, unless a policy is adopted of screening all newsgroups and postings (an absurd and impossible task!) the offensive or illegal material won't get snared.

How can one exercise jurisdictional control over network environments? Anne Branscomb dubs the peripatetic qualities of the Internet as its 'extraterritoriality' and suggests that global standardization of what constitutes acceptable conduct and use of data on networks will alleviate some of these quandaries. In the case of material posted on a BBS or Usenet which breaches local jurisdiction for obscenity, for instance, one is confronted with differing national legal definitions of criminality. In which country does one seek redress of grievances? Can one identify and then obtain jurisdiction over the criminal perpetrator? How can such laws be harmonized and administered globally? (Branscomb 1993: 85).

The line between the public and private domain in networking environments is murky. In the academic context offensive or potentially illegal material on Usenet raises the issue of the public–private debate; for instance there is the problem that the display or discourse of potentially illegal material is conducted in public conferences residing on systems which are university-owned. Should one recognize individual responsibility and control over message content, or implicate and absolve the network provider from liability for messages it allows to be published? In the university context, are students solely responsible for their speech and actions, or are system administrators (and potentially a whole chain of administrators) responsible for irresponsible conduct?

The Computers and Academic Freedom (CAF) draft principles detail how the principles of academic freedom apply equally to academic computer systems. They state that: (1) the principles of intellectual freedom developed by libraries should be applied to the administration of information material in computers (similarly formulated in the American Library Association Bill of Rights, Freedom to Read Statement, and Intellectual Freedom Statements); (2) computer newsgroups should be selected by computer sites the same way that magazines and books are selected by traditional libraries; and (3) that academic freedom applies to student and faculty publications in traditional media, as well as to publication in computer media (CAF 1992). The ALA, interpreting from the Library Bill of Rights, has recently issued draft guidelines for access to electronic information, services and networks.[11] These guidelines stem from the various Usenet controversies on campuses as well as from public policy and parental fears concerning offensive net content.* The new draft guidelines state that:

> Libraries and librarians should not deny or limit access to information available via electronic resources because of its allegedly controversial content or because of the librarian's personal beliefs or fear of confrontation. Information retrieved or utilized electronically should be considered constitutionally protected unless determined otherwise by a court with appropriate jurisdiction. . . . Libraries may discover that some material accessed electronically may not meet a library's selection or collection development policy. It is, therefore, left to each user to determine what is appropriate. Parents who are concerned about their children's use of electronic resources should provide guidance to their own children. (ALA 1995)

As Rodney Smolla has remarked, the impact of technological change on

---

* Hysteria over alleged proliferation of porn on the Internet perhaps reached its apotheosis in the United States with the *New York Post* headline of 9 January 1995: 'COMPUTER SICKOS TARGET YOUR KIDS: Child-porn perverts roam info-highway'; coupled with the introduction in early February to the Senate of the Communications Decency Act of 1995 (S.314). This legislation proposes to place substantial criminal liability on telecommunications carriers (including traditional telephone networks, Internet service providers, commercial online services such as America Online and CompuServe, and independent BBSs) whenever their networks are used to transmit any material which is deemed indecent or harassing. In order to avoid these penalties, carriers would be forced to restrict the activities of their subscribers and censor all public and private communications. See EFFector Online, 8:3 (20 March 1995), available URL: http://www.eff.org.

law and policy is not as rapid as the pace of modern communications technologies:

> forms of communication are converging, collapsing the legal distinctions that once brought a semblance of order to free speech policies. For most of this century societies could draw lines of demarcation separating print media, broadcast media, and common law. New technologies, however, are rendering these divisions obsolete. (Smolla 1993: 322)

Should we treat newsgroups as publishers, distributors or common carriers? Common carriers in the communications industries, such as the telephone companies, are regulated by federal statutes; in the US they are covered by the First Amendment provisions of free speech and therefore not held liable for the content of the messages they transmit. Or does a new hybrid model need to be defined for computer networks? How can you regulate heresy, innuendo and wild and fabulous rantings on computer networks?

Definitions of speech have not kept pace with technical currency. The technical characteristics of media – i.e. spectrum scarcity in broadcasting, have been closely linked with the social characteristics of the media, for instance the prominence of television in our everyday cultural life in formulating laws and policies. However, in the case of computer networking, can we characterize the medium as a 'broadcast' medium?

A recent court ruling in the US treated the operator of an electronic information system (EIS) as a distributor rather than as a publisher, in order to assess liability at the state libel law level. *Cubby, Inc.* v. *Compuserve, Inc.* also set an important precedent by ruling that the system operator or EIS owner could not reasonably be held liable for the content of the messages it carries, given the sheer volume and rapidity of the messages on computerized boards (Cubby 1991).

How can different and often conflicting national laws regarding freedom of speech be harmonized in the global context, when technology seemingly knows no physical boundaries? Once again, we're left with a legal – and perhaps insurmountable – enigma that has no easy resolution. It's also not inconceivable that any global resolutions could smack of subtle forms of 'cultural imperialism', particularly given current discords and tensions over differing cultural moral standards and sanctions.

For instance, the Homolka ban struck a raw nerve south of the border, with many American First Amendment fundamentalists lampooning the Canadian media ban and attacking Canada's different distinctions on free speech. When the April 1994 issue of *Wired* magazine was banned in Canada for its story, 'Paul and Karla hit the Net', outraged editor Louis Rossetto said in a press release that 'banning of publications is behavior we normally associate with Third World dictatorships . . . this [is] an ominous indication that the violation of human rights is becoming Canadian policy' (Hoffman 1994). A detailed listing of electronic sites maintained by *Wired* – an Infobot* e-mail server, a Gopher, and a World Wide Web server –

---

* An automatic e-mail responder.

with various banned details, was also given in the same press release. What Rossetto did not mention, however, is that the magazine was banned not because the article revealed how Canadians were circumventing the ban, but because the article discussed details that were in direct violation of the Kovacs ruling.

US Constitutional expert Laurence Tribe has suggested that the First Amendment provisions be extended into the realm of electronic media by introducing a 27th Amendment, which would read:

> This Constitution's protections for the freedoms of speech, press, petition, and assembly, and its protections against unreasonable searches and seizures and the deprivation of life, liberty, or property without due process of law, shall be construed as fully applicable without regard to the technological method or medium through which information content is generated, stored, altered, transmitted, or controlled. (Tribe 1991)

Conclusion: no closure here

At this point, we're left with some rather unresolved but fascinating problems. We have a raucous technology, Usenet, which respects no boundaries or borders, physical or mental; a diverse community of international users, some of whom can hide anonymously behind a thick veneer of bandwidth; a range of neoteric and nebulous ethical issues; a hot new sub-speciality of the law, cyberlaw, staking out its territory; concerned parents; moral fundamentalists and conservatives; libertarian anarchist practitioners of bestiality (and they do it with duct tape, no less!).

Given the wide scope of material available on Usenet, how can one define 'pornography' and 'sexual harassment'? How can one regulate such 'pornography' in the global context? How can one ensure academic freedom and freedom of speech when university administrators 'censor' questionable newsgroups?

In the last few years, several civil libertarian groups devoted to defending and preserving online rights have been established in North America. The preeminent groups are the Electronic Frontier Foundation (EFF), which supports legal and legislative action to protect the civil liberties of online users; Computer Professionals for Social Responsibility (CPSR), which conducts many activities to protect privacy and civil liberties; and Electronic Frontier Canada, founded to ensure that new communications technologies are protected by the principles embodied in the Canadian Charter of Rights and Freedoms.[12]

What all of these groups agree upon is that the common carrier principles must be extended to the realm of new communications technologies. These network carriers (like the telephone system, which is governed by common carrier principles) would be conduits for the distribution of electronic transmissions, but they would not be allowed to change message content or discriminate among messages. Such a restriction would also require shielding the carriers from legal liability for libel, obscenity and plagiarism. This should ensure the continuance of the free and unfettered communication that is the hallmark of Usenet and the Internet.

Notes

1. 'National Information Infrastructure Agenda for Action,' v.1.0, 15 September 1993. (Available via ftp: ntia.doc.gov, pub/nii agenda.asc). See also the speech by Clinton and Gore (1993). For the Canadian case, see *Industry Canada*, 1994.

2. See also Hauben (1993).

3. A version of the alt.sex controversies, 'Ethical issues in electronic networks: the case of Usenet's alt.sex hierarchy and the Canadian university community', was presented at the Feminism and Technoculture Panel of the Northeast Modern Language Association, 8–9 April 1994, Pittsburgh. A lengthier version of the Homolka case originally appeared in *Proceedings of the 22nd Annual Conference of the Canadian Association for Information Science/Association canadienne pour les sciences de l'information (CAIS/ACSI)*, 'The information industry in transition', McGill University, 25–27 May 1994: 109–26. See also a lengthier overview in 'Ethical issues in computer networks: academic freedom, Usenet, censorship, and freedom of speech' (23 November 1993), located at Electronic Frontier Canada's WWW and Gopher site: URL: http://insight.mcmaster.ca/org/efc/efc.html or gopher://insight.mcmaster.ca/11/org/efc.

4. The long history of the regulation of allegedly obscene literary and artistic work in America has been documented indefatigably by Edward de Grazia; he has yet to consider the issue of computerized pornography. Marcia Palley's recent inquiry into current US debates on sexual material and censorship furthers De Grazia's work but likewise does not touch upon the recent controversies over computer networked material (De Grazia 1993; see also Palley 1994).

5. Dworkin vs. Flynt: this refers to Andrea Dworkin, anti-pornography activist, and her various crusades to rid the streets of pornography; and Larry Flynt, publisher of *Hustler*, one of her targets.

6. Set up in 1993 when Lorena Bobbitt of Manassas, Virginia, went to trial for the highly publicized act of cutting off her husband's penis in a marital dispute.

7. These comments were elicited by posters to the Computers and Academic Freedom (CAF) newsgroup, discussing a recent censorship case at a Canadian university.

8. In *Defending Pornography: Free Speech, Sex, and the Fight for Women's Rights* Nadine Strossen (1995), president of the American Civil Liberties Union, analyses the feminist pornography debates and argues persuasively that censoring pornography does women more harm than good. Her book is an indictment of recent efforts to suppress speech, led by Catharine MacKinnon and Andrea Dworkin, who have helped draft several laws that define pornography as a form of sex discrimination, including Canada's anti-pornography law, Butler v. Regina (1992) 2 W.W.R. 557 (Can.). The book also highlights the recent activities of anti-censorship feminists, led by groups such as Feminists for Free Expression and the New-York-based National Coalition Against Censorship.

9. 'My Canada includes . . .' is a parody of the 1990 Anglophone anti-separatist slogan 'My Canada includes Quebec'. From stem@sizone.jaywon, pci.on.ca. Message-ID: <56yN7B2w165w@sizone.jaywon.pci.on.ca> (Wed. 14 July 1993).

10. Although Gilmore's words are almost biblical in stance, they can be attributed to a quote in Howard Rheingold's *The Virtual Community* (1993: 7). The original hacker ethic, which espoused the belief that 'information wants to be free', has been astutely documented by Steven Levy (1994). See also Ross (1991); Hafner and Markoff (1991).

11. Available electronically from Computers and Academic Freedom Gopher, Electronic Frontier Foundation Gopher. Posted by Edward.Valauskas@ala.org.

12. For information on EFF, contact info@eff.org, URL: http://www.eff.org, or at

Electronic Frontier Foundation, 1001 G St. NW, Suite 950 E, Washington, DC 20001, USA. Voice: +1 202–347–5400; fax: +1 202–393–5509; CPSR, cpsr@csli.standford.edu, URL: http://www.cpsr.orgdu or at CPSR National Office, PO Box 717, Palo Alto CA 94302 USA. Voice: +1 415–322–3778; Fax: +1 415–322–3798. EFC, efc@graceland.uwaterloo.ca, URL: http://insight.mcmaster.ca/org/efc/efc.html or gopher://insight.mcmaster.ca/11/org/efc.

Stanton McCandlish (mech@eff.org) publishes an online directory, 'Outposts on the Electronic Frontier: International, National, Regional & Local Groups Supporting the Online Community', published at the following sites: FTP: rtfm.mit.edu in the file /pub/usenet/news.answers/net-community/orgs-list E-mail: go to mail-server@rtfm.mit.edu with the message (on separate lines): 'help' and 'index'. Also posted on Usenet to various groups, including: comp.org.eff.talk, alt.comp.acad-freedom.talk, alt.politics.datahighway, alt.internet.services, alt.culture.internet, alt.cyberspace, alt.culture.usenet, alt.culture.internet.

Appendix

Popularity of **alt.sex** newsgroups

```
>       + – Estimated total number of people who read the group, worldwide.
>           + – Actual number of readers in sample population
>               + – Propagation: how many sites receive this group at all
>                   + – Recent traffic (messages per month)
>                       + – Recent traffic (kilobytes per month)
>                           + – Crossposting percentage
>                               + – Cost ratio: $US/month/rdr
>                                   + – Shares: % of newsreaders who
>                                           read this group
>                                               + – Group name
>       ↓       ↓    ↓      ↓      ↓      ↓    ↓    ↓         ∨
>    1470000  6439  90%    17    163.1  100%  0.00  12.6%  news.announce.newusers
>    2300000  4136  56%   842  11829.9    3%  0.04   8.1%  alt.sex.stories
>    3300000  4083  67%  2300   4817.8   18%  0.02   8.0%  alt.sex
>    4290000  3966  87%    10    450.5   90%  0.00   7.7%  news.answers
>    5260000  3507  82%    25     67.0    4%  0.00   6.8%  rec.humor.funny
>    6250000  3438  72%    31    377.7    3%  0.00   6.7%  rec.arts.erotica
>    7240000  3275  56%   737  31428.5    5%  0.12   6.4%  alt.binaries.pictures.erotica
>    8230000  3189  83%  2394   3191.3   26%  0.02   6.2%  misc.forsale
>    9230000  3159  83%  2613   4684.5   21%  0.03   6.2%  misc.jobs.offered
>   10200000  2787  80%  2241   6865.9    5%  0.04   5.4%  rec.humor
>   21774000  1007  81%   649   1583.7   38%  0.03   2.0%  comp.org.eff.talk
>   42856000   771  62%    95    226.9   24%  0.00   1.5%  alt.comp.acad-freedom.talk
>   80340000   548  79%     4     77.5   25%  0.00   1.1%  comp.org.eff.news
>  190917000   228  54%     7     52.7    0%  0.00   0.4%  alt.comp.acad-freedom.news
>   25303900    53  15%   232    410.6    2%  0.03   0.1%  aus.sport
>   25313900    53  13%    80    308.4    4%  0.02   0.1%  de.rec.games
>   25323900    53  10%    10     34.0   10%  0.00   0.1%  chi.places
>   25333800    52  40%     9    111.0    0%  0.02   0.1%  biz.zeos.announce
>   25343800    52  18%    32     30.8   13%  0.00   0.1%  ba.sports
```

Note: Usenet Readership Report: October 1993 from: reid@decwrl.DEC.COM (Brian Reid): This is an excerpted set of data.

References

Aboba, Bernard 1993. *The Online User's Encyclopedia: Bulletin Boards and Beyond*, Reading, MA: Addison-Wesley.

Aggerholm, Barbar 1993. 'UW to probe offensive images in computer network', *Kitchener Waterloo Record* Tuesday, 20 July: 1.

ALA (American Library Association) 1995. *Access to Electronic Information, Services, and Networks: An Interpretation of the Library Bill of Rights*, Draft Guideline, (5 March) Washington, DC: American Library Association.

Branscomb, Anne Wells 1993. 'Jurisdictional quandaries for global networks', in Linda M. Harasim (ed.), *Global Networks: Computers and International Communication*, Cambridge, MA: MIT Press. pp. 83–101.

Burnside, Scott and Cairns, Alan 1993. 'Cops seize Teale story at border', *Ottawa Sun*, 29 November.

CAF (Computers and Academic Freedom) 1992. 'Banned Computer Material 1992; Policy – Examples of the Best Policies; Computers and Academic Freedom Statement – Draft'. Archives available at ftp eff.org, or through Gopher.

Canadian Library Association 1985. *Statement on Intellectual Freedom*, Ottawa: Canadian Library Association.

Clinton, President William J. and Gore, Vice-President Albert, Jr. 1993. *Technology for America's Economic Growth: A New Direction to Build Economic Strength*, Washington, DC: White House (22 February).

Cubby, Inc. v. *CompuServe, Inc.*, 776 F. Supp. 135 (S.D.N.Y.1991).

Darnton, Robert 1982. *The Literary Underground of the Old Regime*, Cambridge, MA: Harvard University Press.

Davey, Frank 1994. *Karla's Web: a Cultural Investigation of the Mahaffy–French Murders*, New York: Penguin.

De Grazia, Edward 1993. *Girls Lean Back Everywhere: the Law of Obscenity and the Assault on Genius*, New York: Vintage Books.

De Lacey, Justine 1987. 'The sexy computer', *Atlantic Monthly*, July: 18–26.

Drake, William J. 1995. 'Part IV: Outlook & Conclusions', pp. 301–78 in William J. Drake (ed.), *The New Information Infrastructure: Strategies for US Policy*, New York: Twentieth Century Press.

Duncanson, John and Pron, Nick 1993. 'Computerized bulletin boards abuzz with Homolka trial details', *Toronto Star*, 31 July: A3.

Furniss, Maureen 1993. 'Sex with a hard (disk) on: computer bulletin boards and pornography', *Wide Angle*, 15(2): 19–37.

Globe and Mail 1993. 'Public's right to know gains here, loses there', *Globe and Mail*, 2 December: A1.

Gooderham, Mary 1994. 'College drives sex titles off info highway', *Globe and Mail*, 5 February: 1.

Greenberg, Alan and Hall, Ron 1992. 'What is Usenet?', *McGill University Computing Centre Newsletter*, May/June: 2–7.

Hafner, Katie and Markoff, John 1991. *Cyberpunk: Outlaws and Hackers on the Computer Frontier*, London: Fourth Estate.

Hauben, Ronda 1993. 'The development of the international computer network: from ARPANET to Usenet News (on the nourishment or impediment of the Net.Common-wealth)'. Paper presented at the International Association for Mass Communication Research Conference, Europe in Turmoil: Communication and Democracy in Civil Society, 25–26 June, Dublin, Ireland. Copy available from the author.

Hoffman, Taara Eden 1994. 'Cyberspace cannot be censored: *Wired* responds to Canadian ban of its April issue', *Wired* press release, 23 March.

Horton, Mark and Spafford, Gene 1993. 'Rules of Usenet conduct'. Part of a series of documents compiled and distributed by Gene Spafford 1992/93 in news.announce.newusers.

Hunt, Lynn 1993. 'Introduction: obscenity and the origins of modernity, 1500–1800', in *The Invention of Pornography: Obscenity and the Origins of Modernity, 1500–1800*, New York: Zone Books. pp. 9–45.

Industry Canada 1994. 'The Canadian Information Highway: Building Canada's information and communications infrastructure', in *Spectrum. Information Technologies and Telecommunications Sector*, Ottawa: Industry Canada (April).

Industry Canada 1995. *ISC News*, electronically available: File name: 02–26–95, debra.dgbt. doc.ca File path: /pub/isc/Industry.Canada.News.Releases/1995, Date archived: Wed. 1 March 11:09:53 EST 1995.

Jacqmotte, Benoit and Broadhurst, Michael 1993. 'Homolka newsgroup suspended', *McGill Tribune*, 16–22 November: 8.

Keen, Ben 1987. 'Play it again, Sony: the double life of home video technology', *Science as Culture* 1: 7–42.

Kendrick, Walter 1987. *The Secret Museum: Pornography in Modern Culture*, New York: Vintage Books.

Lesser, Wendy 1994. *Pictures at an Execution: an Inquiry into the Subject of Murder*. Cambridge, MA: Harvard University Press.

Levy, Stephen 1994. *Hackers: Heroes of the Computer Revolution*, New York: Delta.

McLaughlin, Margaret L, Osborne, Kerry K. and Smith, Christine B. 1995. 'Standards of conduct on Usenet', in Steven G. Jone (ed.), *Cybersociety: Computer-mediated Communication and Community*, Thousand Oaks, CA: Sage. pp. 90–111.

Marvin, Carolyn 1987. *When Old Technologies Were New: Thinking about Electric Communication in the Late Nineteenth Century*, New York: Oxford University Press.

Mercille, Raynald (legal advisor) 1993. 'Memo to Ms. Frances Groen, Associate Director Public Service & Collections re: "Foreign press articles – Canadian Ban"', 3 December. Copy available from author.

Micelli, Pat 1994. 'Censorship: it's OK to read about Homolka on computer, lawyers say', *McGill Daily*, 24 January: 3.

Moon, Peter 1992. 'Network sex: is increasingly explicit material on some computer bulletin boards free speech, or obscenity?', *Globe and Mail*, 20 July: 6.

Palley, Marcia 1994. *Sex & Sensibility: Reflections on Forbidden Mirrors and the Will to Censor*, New York: Ecco Press.

Pearson, Ian 1991. 'Terminal sex', *Saturday Night*, February: 19–25.

R. v. Bernardo between Her Majesty the Queen, and Karla Bernardo also known as Karla Teale (1993). O.J. No. 2047. Action No. 125/93. Ontario Court of Justice – General Division, St Catharine's, Ontario, 5 July 1993.

Raymond, Eric 1991. *The New Hacker's Dictionary*. Cambridge, MA: MIT Press.

Reid, Brian 1993. 'Usenet readership summary report'. Palo Alto, CA: Network Measurement Project at the DEC Western Research Laboratory (March).

Reid, Elizabeth M. 1991. 'Electropolis: communication and community on Internet Relay Chat', Honours thesis, University of Melbourne, Department of History.

Rheingold, Howard 1991. *Virtual Reality*, New York: Summit Books.

Rheingold, Howard 1993. *The Virtual Community*, Reading, MA: Addison-Wesley.

Ross, Andrew 1991. 'Hacking away at the counterculture', in *Strange Weather: Culture, Science and Technology in the Age of Limits*, New York: Verso. pp. 75–100.

Sandfort, Sandy 1993. 'The intelligent island?', *Wired*, September/October: 52–5, 116.

Shapiro, Bernard 1992. 'Memorandum to executive heads of all colleges and universities', September. Available electronically at eff.org or Gopher; Message 1992Oct20.181236. 15507@eff.org. Tuesday, 20 October.

Smolla, Rodney A. 1993. *Free Speech in an Open Society*, New York: Vintage Books.

Spigel, Lynn 1992. *Make Room for TV: Television and the Family Ideal in Postwar America*, Chicago: University of Chicago Press.

Stephenson, Neal 1993. 'Smiley's people', *The New Republic*, 13 September: 26.

Strossen, Nadine 1995. *Defending Pornography: Free Speech, Sex, and the Fight for Women's Rights*. New York: Scribner.

Tribe, Laurence 1991. 'The constitution in cyberspace: law and liberty beyond the electronic frontier'. Keynote Address to the first US Conference on Computers, Freedom, & Privacy (April).

Wicke, Jennifer 1993. 'Through a gaze darkly: pornography's academic market', in Pamela Church Gibson and Roma Gibson (eds), *Dirty Looks: Women, Pornography, Power*, London: BFI Publishing. pp. 62–80.

2

The Labyrinth of Minitel

André Lemos

Labyrinth: An enclosure formed of an inextricable network of passages or galleries furnished in such a way that once engaged within, no one can find the single escape except with difficulty.

The gate of the labyrinth

Technology is always full of unexpected events of which various media gives us some privileged examples. The record player was thought of by Edison as a means of recording voices to be preserved beyond the death of the speaker. In June 1878, he declared, 'the principal use of the phonograph is to permit one to write letters, to dictate texts' (cited in Flichy 1991: 52). The use of the phonograph as a musical and an entertainment medium was unanticipated. Similarly, the telephone conceived in the service of commerce became a convivial, domestic apparatus; the computer, invented as an enormous calculator of military ballistics equations, has metamorphosed into a holistic device which is at once both rational and *ludic* (literally: related to play and sport).

After two centuries of modernity, technology has been identified as the accomplishment of the rationalization of the world, as the victory of the artificial over the natural, and as the supremacy of the external object over the subject. It is even held responsible for the displacement of magic-religious thought.* Thus basic aspects of culture are held to have become cut off from 'truth', which is regarded as accessible only through scientific means. The social imaginary thus becomes a foreign territory. The reduction of 'technique' to only the techno-logical (a mix of 'technique' and rational discourse about the world)** can appear only in a framework

---

* This will be referred to as the *imaginary* in this chapter. Developed in symbolic anthropology, the social imaginary is composed of myths, folk tales and key symbols which represent not only 'rules' for living but also cultural resources upon which people draw when confronting issues or developing options on a daily basis.

** Today we take technology as the complete and full meaning of 'technique'. This mix of 'technique' (from the Greek *technè*, art) and 'techno-logy', is a mix of the organized and structured thought of technology, and is symptomatic of the modern condition. From its origins in the fifteenth century, technique has never been isolated and independent of other fields of social activity such as religion, labour and morals. In respect of myth and ritual, Mauss (1962), Spengler (1958) and Ellul (1977) speak of a technology of the sacred. Here, technique is a method for producing results on the symbolic and material level. It is

where technical problems alone are comprehensible. This is to say that when dichotomies are established between the rational and non-rational the separation stops us from seeing the complexity of the situation.

Our understanding of reality has flowed from this modernist identification of technique as inseparable from science, authoritative, homogenizing and autonomous. It is clear that we no longer live in a state of 'magical indifference' (Simondon 1958) in which the technical dimension does not exist except in the context of 'magico-religious' practices and beliefs.* We live in the realm of the object, in the risks and in the paradise promised by the artificial mastery of the world. Modern thought has already illustrated the fear of the artificial – this fear *vis-à-vis* the independence and power of technique. Max Weber, Martin Heidegger, the Frankfurt School, Jacques Ellul, Lewis Mumford and Hans Jonas among others have shown the dangers of technological interference with nature (pollution of the environment) and culture (the instrumental rationalization of life). They have pursued, in a sort of actualization of our Platonic and Aristotelian heritage, this fear of the artificial and this sentiment of the transgression on the divine which is intrinsic to the march of technology.

The radical consequence of this idea of rupture (between the nature and the artificial, subject and object – and here the 'cyberpunks' are the spokespeople) translated into a mixture of fear in relation to the benefits of progress and the symbolic and practical appropriation of new technologies. It there is no future; if old-style History, with its ideological components of progress and reason, no longer makes sense, the only option is to take charge of the technological destiny of the planet. This punk humanization and 'exasperation' of technique is visible in computer viruses, hacking, video gaming, VR, cybersex. In this, cyberpunks represent an attitude common at least in part to all.

If modernity refused the artificial, and deepened separations and dichotomies, postmodernity tries to surpass well-established dichotomies, not in the dialectical sense through sublimation and synthesis, but more in the direction of making a place for dialogical complexity. The notion of the dialogical is used by the sociologist Edgar Morin to show that opposed logics can be integrated in a complex and inclusive 'double logic', and not only in a dialectical synthesis (1986). This perspective moves against the modernist project, which consisted of separating, cutting off and recon-

---

this marriage of science and technique which causes technique to change its role, become redefined and newly understood as 'technology.' Today 'technology' is used to describe the technical processes as well as technical 'objects' (the technology of chemical synthesis in the former case, and the technology of turbines in the latter).

* I'm referring to G. Simondon's thesis according to which the primary relation between people and nature is the 'magical phase', in which the figure and ground (subject and object) are united. This 'indifference' for Simondon is the intimate relation between technique and the world, which exists before the radical separation of technical objects and religion – and it is for this reason that the indifference is 'magical indifference' (Simondon 1958).

structing pieces which had been analytically separated, through a process akin to addition.

We can analyse technical phenomena via a dialectical logic which has enclosed technology in an isolated system autonomous from the other cultural expressions. We will show that one of largest top-down organized 'telematic'* networks in the world, 'Minitel', has not escaped the process that one can label 'technical vitalism' in which the union of new technologies and new media produces unforeseen results and in which the technology takes on a 'life' of its own or is taken over and made to come alive by the diverse forces of social interaction. Thus a rational tool, a computer, or network becomes a symbolic medium and cultural resource. Furthermore, Minitel is even the consequence of this 'social vitalism' which, as Simmel (1990) had shown even in the 1890s, always struggles against the established forms of culture. 'Cyberculture', of which Minitel was and is one of the precursors (in terms of enabling media), is a strong example of these processes.

Minitel

Born in 1981 as a videotext system to give access to an electronic phone book, stock prices, and sports results from home terminals, the austere Minitel has since entered into the mores and the daily life of the French (see Figure 2.1). Minitel was the result of a political economic strategy of the end of the 1970s to place France on the cutting edge of the development of public online systems.**

By 1987 Minitel was 'the world's largest E-mail system, a fascinating mix of socialism and capitalism' (Brand 1988: 25). Today the telematic network has over 6.5 million terminals and more than 1.6 million calls per year

---

* Télématics is a popular term to designate online data access and computing. It is interesting that the French term 'informatique' (translated as computing) blurs computing and the furnishing of information via electronic databases, a much less independent use of technology because the data is provided for the user.

** As a medium of 'cyberspace', Minitel is a hybrid terminal halfway between a telephone and a computer which permits 'actors' access to multiple information sources. One can consult the phone book, book a trip on the train or reserve a seat at the opera, consult databases, send a fax, or explore the *messageries*. To be connected to a server implies that one must 'navigate' by the options provided and immerse oneself in the 'cyberspace' by means of an assumed character (*personage*). To receive electronic mail, one opens a *boîte aux lettres éléctronique* (BAL) with a '*pseudo*'. This pseudonym and a password are obligatory. The 'pseudo' remains a 'pseudo' even if one uses one's true name. Here the 'simulacrum' is law because along with anonymity of online exchanges, the communication act is structured with the accepted risk of the *lie* – of falsehoods and deception. The game of phantoms is the rule. For example, one muses, 'I could even put my real name because for the other person this will always be taken as a "pseudo".' Through the anonymity of this *téléaction*, 'I can be the man (or the woman, or both persons) that I want to be.' The password (*mot de passe*) is a personal code which supposedly guarantees the inviolability of these private exchanges on the BALs.

Figure 2.1 Minitel terminals

Source: Courtesy of France-Telecom, 1994.

(45 per cent for the directory), 113 million connect hours (of which 80 per cent are for *messageries* or commercial bulletin boards and chat lines), over 4,200 serves, 24,000 access codes and a budget of around 6.7 million francs (Ceria 1994; *Le Monde Informatique*, 1994).

As far as technological development is concerned, France was the first to develop a public telematic system and to use a high speed network (Transpac) with relative success.* Minitel became a symbol of France – the France of the recent architectural mega-projects in Paris (renovations and expansion of the Louvre, l'Arche de la Défense (a building in the form of a cube-like arch) which terminates at the axis of the Champs Elysées), among other developments, is equally the France of the 'Grand Réseau Télématique'. However, and as we will soon see, the system was hampered: 'a slow decision-making structure, a relation too marked between industry and the state and an almost non-existent confidence in a youthful and innovative spirit contributed to the loss of its position in the actual development of computing' (Hauter 1993). In the age of information superhighways, the French telematic system now appears outmoded and new efforts have begun to attempt to better adapt it to new technologies.

The construction of the labyrinth

Like all the technologies of 'cyberspace', Minitel was born out of the convergence of telecommunications and computing, or more exactly, from the marriage of the telephone, the television and computers at the Centre National d'Etudes de Télécommunication (CNET) and the Centre Commun d'Etudes de Télédiffusion et de Télécommunication (CCETT) in 1972. It is the product of different sets of 'enabling technologies' (Rheingold 1991). Possibly this is why Lagneau refers to Minitel as 'a hybrid, a travesty of a castrati', the result of 'the seduction of the technological travesty' (Lagneau 1992: 174). For Guillaume (1982), the 'teletechnologies' are characterized by the circulation of spectres and 'teleaction' (computer-mediated action at a distance, a slightly lesser form of 'telepresence'). The spectres are the users' doubles, which circulate in the networks like phantoms. Furthermore, this virtual double is not an exact copy of its master. It is a travesty and hijacked double, a double which cannot have the physical, social or moral ties of the master. Minitel is a space of circulation, of production and the extinction of virtual and

---

* The French telematic system depends on three national networks: the RTC network (or *Réseau par téléphone commuté* – basically via computer modem over regular phone lines), Transpac and the rented lines of private providers. The RTC system is an automatic, multi-line system (like a PABX) with a low speed for information transfer (100 to 2,400 baud). The private lines are rented directly from France Télécom and the Transpac network was created at the close of the 1970s to optimize the transmission of data and the development of packet switching, the notion of virtual circuits and billing on the basis of the volume of data moved over the lines.

phantasmagorical spectres. In 1968 barely 16 per cent of homes in France were equipped with a telephone: France was in the process of falling off the technological train of history. To respond to this situation, Valéry Giscard d'Estaing announced the creation of the 'Telephones for all the French' programme in 1974. Gérard Théry, Director of the Division Générale de Télécommunication (DGT) which is now France Télécom, launched a project to create a public online phone book.*

At the 1974 'Salon Sicob' trade show, TIC-TAC, a broadcast videotex terminal was presented, using a television and keyboard. Through it, one could consult news-wire, stock market, and phone book information as well as play games. The Giscard government adopted this as the basis for future telematic developments.[1] The strategic need for the 'informatization of French society' was made more explicit in the development of an experimental system for the town of Vélizy (near Paris) in 1977 and later documented in the Nora and Minc report (1978). The logic of the technocracy in place had been overtaken by the exploding development of computing. Thus they anticipated 'an infinity of small machines . . . efficient and cheap: they could become synonymous with liberty. Mass activity will succeed an elitist technology' (Nora and Minc 1978:17).

Nora and Minc thus proposed a broadly public teleinformatics, named telematics to distinguish it from the professional usage of 'teleinformatics' (*téléinformatique*), and the development and operationalization of the Télétel system (the name of the technical protocol which was later to become known as Minitel) as a strategic element in maintaining the French position in broadly distributed online information systems. The success of the demonstration of Télétel at the Palais de l'Elysée (the President's Palace) in 1980 ensured the continuation of the project and was the beginning of the first public experiment in consulting an electronic phone book in Saint Malô beginning on 15 July of that year. The press, however, identified telematics as a potential danger, a sword of Damocles. Fearing the 'death of paper' (the term is from one of the conceivers of the system, Gérard Théry), the new 'useless gadget' (*Le Monde*) might eventually substitute telematic practice for the writing of journalists.

The left took power in 1981. Roger Tallon, designer of the TGV trains and of the new terminal, proposed the name Minitel. The Ministre des Postes et des Télécommunications officially opened the Télétel experiment in Vélizy, a suburb of Paris, where 2,500 homes were equipped with a decoder to consult about 20 services via their televisions. The results, however, were unsatisfactory: 20 per cent of the users were responsible for

---

* This was envisaged as similar to the Prestel system which came on line in the late 1970s in the UK. This system used a decoder and television to display information sent by telephone. Prestel is thus an interactive videotex rather than a broadcast videotex. There are many videotex systems in Europe, North America and Japan including BTX (Germany), Telidon (Canada), Captain (Japan), Nistel (Belgium), VTX (Switzerland) (Saboureau and Bouché 1984).

60 per cent of the connection time and 30 per cent of users ignored the device (see *Libération* 1991).

In parallel, three local telematic projects were developed in Strasbourg (GRETEL), Grenoble (CLAIRE) and Nantes (TELEM). At the end of 1981 the messaging software (a type of bulletin board system or BBS) for the GRETEL system was pirated by some users planning to communicate between each other in real time. Through this *détournement* – literally, a 'hijacking' was born the *messagerie*.* By hacking and then making available the bulletin board software, a counter-current to the French technocratic approach produced a usage of the system which was never a planned objective. Direct communication – the equivalent of Chat – became the principal activity on Minitel networks. In the spring of 1982, a *messagerie* came on line in Vélizy as a sort of 'forum' for dialogue through a system of electronic mailboxes (*Boite aux Lettres Electroniques*: BAL). In June, participants in the OECD Versailles Summit talks were networked with 250 terminals in 35 locations with three services (*Journal du Sommet*, real-time information, and *Guide du Sommet* with 8,000 electronic 'pages' of information). In front of over 3,000 journalists, the demonstration was a success.

With the conclusion of the Vélizy experiment (December 1982) the free distribution of terminals was started. By January 1984 there were already 145 services available. In 1983 another experiment at Ille-et-Vilaine (Bretagne) with 150,000 users began. The free terminals allowed one to consult a set of data banks on telephone services including the phone book. The success of the implementation of the electronic phone book and the free terminals was crucial to the expansion of the Minitel network throughout France. What was still lacking, however, was commercialization: a system to make it possible to bill for services with each month's telephone bill.

In February 1984, the Kiosque system – with images of an open-air pavilion, hence a kind of electronic and social 'place' – was opened. Kiosque allowed services to be billed for and in 1987 the next generation, Kiosque multipalier, allowed France Télécom to include within telephone bills, Minitel billings on the basis not only of the service used but of connection time, independent of distance.

The Télétel system allowed for the classification of services with an identifying number for each type of service:

3611 – the electronic phone book (free for the first three minutes);
3613 – Télétel, allowing international e-mail at 90 francs per hour (approx

---

* The *messageries* include games, dialogues in real time and postings. The servers used for erotic bulletin boards work are classified under the same field (i.e. *messageries*). Thus the *messagerie rose* is the same software system. Over time, this appropriation would profoundly modify the role of Minitel within daily practices. Minitel would become 'a means of permanent connection to a world onto which one could open onself only when one desired' (Marchand 1987: 11).

US \$15 per hour) but where costs are normally paid by the service provider, not the user (similar to a 1–800 call in North America);

3614 – Télétel 2, where the connect time is billed but not the service;

3615 – Télétel 3, known as the *kiosque grand public* where both the connect time and the service are billed;

3616 – Télétel 3P, for professional use;

3617 – Télétel 4, for professional use;

3618 – which permits communication from one Minitel to another;

3628 – data banks;

2629 – data banks.

Thus, the success of Minitel can be attributed to the free distribution of terminals and the commercialization of tele-informatics through the Kiosque system. The strategy is almost the same as for video games: the console or player is relatively inexpensive but the purchaser also becomes a consumer of game cartridges. In the Minitel network, free terminals were intended to stimulate and develop the consumption of online services. This was successful.

From another point of view, the almost imperceptible change in the nature of Minitel's use, that is to say, the transformation of a service-oriented media (consultation of the telephone book, stock market quotes, etc.) into a 'contact' media which is convivial, ludic and erotic allows the creation of new networks of social interaction (sociality) and an explosion of services. The service-provider no longer furnishes only a simple message (for example a stock quotation), but a range of more or less flexible possibilities. The consumer is no longer a passive receiver, but a producer and creator of information.

The technocratic strategy always insisted on increasing human–machine interaction on the basis of a model of the ideal user (rational, austere, individualistic). Now, the networks of socialization created by these real users, at least in the case of Minitel, have demonstrated that the ideal user does not exist and the recreational applications have a much more important role (see Charon 1987: 112). From 1985, the logic of the ludic and the convivial have taken the foreground. The Télétel system allowed the expansion of the game services, social bulletin boards and the first erotic bulletin boards or *messageries roses* – the 'Pink Minitel'.* Claire Ancelin notes, 'the public has not hesitated to manifest tastes often opposed to those foreseen by experts, this public has not hesitated to make a serious information tool into a frivolous communication tool' (1987: 94). A Louis Harris France poll found that in 1991 89 per cent of the French were against prohibition of the *messageries rose*.**

---

* As Marchand (1987) explains, the word *rose* (pink) was taken as a parody of the symbol of the Socialist Party (a rose) which took power in 1981.

** In 1986 the first roadside billboards for the *messageries rose* appeared (picturing, for example, a robust male or a woman with slogan '3515 BUSTY', the online address of a *Mintel rose* chat service). French traditionalists were outraged and Charles Pasqua, acting Minister of the Interior, attacked the gay *messagerie* Gay Pied. Worse, the French state

To return to the initial argument of this chapter, the phenomenon of the *Minitel rose* is in reality a social expression of the vitalism which struggles to tame technique. Sex, which is nothing new, is one of the most effective means of appropriation of new media. This has recently been the case with video and its X-rated films, or CD-ROMs and virtual reality and its games and interactive cybersex.

Besides sex, swindling and other rackets entered the scene. In 1989, the Ministry of Equipment at l'Arche de la Défense (Paris) noted that its telephone bill had doubled because three guards had left their Minitels on all night connected to a telematic service. Technics demonstrates its 'Dionysian' character. In Nietzschean terms, Apollonian, ordered, reason is hijacked by the 'demon' of the playful, ludic, Dionysian.* Soon linked to prostitution and electronic crime, the Minitel became the object of moral sanction. Aggravating the situation, the servers engaged veritable informatic professionals, or *animateurs*, to pose as users of the boards and chat services and thus to animate the discussions: a new virtual class of service workers. Why? They are there to increase the amount of time spent on line. Users lost confidence and the *messageries* collapsed.

The reticulation of the labyrinth: alternative networks

In parallel with the Télétel system, the Minitel terminal gives access to alternative servers via the telephone (the RTC, *Reseau par Téléphone commuté*). These services provide a type of BBS, on which service is free as on the 3614 services of Télétel. Thus, Minitel encouraged the formation of an alternative network. Symbols of the French cyberculture, the *fanas* of informatics and the creators of the first BBSs in France formed the first alternative services via RTC in the early 1980s. Their objective was to develop the alternative usage of telematics, thus of Minitel (taking advantage of the success of the freely available terminals), and to engender a discussion of the mutations linked to informatic technology and its sociocultural aspects.

Like a BBS, or even the Télétel services (with the difference that it is much cheaper because one pays neither the cost of connection time nor for the service), the RTC servers provided a space for discussion (with many thematic online forums), e-mail communication through an electronic mailbox system (BAL and chat), and electronic downloading of software.

---

gains 36 per cent of the total charges paid. Taxes on all the *messagerie* services became the order of the day. France Télécom has no way of distinguishing between the *messagerie rose* and any other board or *messagerie*. In 1989 the government tax was 30 per cent and in 1991 a 50 per cent tax was imposed in the hope of eliminating all *messageries*.

* Apollo and Dionysus are the metaphoric figures used by Nietzsche to differentiate the plastic arts (order, measure, reason, etc.), central to the myth of Apollo, from non-plastic arts (polymorphic, unquantified, irrational, drunken) centred in the divine figure of Dionysus. (See Neitzsche, 1977).

A communal character developed on these services. Normally, an adolescent *bricoleur* with an Amiga computer would create an alternative server. This new **sysop** (system operator) is thus visited by a relatively loyal public, who share common ideas and live the experience of being together, even at a distance. In a small, alternative *messagerie* the affinities between the members are more structuring of the interaction (some are more technical, others more ludic or leisure-oriented) and this allows us to speak of a true community, even if it is electronic and virtual. There are more than fifty RTC servers in the Paris region, with diverse characteristics: some oriented to gaming, others to downloading, travel, virtual reality; and others are principally *messageries*. In perceiving themselves as actual examples of and sites within cyberspace, some services give free access to newsgroups on Usenet (the alt. hierarchy, for example). With the limited Minitel, one can even, for a small subscription fee, gain access to Internet to send and receive electronic mail or subscribe to a *lettre spécialisée* – a list server or mailing list.

The logic of France Télécom was thus to promote the use of the Transpac network for the transmission of data and to limit the RTC to voice telecommunication. However, this has been turned upside down, as the effervescence of the alternative networks on RTC have redirected the use of the simple Minitel to their cheaper and more sociable or 'communitarian' services than those provided by the Kiosque system.

Hide and seek: the *messageries*

Interactions on the *messageries* are more and more related to communication as a game. Laurel observes something similar in the human–computer relationship of users when describing this as a 'theatrical interface' (Laurel 1993). The users or *Minitelistes* are truly 'players' in the development of the system. The Minitel cyberspace is thus a complex ecosystem where the macro-system (the network administered by France Télécom) and the micro-system (the daily dynamics of users) are interdependent. This ecosystem is constructed through the dissemination of information, through the flux of data.

Telematic communications, at least so far, depend on the written word and not on the spoken word. These are words without voices which people the Minitel ecosystem. On the bias of the written word, this ecosystem evolves and becomes more complex; it becomes the result, always unpredictable, of the synergy of the flux of letters, of figures and of words, which traverse the 'organism-network'. As Burroughs writes, 'words are micro-organisms, living dust-specks which alone assemble and organize, up to the differentiated levels of meaning, the electronic revolution' (cited in Virillio 1989: 74).

In contrast to a hieratical and closed system, the Minitel cyberspace creates – through multidirectional communications, through the exchange between points of communication, and through the circulation of virtual spectres – a complex ecosystem. In this virtual world the development of the 'Game' (because here one can speak of a veritable game of and in communication) does not belong to a central entity but to a networked organism which is constructed out of the circulation and through the augmentation of informational flux.

The personality of actors is fluid and ephemeral because one can choose the representation(s) of oneself, one can appeal in several 'electronic tribes' (several servers or BBSs) as a sort of 'tele-appearance' lived at a distance. In this case, something like political party membership is not a model. One can note the frequent micro-political, everyday effervescence directed towards the problems of daily life or simply oriented by the desire to pass the time or exchange frivolities. Here, the communicative game is played by personae which are represented through pseudonyms and escape the weight of individuality. A persona can be thought of as fused with other virtual spectres of this cyberspace. This community of spectres, as Guillaume (1982) puts it, can not be unproblematically understood as a 'real community' because, as Thayer argues: 'the meaning of things is given by the function that we believe that they fill in the course of the social enterprise in which we believe we participate' (Thayer 1990: 89). While both are communities, life online is not the same as a propinquitous, face-to-face community.

The idea of community is above all a modern notion, an invention of modernity, because it is only with the appearance of new forms of social organization that the previous model (the community) could be identified and examined. Social thought from the sixteenth to the eighteenth centuries developed a theory of society which was not at all based on 'natural laws'. For example, consider their central terms: the corporations, the family, guilds – in brief, the community (Nisbet 1970). It can be argued that concept of 'community' is created in order to displace modernity from the project of 'society'. In this sense, 'community' now signifies a social collectivity (often primitive or religious) in which the contract, institutionalization, a common project, a certain utopian optimism, the appearance of proximity, a physical territoriality and forms of communication which are direct or almost unmediated, prevail. It is this idea itself of community, in its modern connotation, which makes the effervescence of the new (non-modernist) forms of electronic community incomprehensible in the terms of the modern 'community'.[2]

Institutionalization becomes 'tribalism'; the contract, empathy; the utopian optimism, non-finality; the future-orientation becomes an urgent present. Appearance stretches itself towards appearance which, without substituting for the face-to-face meeting, can be experienced at a distance, as a type of tele-appearance. The collective project, understood in modernity as political engagement, with specific ends in accord with a pre-established global project, is transformed into common interests which translate in turn into action within the sphere of the banal and everyday rather than political engagement. The sentiment of exclusive appurtenance stretches into multi-appurtenance wherein the individual even if individualistic, participant and actor can 'navigate' within groups. 'Engaged exclusivity' (e.g. of the political party and its members) becomes 'ephemeral inclusiveness' (e.g. Usenet alt. groups, its posters and lurkers).

The concept of territoriality and neighbourliness detaches itself from the constraints of physical geography to become a symbolic territoriality which is no longer dependent on physical proximity. More enlarged thanks to information technologies, 'symbolic territoriality' can be formed at a distance via ties to a symbolic 'empathetic proximity'. This is understood to be comprised of social relations even though race, sex or social status remain fundamental. This sense of proximity thus derives from the collective interest, from shared tastes, and from common ideas. Empathetic signifies the identification of one with the other, to the quality of being moved by the other. This 'empathetic proximity' is one of the most striking characteristics of cyberspace in which physical constraints are abolished.

Since the beginning of this century, forms of communication have been augmented by communication technologies. Speech, gestures, writing, sounds have continued to exist perhaps stronger than ever. However, today these forms of communication can be conveyed digitally and through the compression of data which in a certain manner dematerializes and deterritorializes these older forms of communication at the heart of community interaction. Taking into account the electronic community, one can say that the modernist *idea* of community is outmoded (even while communities themselves still exist and will continue to exist).

Out of the labyrinth

A technology is not adopted alone, and often users succeed, through the most unexpected means, in giving vitality and force, in hijacking and even re-enchanting the cold machine. According to Felix Guattari: 'one cannot hope for positive repercussions from new technologies except on the condition that they will be taken up in the creative practices of individuals and collectivities' (Guattari 1991: 2). He cites the example of Minitel in which the practice of *messageries* was made possible through such a hijacking. In the Minitel cyberspace the most interesting evolution is that of the practices of users. Like a sort of humanizing contamination unleashed on the artificial, in a small space of time the Minitel cyberspace will be polluting and polluted, impregnated by the subterranean and banal practices which structure everyday life (games, violence, sexuality). In complex societies, new technologies – the result of micro-computing – favour most often tactility and proximity, which are characteristics of interaction, rather than tending to isolation and homogenization. This contemporary society is the offspring of a 'concurrence between archaic elements and technological development' (Maffesoli 1993: 205).

As the Minitel experience has demonstrated, paradoxical as it seems, sexuality and its perversions, violence, the desire of the game and dream, the sources of the irrational and the imaginary are conveyed and even stimulated by technical objects and media. They emerge as central even within the pretended incarnation of instrumental reason which in a moment of history has disenchanted the world. It is precisely this 'conflictual integration' which structures life in complex societies today. Perhaps the formula of Naisbitt says it all: '*high tech, high touch*' (cited in Brand 1988: 26).

The 'touch' in Naisbitt's formula is charged with symbolism. It is the action of a symbolic transfer of our desires towards the machine. The act of pushing a button is the primordial source of information and the first point of a humanizing inflection. This act is the starting point of a process of sacralization of the object and of the profanation of the sacred by the object, in a new form of everyday hierophany. This act enacts the processes of successive sacralization and de-sacralization, turning them into a social drama – a process which Acquaviva (1967) calls 'dis-sacralization'.

However, as we have seen, Minitel was above all conceived as an objective terminal, something cold and austere, directed toward accessing useful informaion. It is, even today, a limited machine, with barely satisfactory graphics and a low speed of information transfer. Despite all this, Minitel has changed everyday life in France.*

That cyberspace called Minitel has changed, *augmented* reality (Kellog, Carrol and Richards 1992); it adds to our cultural environment three new elements: the virtual flux of digital information, the *messageries* and interactive games. Minitel has been the first public experience with computing in France and, as such, it has without doubt been the principal factor in the 'appropriation' of informatic practices and their sociocultural content. This appropriation isn't only a technical appropriation (in the sense of learning the correct use and mastery of the terminal), but is rather a symbolic appropriation, in which actions have repercussions in 'real life' because those actions are productive of meaning.

To judge by the clear majority of uses of the system for interaction and postings via the *messageries*, it is the ludic, convivial and sexual which are unleashed on the apparatus and which have been the means of this techno-symbolic appropriation. Now, through Minitel, the most banal movements and trends within the everyday life of the French have, even without them knowing it, altered the face of the technology. In this, they take up, concretize and throw into circulation the abstract notions of cyberspace

---

* Today, Minitel seeks its place within the global trend toward the creation of information superhighways and one could even say that Minitel is now the prison of French telematics. Thus, to respond to the demands of information superhighways, France Télécom is preparing the creation of a new code – kiosque micro – accessible through a modem and micro-computer. For mid-1995, a new 9,600 byte-per-second terminal – the Télétel Vitesse Rapide (TVR) – is planned with some multi-media capability.

(specifically, virtuality, real time, navigation, immersion, virtual inter-action (*téléaction*)).

The 'formist' perspective of Simmel (1990) foregrounds the changing forms taken by the same dynamic impulses towards social interaction across cultures and histories. He shows that 'the life of life' (social vitalism) will always struggle against the established, ritualized, forms of culture, that every crystallization of a cultural form elicits a 'negative' force, a face which will destabilize and reorganize social life. These forms, for their own stability, are directed towards temporal permanence. However, the disruptive and dynamic character of social life unforeseeably restructures and reorganizes all old figures. Minitel has not escaped this vital dynamism. From a cold and objective instrument, it becomes convivial, interactive, amoral and ludic. Social life thus restructures the 'Minitel form' which integrates these alterations and is thereby reorganized.

The *messagerie* or bulletin board is the most expensive in terms of connection time and is also the aspect of Minitel which raises the most interesting sociological questions. The convivial use of Minitel, as we know it today is the result of a *détournement* (the pirating of the software), of the social appropriation (usage of the machine and the network outside of those uses in the instruction manual) and of desire (for communication which is multidirectional, ludic and erotic). This strange mixture of technical rationality and of the social imaginary makes the analyses of Minitel and its associated technological phenomena more complex and stimulating.

The new technologies which fill our lives day by day are located within this same social ambiance. The newborn global cyberculture appears to be the result of the unprogrammed encounter between new technology and a 'sociality' which has escaped, or been overlooked in modernist paradigms of social scientific understanding (Maffesoli 1979). The Minitel cyberspace has become almost a 'temporary autonomous zone' (Bey 1991) – a virtual space which is 'self-organizing' (Morin 1986), a sort of plateau, a 'rhizome' where the interconnections and multiplicities even change the nature of the media such that it metamorphoses into a medium of contact (Deleuze and Guattari 1980: chs. 1 and 2). On this plateau, users are virtual nomads, phantoms who circulate in the structures of the labyrinth.

The *coupure* (the cut, separation, analytical dichotomy) of modernity is no longer the default approach, and – even if the artificial–natural problematic is still the order of the day – the users/actors transform the terminal into the instrument of their desires: desire for instantaneous communication, for information, for sex, for camouflaging their bodies, for disguise and identity through pseudonyms, for games, and for communal sharing. The discharge into the cold terminal are these micro-movements which make up the complexity of contemporary social life. They 'use computer technology to personalize and deeply humanize absolutely everything' (Negroponte cited in Brand 1988: 7).

It appears that contemporary technology is far from forming an independent and isolated system (Ellul 1977), which is all-powerful and homogeniz-ing, preoccupied with the mastery and domination of the world.* Contem-porary technology is embraced, diverted and reappropriated by everyday life. In any case, one can say that the domination and mastery of nature has already happened and, today, the stakes are more oriented in the direction of the conquest of new symbolic territories. It is not by chance that the construction of images and virtual worlds, multi-media, electronic games and cybersex are part of the motivating principles of the new technologies (images of synthesis, cyberspace, virtual reality, expert systems, cryptography, software). Through micro-deviations such as the *messageries*, contemporary technology appears to have been *re-enchanted*. These are the microscopic actions of everyday life which nonetheless refuses positive contracts, the totalitarianism of reason and blind obedience to the dictates of the pre-ordained and official use of things.

Notes

1. Bourgault defines telematics as the 'group of computer-based services which can be furnished through a telecommunications network' (Bourgault 1989).
2. This is discussed elsewhere. See Lemos (1994: 253).

References

Acquaviva, S. 1967. *L'Eclipse du sacré dans les civilisations industrielles*, Tours: Mame.
Ancelin, C. 1987. 'Services videotex grand public, la naissance d'un secteur économique,' in M. Marchand (ed.), *Les Paradis informationnels. Du Minitel aux services de communication du futur*, Paris: Masson et CNET-ENST.
Benedikt, M. (ed.) 1992. *Cyberspace: First Steps*, Cambridge, MA: MIT Press.
Bey, H. 1991. *TAZ: The Temporary Autonomous Zone. Ontological Anarchism, Poetic Terrorism*, New York: Autonomedia.
Bourgault, P. 1989. *Minitel et micro: la 'french connexion'*, Paris: Sibex.
Brand, S. 1988. *Inventing the Future at MIT*, New York: Penguin Books.
Ceria, Ugo 1994. *Il gesto telematico. Minitel e interazione sociale*, Milan: Università Cattolica di Milano.
Charon, J-M., 1987. 'Teletel, de l'interactivité homme/machine à la communication mediatisée', in M. Marchand (ed.), *Les Paradis informationnels. Du Minitel aux services de communication du futur*, Paris: Masson et CNET-ENST.
Deleuze, G. and Guattari, F. 1980. *Capitalisme et Schizophrenie Vol. 2. Mille Plateaux*, Paris: Editions de Minuit.

---

* It comes as no surprise that Minitel is to turn into a sort of micro-computer. There are two tendencies in this development. First, as we have seen, the Minitel terminal will be 'extended': it will become more rapid and have multi-media functions. On the other hand, the *Kiosque micro* system will permit the connection of home computers. The creation of France Télécom Multimédia will test the market with multi-media services from the fall of 1994. An alliancce with General Magic is planned to give the future terminal the technology of 'agents' which will permit the consultation of several databases with one call. The second tendency at France Télécom is the popularization and development of a network known as Numéris (ISDN with a data transfer rate of 64K bps) to deliver public services at a better rate. This expansion is planned for the end of 1996 – something to look out for . . .

Ellul, J. 1977. *Le Système technicien*, Paris: Calman-Levy.

Flichy, Patrice 1991. 'L'Historien et le sociologue face à la technique', *Réseaux CNET*, 46/47 (March–April/May–June): 49–58.

Guattari, F. 1991. 'Pour une éthique des médias', *Le Monde*, 6 November: 2.

Guillaume, M. 1982. 'Telespectres', *Traverse*, 26, Paris: Centre Georges Pompidou: 18–28.

Hatem, F. 1993. 'Informatique: la crève coeur français', *Libération*, 9 November.

Kellog, W.A., Carrol, J.M. and Richards, J.T. 1992. 'Making reality a cyberspace', in M. Benedikt (ed.), *Cyberspace: First Steps*, Cambridge, MA: MIT Press: 411–31.

Lagneau, G. 1992. 'Le Minitel, un mariage mécanique', in A. Grass and S. Poirot-Delpech (eds), *L'Imaginaire des technologies de pointe au doigt et à l'oeil*, Paris: Harmattan.

Laurel, Brenda 1993. *Computer as Theatre*, New York: Addison-Wesley.

Le Monde Informatique 1994. *Autoroute de l'information pour aller où? Quand et à quel prix?*, 597 (July).

Lemos, A. 1994. 'Les communautés virtuelles', *Sociétés*, 45 (September): 253ff.

Libération 1991. 'Moi, le minitel', *Libération* supplement, 20 November.

Maffesoli, M. 1979. *La Conquête du présent: pour une sociologie de la vie quotidienne*, Paris: Presses Universitaires de France.

Maffesoli, M. 1993. *La contemplation du monde. Figures du style communautaire*, Paris: Grasset.

Marchand, M. 1987. *La Grande aventure du minitel*, Paris: Larousse.

Mauss, M. 1962. *Sociologie et anthropologie*, Paris: Presses Universitaires Françaises.

Morin, E. 1986. *La Méthode*, 4 vols, Paris: Seuil.

Nietzsche, Frederich 1977. *La Naissance de la Tragédie*, Paris: Gallimard.

Nisbet, R.A. 1970. *The Sociological Tradition*, London: Heinemann Educational Books.

Nora, S. and Minc, A. 1978. *L'Informatisation de la société*, Paris: La Documentation Française.

Rheingold, H. 1991. *Virtual Reality*, London: Secker & Warburg.

Saboureau, J-P. and Bouché, G. 1984. *Guide pratique du videotex et du minitel*, Paris: CEDIC/NATHAN.

Simmel, G. 1990. *Philosophie de la modernité*, Paris: Payot.

Simondon, G. 1958. *Le Mode d'existence des objets techniques*, Paris: Aubier.

Spengler, O. 1958. *L'Homme et la Technique*, Paris: Gallimard.

Thayer, L. 1990. 'De la communication et de l'existence de l'esprit humain,' in *Colloque CERISY: Technologie et symboliques de la communication*, Grenoble: Presses Universitaires de Grenoble.

Virilio, Paul 1989. *Esthetique de la disparition*, Paris: Galilée.

3

Cool Runnings: The Contradictions of Cybereality in Jamaica

Joerge Dyrkton

The more I consider things the more I find that I'm only a social critic by accident.

John Galsworthy *The Forsyte Saga* (1949: ix)

Jamaica, the third largest island in the Caribbean, is a land of many contradictions: for example bobsledding and more recently e-mail. Known also for its beaches, ganja, Bob Marley, and even Miss World, Jamaica is considered by its nearly 3 million inhabitants to be the first among Third World nations. Its democratic system, however, is enforced by gun crews ('Dons' fighting for turf) at election time, which adds to a frightening annual death toll figure. Life for the average Jamaican is also disturbingly poor. The minimum wage is a mere US $8.00 daily.

How can computer networks function in a country beset by tropical conditions and Third World problems – where water supply can be down for days; where roads are repaired only when dignitaries come to visit; where the streets of downtown Kingston are dominated by men steering go-carts; where rain stops everything, including postal services; where mail between China and Canada is faster than that between Jamaica and Canada?

Jamaica's infrastructure is devoid of much rationalization; roads are chaotic, pot-holed and dangerous. Impatient bus drivers leapfrog one another regardless of traffic conditions. Buses are normally crammed with people, and increasingly dangerous. Violence – homicidal and domestic – usually headlines both radio and newspapers.

Everywhere the regular support system is breaking down,[1] and now e-mail comes to the rescue. Donkey carts can be seen on the roads quite regularly, passing by the university. My female house 'helper' (who has no telephone) does not use a washing machine: she does it all by hand. The average car in Jamaica (certainly if one considers taxis) is thirty years old, usually without proper brake lights and in dire need of repair.

E-mail demands cyborg technology and the latest in equipment. This is seemingly quite incompatible with the spirit of Jamaica. Miami is only two hours away by plane, but it is a world apart. Anyone who has been to Kingston airport will notice that the arrival and departure television screens are behind schedule by several days: today's flight arrival time will appear in two days' time. Also there are no working intercoms. Anyone who has used a bank's automatic teller will notice that computerized statements will differ depending on which machine has been used, which will differ again from the passbook statement.

Today, Jamaica is trying to move by leaps and bounds away from the chaos of a collapsing infrastructure and closer towards First World electronic communication with computer network links, fibre-optic cable, and baffling bridge rooters. The University of the West Indies, founded in 1947 as a college of the University of London, is at the centre of this transition. Composed of three campuses, Mona (Jamaica), Cave Hill (Barbados), and St Augustine (Trinidad and Tobago), the University of the West Indies is linked to the outside world by the UUCP Computer-link Network.

In June 1991 the Organization of the American States (OAS) approved the creation of the Hemisphere Wide Inter-University Scientific and Technological Information Network. CUNet (The Caribbean Universities Network) is under the initiative of SIRIAC (Integrated Informatic Resource System for Latin America and the Caribbean). The Caribbean and Latin America were the largest block remaining in the world unconnected to e-mail, and SIRIAC was the project designed to bring this part of the Third World into the twentieth century. The secondary purpose was to bring regional integration to the area and to promote greater information exchange and sharing, thereby stimulating the ever-expanding 'global village'.

The OAS funded the initiative and agreed to pay for the interconnection equipment: between 1991 and 1994 US $40,000 was spent on networking equipment in Jamaica alone. Any upgrading was to be paid for by the member universities. CUNet was originally composed of fourteen different countries. The initiative behind CUNet is to contemplate 'the integration of the Caribbean Region countries, regardless of political situations and cultural or linguistic aspects'. These countries include Antigua and Barbuda, Barbados, Bahamas, Belize, Dominica, Grenada, Jamaica, Puerto Rico, Dominican Republic, Saint Kitts and Nevis, Saint Lucia, Saint Vincent and the Grenadines, Suriname, and Trinidad and Tobago. Today a total of twenty-four Caribbean countries are involved, including Bermuda, Cayman Islands, Cuba, Guadeloupe, Guyana, Haiti, Martinique, Montserrat, Virgin Islands (British) and Virgin Islands (US).

E-mail

The first e-mail site was established at the University of Puerto Rico. CUNet is coordinated by the CRACIN (Corporation for the National Academic, Scientific and Research Network of Puerto Rico) and OAS along with other members. All twenty-four Caribbean sites dial into the

Puerto Rico station to relay and receive their e-mail messages. Today the University of the West Indies at Mona aspires to be an active internet site on its own, with First World links to the Sprint network in the United States.

Known commercially as the Convex* but more acceptably – and in admiring tones – as the Supercomputer, it represents the future of the University of the West Indies. The supercomputer arrived on 22 June 1992 with apparently little fanfare, perhaps because it was originally purchased for commercial digitizing. Within 300 metres of this supercomputer, on the outer perimeter of the university, is a shanty town bereft of running water, electricity and proper sanitary facilities. The university is subject to the occasional vagrant from the shanty town often searching for scraps of wood to repair his home. The campus is like a compound, a preserve for the few who can afford to be educated. The ring road, lined with cars, much as the wagons circled in a laager, is the first line of defence.

Jamaican e-mail has passed through three definite stages since 1991. In the first stage the single e-mail computer could be found near the principal's office and in the room of Keith Manison. Manison is the computer planning officer, an electrical and computer engineer and 'broad dreamer', appointed to make e-mail a functioning reality and who wants to see a computer at every office desk. The first e-mail computer was a PC donated to the university by Advanced Integrated Sytems. Software was supplied free by the OAS, and the modem was supplied by Manison himself to speed things up. When Manison took office in 1991 there was not one iota of computer infrastructure at the university. In order to send e-mail in the early days, one had to put one's message (assuredly academic!) into an ASCII file and leave the disk with him to be sent off.

E-mail was rudimentary and awkward, yet messages could be sent. But there was never any guarantee that they would be received efficiently. Faculty were beholden to Manison to retrieve and notify them of incoming messages. After a few short weeks, however, the computer had been moved to a small corner in the office, and faculty could work at the e-mail themselves. After nine months of this quasi-inaccessibility, the computer was moved to a more appropriate space, the Computer Science building, thus initiating the second stage.

Cool and air-conditioned, the Computer Science building was unlike most other buildings in Jamaica or at the university. It was easy to escape the heat, the life of the Third World and sit bewitched by this link to the heart of civilization. At one and the same time Jamaica seemed to offer a peculiar mix of sun, sand and aspirations towards high-class technology. But in Jamaica even technology suffers from that great tropical disease: the ideology of delay. Jamaicans dote on slowness – in the shopping queue, at the bank, and in opening offices. There is little, if anything, that functions

---

* Technically, it is a Convex 3440 with a 4 dual vector/scaler processor and 1 GByte of RAM and 28 GByte hard disk storage.

on time and efficiently. Life is simply – and is supposed to be – slower in a tropical paradise. Even e-mail messages appeared to be delayed.

For the whole of the university in 1993 there was only one terminal. Imagine the congestion at peak hours. Luckily faculty had some priority. But it was a good way to meet people, standing in a queue. . . . When I first arrived at the university in the mornings I remember reaching the Computer Science office before 8 a.m. in order to have the most uninterrupted minutes available to me. Forget about dialling into the university modem from your own computer. Forget about Internet and the immediate delivery of messages. Just write your message (you could use ASCII files) and wait for it to be sent out – within a few days. Once or twice a week someone in the Computer Science department would trigger the dial to Puerto Rico, where they have a satellite dish, and relay the message out via them. Delay lay at the heart of this system.

E-mail at this time was dependent on regular, undedicated phone lines. Each call to Puerto Rico is long distance and uses valuable credits allowed to the University by the Jamaica Telephone Company. If the Computer Science department used up its weekly quota, it could not send or receive mail; e-mailers would have to wait until their quota was restored. If there was an incoming call while e-mail messages were being sent out, all e-mail sending procedures would halt and operators would have to dial again. If the mail message was too large (i.e. too many pages) – either sending or receiving – it could block the line and prevent any other mail from entering the system. This happened in November 1993, and we were stuck with an unusual situation: we could send mail regularly, but we could only receive mail that was a week late, telling us about events that happened – in computer terms – in the Stone Age. It was as if e-mail had to go through customs on its way into the country. Fortunately that appears not to have been the case.

'E-mail seems to work everywhere but in Jamaica', correspondents complained. And there was not much privacy either. The computer terminal was at the end of a small, poorly lit room with the screen facing any onlooker's glances. Whenever the word 'love' or 'my dear . . .' appeared on screen one felt the pressure of a thousand prying eyes. Why not use a Valentine card? Because the post was staggeringly slow. How could a university lecturer embarrass him/herself with such 'hot' intimacies on the screen? Why was s/he not using the terminal for more 'cool' academic purposes? The cool language of networking seemed to under-estimate e-mail as an important personal device.

In the third stage, e-mail was linked to the supercomputer. Eventually all PCs on campus should be tied into a campus network. Manison envisages everyone with a terminal on their desk, and Internet at the high-school level. Another goal is to promote regional integration, so vital to a university whose campuses are hundreds of kilometres apart. Machines should be able to communicate with each other. Academics will be able to link interactively with overseas computers and download files on Internet

(File Transfer Process – FTP). Perhaps its most pedagogical use is for the UWI Distance Teaching Network, where all fourteen English speaking islands will be linked by Internet.

It has to be admitted that there is a certain irony about putting e-mail into Jamaica. Offices are now being wired up for e-mail when they don't even have phones. Presumably this is the solution to the tiresome problem of installing proper connections for them in the first place. The phone system at the university is archaic. In order to dial in or out (unless you have a rare direct line), you must dial through the university operator. The phone system involves long waits and frustrations and is often a fruitless exercise. While you may not be able to phone a local taxi, you can e-mail to New York for one!

Telecommunications in Jamaica are limited, as they are run by a monopoly, Jamaica Telecom, a subsiduary of Cable and Wireless, with little interest in upgrading. They have not invested in fibre optics anywhere in Jamaica. At most, they appear more interested in basic service. It takes at least three months to order a phone, if you are lucky. The solution, as I discovered, is to indicate on paper that you are prepared to spend large amounts of money on your monthly calls, whereupon a telephone is promptly delivered to your home.

At the level of senior political and telephone policy-makers – this was aired on an important public radio interview programme (and garnered from talks with the Convex computer engineers) – there seems to be tremendous confusion (unlike in North America) concerning the roles of 'voice' phones and 'data' phones. They seem not to realize that today's technology recognizes no difference between voice and data. The 1993–94 Jamaica telephone book is the first to mention fax machines, and its policy is 'to allow customer owned fascimile machines to be interconnected to the telelphone network'. In all cases the fax machine must be registered. In order to avoid the 'systems-cracking' craft of the Jamaican mind, all long-distance calls require the albatross of an ICAS (international call authorization system) code before the call can be made. This code can be activated or deactivated; in either case it requires a further password and a personal identification number, such as that from a passport. One must hide all documents when one deactivates the long-distance phone access and bring them out again for the next overseas call.

The ICAS code also frustrates the use of the fax message beyond the island. A computer with a fax facility, for example, cannot send an international fax because the computer dials the number too fast for the telephone, which is waiting for a special dial tone. Cellular phones too are allowed on the island but with each monthly bill the connection is terminated; presumably the Jamaica Telephone Company fears that 'mobile' users are apt to leave the country without paying their bill.

Another problem with the phone system is that there is no direct line to the modem pools from campus. It is easier to dial into the Convex from outside than from inside the campus: it is easier to get Convex connections from off campus even though the computer is on campus. Faculty – those who can afford them – are invited to bring their nice new computers on to campus, where they are even more likely to be stolen by budding cyberthieves.

A central dilemma is that Jamaica remains ill prepared for the computer age, something that requires technological support and software literacy. Jamaica is nowhere near achieving universality in primary and secondary education. A country which can hardly distinguish its patois from standard English – because schools here do not teach 'English' as a separate language – seems most poorly placed for the computer. This central problem in Jamaican culture leaves the country badly equipped to face the twenty-first century, and it figures very highly in the problems of higher education generally. All freshman students at the University of the West Indies (Mona) are required to complete a course in English grammar and language. Will the move to high computer technology polarize the national literacy problem? Will it create an elite of computer literates and an ever-growing mass of unlearned non-users?

This problem is avoidable at the Barbados and Trinidad and Tobago campuses, where English is taught in schools separately from patois. These campuses of the University of the West Indies do not have to ensure that their students are functionally literate in English. The Mona campus, situated on the site of the Mona slave plantation, appears to feel the need to struggle with the memories of the past, which is suitably ironic and postmodern.

This brings to mind another use for the supercomputer in a country so dominated by its memories. Simple file cards are an extension of mechanical writing and electronic sequencing. The revolution of the electronic memory has made its spectacular mark in the twentieth century. The acceleration in technology – and technological history – since the 1960s has facilitated the development of an automatic memory. Memories register data, and we can preserve the results. The memory of humans is considered fallible and unstable, whereas the memory of machines (following Pascal's invention) shows great stability. Will the computer become the repository of the island's collective memory (Le Goff 1988)? This could be deemed a positive benefit in bridging the gap between social classes.

Another problem is that the major e-mail users in Jamaica usually come from the First World, like myself. They are those who have experienced its delights in the industrialized nations. E-mail in Jamaica requires a major cultural shift and a huge educational programme in order to teach those born and bred in Jamaica to become more familiar with it. Native Jamaicans need to be taught, not to be intimidated, by the software and computers. The corollary of this problem is that most e-mail messages leave the Caribbean for the the United States and Europe and do not remain within the region. This suggests that there is currently very little regional communication, the very purpose for installing the network in the first place.

How effective is e-mail in the practical sense? How does this electronic interaction compare with the face-to-face reality of everyday life? When there was one terminal for the whole of campus those who waited to use it socialized in the ever-growing queue. We knew each other and we met regularly, almost daily. When the computer did not run fully, we abided by a set of artificial social relationships which no longer exists. Now, on the Convex, we no longer see each other, and know each other only by name as one of the list of users. There are about two hundred users at the university, and perhaps it is too early to tell how interaction is being shaped by the Convex, but it is agreed that users communicate more often among themselves than with non-users.

Most non-users seem surprised to learn that Jamaica has this advanced technology already installed. Those who first used e-mail on the Jamaican system would often call by phone to check if the recipient actually received the e-mail message. When I agreed to write this chapter I spoke with Jeremy Whyte, the technician behind the Convex and e-mail links. Using two of his e-mail addresses (one of which responded: 'no such user') I was unable to get an answer over two or three days. Was he overloaded with requests? Is it possible that when we are all on e-mail – and overloaded – we will have no communication at all? Was my message purged perfunctorily? Did the immediacy of the request force him to throw out the message, instead of putting it in a stack as one did with old letters? No, I had to walk to his office for face-to-face introductions and an interview. A Jamaican, he clearly enjoys his work and has pleasure in explaining it. He stuttered, and I could see in his thoughts: 'It is almost First World.' He was a man proud of his share of achievements, from ground level to e-mail in three short years.

E-mail is a hermetic pleasure in a land which avoids the hermetic. Offering release from the tedium of daily life by the elevation of the electronic senses, it is a blissful search for the unusual outside of the ever-present world of sunshine and beaches. This research paper was, for the most part, a tropically air-conditioned field study. If technology and its techniques are above all social productions, as Pierre Lemonnier argues, then how can we reconcile techniques of First World culture and Third World society (Lemonnier 1993: 2)?

This chapter has not been a study of the effects of technology on society; nor has it been an extensive search into how academic groups communicate with their new e-mail tools. Rather, it has been an examination of contradictions: simple tools like Jamaican taxi meters are non-existent because they have been unable to keep up with inflation. It is often impossible to understand the patois of a grocery clerk and it is often just as difficult to understand the technological words of Jeremy Whyte. Everyday life for many Jamaicans is so miserable that the advent of e-mail looks like just another misunderstood 'white-man thing'. Few native Jamaicans can use the e-mail beyond the Mona campus because they need to be off the island and to be sufficiently educated to get the appropriate contacts.

E-mail represents a significant advance for the university as a place on the margin in the Third World (which now outperforms Finland in networking) but it is also a political tool in a very polarized, hierarchical society. E-mail can only exacerbate the gulf between classes; while it may help to rationalize the telephone system at various locations, it will not help realize appropriate sanitary facilities. The financially comfortable will learn to speak with computer literacy while the poor will continue in their world apart, just next door. The juxtaposition of a certain 'cool running' with every conceivable type of social ill in this tiny island conjurs up images of postmodernism becoming ever more the Third Word computer chip blowout between 'marginal' slums and megabyte slickers.

Jamaica needs higher-level technology, but e-mail is too cool to bring about improvements in unemployment or other immediate social gains. It represents stronger links to the First World rather than the Third World. In Jamaica the breeze of the computer fan empties itself into an abyss of unrelenting everyday life. The mundane must be confronted. Staring into the radioactive glare of the monitor cannot be good for the eyes. But it must be done.

Epilogue

Since writing this chapter the author has returned to Canada where he is affiliated to the University of British Columbia. His use of e-mail has dwindled to nothing, given the fact that his new home university charges faculty and other users for all e-mail messages. The University of the West Indies, however, does not charge its users and pays about US $4,000 per month in telephone costs. The author's one remaining contact in Jamaica has a brand new modem but he does not know how to use it yet, apparently. Another contact (who never used e-mail on the island), now in England, has access to e-mail, still does not use it, or so it seems. The author is more electronically isolated in Canada than when he was in Jamaica.

Notes

The University of the West Indies can sound very tempting, especially to those who come from temperate climates. I answered one of the many advertisements UWI at Jamacia puts out for lecturers, hoping that I would find my place in the sun. Little did I know that it would be the 'cool runnings' that would both sustain and frustrate my stay on this tropical island. The author would like to thank Nick Saunders – who does not use e-mail – for his many ideas and suggestions.

1. Consider the toilet facilities in Whitfield Town, an inner city area of Kingston, where life is less than equitable. In 1982, the last available census, a mere 3 per cent of the 905 houses used a pit; and another 19 per cent used a WC not linked to a sewer; while 46 per cent used a WC linked to a sewer. Significantly, 32 per cent of the households did not identify their type of toilet facilities. This area is known for its sewers breaking down – and taking months to

repair. When there is a shortage of water, residents can be seen fetching it with pots and pans from the nearest primary school. If this is everyday life, albeit some of it statistically of a decade ago, how can Jamaica prepare for the technological age? I am grateful to Novlet Smith for supplying these census statistics (Smith 1993–94).

References

Galsworthy, John 1949. *The Forsyte Saga*, New York: Charles Scribner.

Le Goff, Jacques 1988. *History and Memory*, trans. Steven Rendall and Elizabeth Claman, New York: Columbia University Press.

Lemonnier, Pierre (ed.) 1993. *Technological Choices: Transformation in Material Cultures since the Neolithic*, London: Routledge.

Smith, Novlet 1993–94. 'An assessment of the contribution of the Canadian Jesuits to the social life of Whitfield Town Community in Jamaica, 1986–1993', Hons thesis, Caribbean Studies, University of the West Indies.

4

Is there a Body in the Net?

Katie Argyle and Rob Shields

'Cow' emoticon (Tilenius 1989)

Technology is often viewed as source of separation between people, a barrier. No longer do we meet in person, but we talk on the phone. We watch performances on television, we fax each other, and we communicate using computer modems hooked up over telephone lines. Conversations are held with distant and absent others (Shields 1992). Alienation and dehumanization. A separation of body and mind. Nonetheless, 'presence' doesn't just vanish. Technology mediates presence. Within computer communication technology, there are ways that allow us to be present to each other, with our bodies, interacting in a holistic manner.

Bodies cannot be escaped, for we express this part of ourselves as we experience together. Although some attempt to conceal the status of their bodies, it is betrayed unless we resort to presenting another kind of body in our communications. There is no loss of body in and through virtual reality technologies. While we may 'lose ourselves' in a good book or in the trance-like state of online interaction, we know that this is a change of consciousness: something in the mind, not the body. Not surprisingly, the simple dichotomies of online versus everyday life, of the virtual and the real have been the fodder of both the ecstatic boosters of computer-mediated communications and the dour critics of the time 'lost' to virtual simulations of neighbourhoods and to online interaction. Instead, bodies and everyday lived experiences are both the content of Internet communication (in the banality of the gossipy postings or the discussions of sex) and contiguous with its use (in the form of users' bodies). Internet itself is part of everyday life; it is part of the most banal aspects of social interaction.

Katie's experience

I started BBSing in August 1991. I called 'Technical Magic' (TM), my first 'board' or bulletin board service (BBS), with my computer's modem, over the telephone line.* My brother, who had just moved in with me, brought with him a computer. Before he got up in the morning, he turned the computer on. He was enraptured with this thing. He laughed a lot while using it. I thought he'd never make any friends in a new city if he stayed in the house all day on that thing. One day he announced he was meeting a group of people for drinks, and could I give him directions? I was baffled. 'Who are they?' I asked. 'They're on the computer, you know, the BBS. Told you Katie, you should try it, it's really fun.' I did. What persuaded me was the joy and the laughter and the relaxation of his body.

I am not familiar with the electronic. It is somehow unapproachable. I can't see the parts move. I feel no connection to it. I soon met a variety of users on the board (the **BBS**), complete with pseudonyms, and had become intimate with them through the **Chat** mode; a private channel where you can talk about anything and everything. Sex, sadness, elation: the important trivialities which make everyday life are opportunities for contact, for people to make themselves felt-presences to others, translating themselves from absent and abstract computer addresses into engaged interlocutors. Online I was myself, pseudonym **Kitty**, and could have easily presented myself as one or several other fantasized personae. Many people trusted this 'other' that I gave them of myself, and they revealed parts of themselves to me in turn. What we exchanged was *real*. I felt it in my body that they were honest about the facts of their lives, their confusions, their dreams, as I was. I was very concerned with being authentic and true to my real self via this electronic persona I was projecting, though I could not resist using the cover to heighten aspects of myself that I thought a bit inappropriate in person.

Each area, each selection on the menu, of the BBS offered something to do; but for me, it was the interaction, the intrusion into my world, my line of vision, of an other sending me a message that I had to respond to, decipher within my body as to whether this should be dealt with or ignored, and to try to filter the reality from the masks. It was as captivating as my brother told me, and the world in there was huge.** All I needed was the

---

* I called the board one morning in August. Feeling very sick with a high fever, alone at home, I entered what was a new world for me: an alternate world occupied by many individuals though I could not see their bodies. Not knowing what I was doing, I tried everything. I got frustrated with the computer stuff, the codes of language that were required in order to manoeuvre through that place, but people were sending me messages. The screen was *moving* and I wasn't doing it. I could only react to the stimulus they presented, and answer the questions, and question if it was real . . . could this be possible? I felt palpably weird. It was as if every idea that I had about communication, about speaking, about writing and being heard in what I say, was in question. The sheer strangeness of these others, curious to discover who I was, another user on their computer screens, heightened my need to understand.

** Once, we visited the Bulletin Board's office. We were led up a carpeted staircase. I trailed behind, wondering what this would do to my perception of the BBS world. What would I find? I thought it's got to be huge, like those big spewing smoking machines, but it's a computer, so . . . it's small, not too small, and probably there are three or four of them. I was sure that the system must have at least these many parts to contain us all, the users,

language to allow me to move at will, and the courage to test what I felt, to say what I meant, and to allow this from others.

Like Technical Magic (TM) and other BBSs like Prodigy and Compuserve or even Internet generally, typical options are offered to the user, often in the form of a menu: games, special interest forums, registry, electronic mail and teleconference. It is in teleconference that individuals interact with each other as if they were having a conversation. Users type in what they want to say on their keyboard, and it is transmitted to the other users in teleconference, so everyone can see what you are saying and respond to it or not. In this manner interaction occurs amongst groups of individuals.

Teleconference appears as a section of the board, even if its reality is just a branch program being run which focuses on real-time interaction between users. Other options enhance your experience there. All users have access to an 'action list' comprised of action words to aid communication between users. The words are inserted into conversation to help express what the user is trying to convey. If we are trying to express our emotions, and to read the state of the others involved, how will it be possible in an environment that seems to separate us from each other in a physical sense?

Generic actions

Emotions are expressed through behaviour including 'vocal qualities, body movements, and facial expressions' (Sdorow 1990: 363) None of these elements can be used during a conversation in teleconference.

> These restrictions pose a dilemma to the users of a system that must be overcome. Communication researchers looking at computer mediated communication (CMC), have noted that users have adapted to the medium. It has been described as an altered state of communication . . . CMC may change the psychology and sociology of the communication process itself . . . CMC may very well be neither conversational nor written, but a 'new linguistic entity with its own vocabulary, syntax and pragmatics'. (Rice and Love 1987: 86)

One avenue to creative self-expression on TM is the **action list**. These words can be used as written expressions of body movements and/or functions, including facial expression and vocal intonation. Many of the words given in the list have as a primary focus an action that puts them in physical contact with another user. For example the words **squeeze, hug,**

---

one and others, within its physical boundaries. 'Well Kitty, here it is . . .' Where? My brother was oooing and ahhing and saying it was amazing. I was looking around. There was nothing big here, nothing. I saw a computer that looked like the rectangular box that my monitor sits on, but there wasn't even a monitor. They gestured for me to take a look. Look at what?

nibble, tickle, all cause the computer to ask me who I want to do this to. Other words such as **smile, frown, grin, smirk**, are directly related to facial expression, while **groan, cry, snicker** or **sigh** give clues to how I would say the words I have placed on the screen.

Could users, in this way, place physical elements into their encounters with each other? Would these words have the same effect upon the user as face-to-face contact? To take action words one step further, most tele-conference systems offer 'generic actions', or GAs for short. The easiest way to think of a GA is to replace the initials with the user's name. TM is a commercial BBS. When users become paid members, they are allowed to have generic actions, otherwise they are limited to the action list. GAs are a very popular feature, and much sought after. A GA allows a user to move their electronic body as they choose. '**ga is just playing . . .**' tells the others that I am moving about in this type of manner, or that my attitude is playful, giving them clues as to what I am feeling as I write/respond to the conversation. With action words, the computer has a predetermined expression that is given when a word is selected, but a GA leaves this up to the user. If a user types,

handshake Kitty

as another user named **Rubber** did to me, everyone would see:

Rubber is shaking hands with Kitty

while I would see,

Rubber is shaking hands with you,

and when I return the handshake, I type, '**handshake Rubber**', and I see,

. . . Shake, shake.

representing my body touching **Rubber**'s and shaking hands. In these ways the presence of the body most obviously appears. Body actions and corporeal engagements scroll by on the screen minute by minute: **Rubber shakes hands with Kitty; Snakeman blows a kiss to River; Fido winks to Rubber**; and I type, '**grin Rubber**' to introject not just words or commands but a *gesture* and so further animate the scene of personae, and sometimes obey my own stage directions. The screen responds,

Smile

And, spontaneously, I do.

Although technology has a mediating power – and it sometimes doesn't work: the system crashes and communication stops – the communicative interaction is not 'in' the machinery. It is rather shared between persons and interpreted by each interactant. We experience the system through our bodily systems, and we exchange this experience with others through the communication of the network. The traces of others are carried within us physically as we experience together.*

Could this electronic network hold the physical and the intellectual elements of human beings at the same time? Was it a myth that we are separate from the machine, the computer; that it is cold, hard, circuitry that cannot be penetrated by the user? That it mediates us, not we it? Or could there be a way that individuals leave bits of themselves on the system, to communicate, and enhance our presence, leaving lures to catch the attention of another even while we carry on with our day-to-day lives. And, in such exchanges and postings, do we not bring all of ourselves to the task of communication, unable to separate the body from the mind, the physical from the intellectual, the head from the heart? Are we whole, or do we withhold parts for when we gather in the flesh?

Some of course do, fetishizing the body and turning 'flesh-meets' into mere embodied footnotes to the dialogical interaction on Internet. It becomes possible to foresee a day when face-to-face bodily encounters are reserved for those moments when the body is absolutely necessary: medical examinations and operations, insemination and sexual events in which touch and bodily contact will have become fetishes. But is such a dystopic vision likely?

Hotchats

The bulletin board service called Technical Magic is a meeting place for individuals. There are computer interactive games, electronic mail services, special interest forums devoted to specific topics of interest, as well as teleconference services allowing system users, or 'users', to talk to each other at the same time. The main focus of Technical Magic is entertainment, conversation, social activity and interaction.

BBSing, as this activity is called, would seem to be very cut and dried. Write a message, leave it, someone else reads it, they post a reply, and so

---

* They opened the body of the machine and pointed to something in there. What? Nothing was moving . . . I couldn't see anything. I was searching for this place, this space that was so huge, so boundless, and looking for all the people I had met there . . . where were they? I could see no traces of their bodies here . . . surely there had to be more. Bravely I admitted I couldn't see 'it'. They pulled out a flat greenish-grey rectangle, maybe two inches square at the most. It had circuits on it, electronic components, and numbers, and lines, and they further directed my attention to one small part, one chip. That was it, they said, that was the heart of the BBS. The heart? It didn't beat, didn't move . . . I could not fathom the two realities. This chip, no bigger than a dime, was responsible for my new world? This is where the bodies of those others, and of mine, were held?

The material, the physical environment of the electronic system was insignificant compared to my experience of the BBS. Indeed, thinking about it seemed very disturbing. The presence of the 'alternative reality' was an anticlimax. Its 'exterior' didn't compare to what it was like when experienced electronically from the inside. I knew, that if this chip was not where we all were, then the experience was in me. And in the others. We all hold the board within ourselves.

on. Deliberate steps, one after the other. An ordered sequence. Nothing required other than to read and to enter a reply to the system via a computer keyboard. The only physical contact being the writer/responder touching the keyboard to create the words that enter the screen. No physical contact with the person being written to. What is the purpose of the communication? Why do we write? To touch someone else; to communicate; to give of ourselves. Are we really able to eliminate physicality so easily, or does the system give us pathways that are wide enough for us to leave parts of our physical selves to help reach each other?

Technical Magic, the Ottawa BBS described above, only allowed twelve callers to be on the computer system at the same time. It has now been supplanted by larger and more sophisticated boards such as the National Capital Freenet in Ottawa. One of the world's largest public access, non-commercial computer services, this allows numerous simultaneous callers to connect via telephone and even more via the Internet. Freenet is a community initiative based on computing facilities at Carleton University in Ottawa. Other Freenets include Cleveland and Victoria, British Columbia with the idea being duplicated in many cities. A Freenet BBS encompasses all levels of the community with access to the system set up in public places like libraries, schools (all levels), and shopping malls. Other Freenets exist in Youngstown, and Cleveland, Ohio, in Victoria, British Columbia, and future sites will be erected in California, Finland and New Zealand, to name a few. There are over 70,000 active subscribers linked to innumerable others distributed throughout the world on other branch networks of Internet. However, the principles and options are the same on both systems. The idea of such a vast communications net, with links to the world, and free access to the user is hard to fathom. Only the geographic distribution of Internet emphasizes the differences between users who are typically students or researchers who access the Internet through the mainframe computers and computer communications links paid for and maintained by universities, government offices and companies. Typically, Internet has flourished because users could make personal use of computers and e-Mail facilities which are paid for at a bulk rate rather than a charge-per-use basis. Economically there is no difference between one message a day and one million messages a day. The crucial difference between current computer communications systems is that they function on a continuous 24-hour basis rather than as message-sending devices which access communications networks only as needed, like telephone and teletype. Furthermore, much of the physical infrastructure such as satellite and microwave transmission networks is often funded by state research and development grants. The major cost is the installation of the necessary cables and local-area networking of computers in an institution's buildings.

Teleconference allowed two users to enter **Chat**. One user will invite the other to 'chat', and the invitation is accepted or rejected. If the answer is yes, the pair find themselves in a private section, where whatever they type to each other appears on the screen as they are typing it. There are no delays between when you finish a sentence and when you see it. A slow typist is a frustrating experience, as you can see them searching for the letters to complete a word, or backspacing to erase bad spelling (appearances count even here), and chances are you already know what they are trying to say.

No one else is allowed entry to this space while the two of you are there. For this reason, **hotchats** are held here. Hotchatting is using the **chat** mode to talk to each other about sexual fantasies, with each other in the past, present or future. The language is detailed, graphic and expressive, to try to transmit sexual activity over the computer. An article in an issue of *Mondo 2000*, a magazine dedicated to exploring the 'new edge' of popular culture, oriented towards the computer literate, gives a description of online sex:

> Why, you might ask, would any sane person drool over typed text on a crummy low-res monitor? . . . You see: on any adult BBS the Desired One is waiting – guaranteed . . . The good part of online surreality is that you may meld to the psychic core of that other living, breathing tax-paying person in Kalamazoo . . . (Petrek and St Jude 1992: 114)

You might feel as if you are having sex, in your body, forgetting that there is a computer mediating the encounter. Hotchats, as I have experienced them, have left me with all the emotions and physical arousal of a sexual act, but when it is over, my sense of aloneness is heightened. To break the connection seems more painful than fulfilling.

Emoticons

In electronic mail and postings to Usenet groups and special interest forums, users do not interact with each other; instead, they are responding to ideas left by others on specific topics, or in forums with a pre-determined subject, from *Star Trek* episodes to a particular programming language, or Harley-Davidson motorcycles. Private correspondence with specific individuals are held via electronic mail. These are responses which only the addressee will see. In forums, anyone can answer, and all will see the response. Here there are no action commands to express the state of the writer at the time of the post. Instead, other avenues have been utilized to express meaning at a deeper level.

Communicators add words in brackets to denote voice inflection, or body movements appropriate to the message. In an exchange between users on TM, Midnight-Black Wolf writes to Sindara that he is not sure what to answer to a request, pressing the point by adding,

> <shrug>

after suggesting she 'do' his driveway in exchange for a modem. Her reply is,

> Dunno. I don't do driveways..(LAUGH).

The bracketed words bring the body into the exchange, punctuating conversation with an action. Emoticons are another way that physical expression is captured on the computer net. *PC Magazine*, in its August 1992 edition, in an article entitled 'PC Magnet', explains emoticons as follows,

> An emoticon is an emotional icon, or a pictorial expression of the emotions of the moment. These are most commonly created on one line using the symbols on the keyboard. (Fudpucker 1992: 557)

Emoticons are read sideways. :) is two eyes and a smiling mouth. :> is a variation of the smile.* Why have these emoticons, bracketed expressive words, action words and GAs appeared on TM and other BBSs? They are not isolated events, but are used with regularity during communication. The type of communication that is found on TM, especially in teleconference, is very fluid, evolving, and in the moment. Computers are known for their state-of-the art, up-to-date reputation, with little tolerance for outmoded equipment. This attitude is reflected in the talk found on the system. There is a flow to the discussions, one sentence leading into the next, sparking the response of one or another.

The flow

Where does the flow come from? It starts in the body of one user, mediated through others, who are witnesses to the words placed into their presence. Perhaps a flowing expressiveness is the natural way for us to reach each other: a dialogical mixing of bodies occurring regularly, with a lack of boundaries when we meld together during talk. Desire circulates in the form of queries expressing users' curiosity, in 'flames' expressing spontaneous judgement, in the infectuous witicisms by which users respond to each other, and perhaps most important, the downloadable images of porn stars and celebrities.

Luce Irigaray, in her book, *This Sex Which Is Not One* (1985) argues for a way of speaking with the body and a theory of language which includes it. The body does not disappear when people exchange thoughts, words and feelings but is present always. There is a multiplicity in communication, without the polarities of you and me. Instead what occurs is a mixing of all, at all levels of our existence. In this way, there would be no separation between communicators. TM, and its computer environment, would not be a barrier, for whenever people come together to speak, there can be no one or an other, but a multiple of layers, a multiplicity, that forms the experience for the whole, including the physical, which cannot be sifted out.

---

* There are lists of emoticons that are freely available on the net (ewtilen@pucc.BITNET). Variations place symbolic bodies on the screen, even those of cows (see p. 102).

We never separate simply: a single word cannot be pronounced, produced, uttered by our mouths. Between our lips, yours and mine, several voices, several ways of speaking resound endlessly, back and forth. One is never separable from the other. (Irigaray 1985: 209)

As she says, a single word cannot be produced by our mouths; our bodies cannot function and stay separate if we wish to be understood (pronounce), to be creative (produce), and to be heard (utter). When we are together (between our lips), there are several voices, and several avenues for the multiple voices we have, including the physical voice and what it may add. These encounters have a life of their own, back and forth, a mixing of all the participants on all levels. This type of communication must be fluid enough to encompass subtle shifts amongst the users and to respond, always changing to keep pace.

The result is a mixing of voices so that the conversation is literally 'many voiced' or heteroglossic. Computer-mediated communication is similarly many-voiced, made up of intersecting dialogues which are the sum of the inputs of each participant, but where the final product is controlled by no single user. Research on computer (tele)conference messages indicated 'a stream of consciousness flow of thoughts',

that exhibited creativity and spontaneity . . . and experienced users develop an ability to express missing nonverbal cues in written form. (Rice and Love 1987: 88, 89)

Nonverbal cues or body language? There is an ability to transmit the body in the writing itself, according to some researchers. Adding to the idea of stream of consciousness writing, with its endless movement from one thought to the next, is Irigaray, using the metaphor of lips in action, of 'two lips kissing two lips', or bodies meeting, sharing together. She says there is no end to what occurs between us, no limits. 'Between us the house has no wall . . .'. There are no barriers when we speak, we always mix with each other. 'When you kiss me, the world grows so large that the horizon itself disappears.' We are all-consumed by our activities together, without an end in sight; just movement (Irigaray 1985: 210).*

Henri Bergson also argues for a multiplicity of expression. In *Matter and Memory* (1978), he writes that memories may not live in the past: indeed the past is gone as a construct, and what we have is a now. In our perception of the moment, memory comes to life through our activity as a self that draws on the whole of our experiences: 'Every perception fills a

---

* Irigaray's comment that the world grows so large when we speak is how I felt upon entering the world of TM, and my perception that the actual physical environment of the BBS had to be huge, a big machine, or several smaller ones linked together, to contain the world that has no end. This would also explain the strange feelings I had when my perception was proved wrong, and the BBS was a small chip. The reality of the chip did not match the reality I had felt. It also corresponds to the anonymous hotchatter in the *Mondo 2000* article, whose goal was to pass through and meld with someone, which is possible if there are no walls. The constant movement, the fluidity of conversation, and the flow of bodies in communication all argue for the presence of bodies on the net. But how else could the body appear?

certain depth of duration, prolongs the past into the present, and thereby partakes of memory' (Bergson 1978: 325).

If the present partakes of memories, then when someone writes of an event that has saddened them, and they add :(to the end of the statement, do we not then 'see' the sad face, hear the sad words and possibly feel sad along with the writer? Or, when Skipper writes that,

... I am a dirty old man sometimes ... <grin>,

can we not 'see' the lecherous grin and feel what this person would be like, drawing upon our memories of encounters with individuals of this type?

To be in the present, writing, speaking and perceiving in the moment, is to be able to respond, to be active in the now. The present, writes Bergson, 'is that which acts on us and which makes us act, it is sensory and it is motor; – our present is above all, the state of our body' (1978: 320).

The state of our body

In teleconference, in forums and electronic mail, we write in the present. We are acting upon words that make our body move to respond, and which in turn cause others to do the same. The body has resources and multiple levels to draw from when acting, including memories, that help us to identify what we are feeling, and what we would like to convey. It is a whole expression that seeks to convey the whole picture, including the physical state from where it originates, in order to communicate accurately with others. This is not an activity that stops and starts, but it is continuous, for there are always encounters in our environments causing us to react to their presence. How else may we see the emoticons, the words in brackets, the generic actions and the action words? Perhaps they are clues that lead us back to ourselves, back to our bodies to try to understand what it is that a person is trying to say. What more may be contained in the words written? Jane Gallop, in *Thinking through the Body* (1988), writes of Barthes and his work on photography, *Camera Lucida* (1981) that the photograph has a '*studium*', which is the 'theme or subject of the picture, what the photographer is trying to say, but it also has to do with ideas and general culture' (1988: 151). Although this may be interesting, it is a second element, which breaks through the *studium*, that is not in the representation, but something more, that catches his attention: 'it goes off from the scene, like an arrow, and pierces me' (Gallop 1988: 151).

She calls this the *punctum*; it is the part that reaches us: 'I animate it and it animates me' (Gallop 1988: 154). It makes us react with movement. There is a mixing of the viewer and the other that is both within the photograph and outside of its boundaries. We look, and we enter the scene and it enters us, it pierces our bodies. It is this sense of something more that causes a desire to try to find it, to seek it out. The idea of the representation 'works the same for the book, the screen and the picture'

(Gallop 1988: 151). I believe we can also apply it to computer-mediated conversation, for it appears on a screen, has pictorial elements, and text. In this space we confront the paradoxes of 'dependence and independence, nature and art, nature and the real, what I add and what is there already, what animates me and what I animate' (Gallop 1988: 160). The multiple layers of interaction, of giving and receiving, are clearly evident in her words. She gives from every aspect of herself to 'this space', and receives more to continue the process.

There is a strong desire in the users of TM and of Internet for the physical. I have noted on many occasions that new users will leave the system if they do not participate in 'events' that bring them together in a social setting to meet each other in person. Also, due to the use of pseudonyms, and the inability to physically check whether the gender that you present on the board is consistent with your physical body, users often ask each other if they have met the new user. Often, there will be mistrust as to whether this user is 'real' until there has been physical verification. This also happens when a user has multiple pseudonyms, with varying genders. Physical contact is the determining factor of reality.*

If we could eliminate the body, then maybe we wouldn't need to be face to face. But the need for face-to-face contact suggests that the body – ours and theirs – is a central stake in our, so-called, virtual neighbourhoods.

A physical encounter has often translated within my experience into a greater willingness to use emoticons and bracketed expressions on the BBS with users that I have met in person. Although I do employ these physical elements with users I have never met, it is with less frequency and spontaneity. Several electronic encounters may be required to build up the level of trust that allows deeper communication.

If we believe that the body must be present in a physical sense to be a factor amongst individuals, that there is separation, and that we can communicate from one level without other levels being present, then it will be very difficult to find physicality on a computer net. The body is not there. The screen, keyboard and monitor are physically in contact with the user, with the flesh up against barrier after barrier. But if we argue for a multiplicity, multiple layers of being, a way to be in the body at all times, to express the whole of the person so there can be no separations, and we view the human as an extremely creative entity wishing to touch its fellows, then how can we eliminate the physical at all?

---

* I had felt that the idea of events was particular to boards like TM that are primarily social gatherings. However, I attended a meeting of the university and community-sponsored National Capital Freenet Project, an information session to discuss further development of the Freenet. Despite the technology that permits it, Dave Sutherland, facilitator of the meeting, said, 'We will hold a meeting the first Tuesday of every month, so we can keep in contact with each other.'

    Did he mean physical contact? I asked him about the statement, and he replied that 'People seem to come out for face-to-face things, though we shouldn't need them, given the media.'

As Ann Game asserts:

> . . . experience need not be equated with presence. Once we think of mediations as constitutive, as having immediacy in the body, 'experience', understood here as unconscious, marked by memory traces and bodily, becomes central to the critique of presence. (Game 1991: 147)

Memory traces, called up by the body, parts of the body themselves, allow us to experience with our physical selves and all the other multiple layers that constitute us in ways that do not require us to be in the flesh. I believe that we meet in the flesh to satisfy our desires to be together, but we also deposit physical bits along the pathways of the BBS that have been made wide enough by the users themselves. For it is the users who have created emoticons, bracketed expressions, a need for GAs and action words. I have only been able to touch on elements of the BBS that could use further study, such as pseudonyms, events, sexual encounters, and the desire for these. Indeed, desire for electronic encounters could occupy many studies. By showing that there are multiple layers in an electronic network, perhaps I have also shown that it is a rich landscape whose fascination is not due to the technology itself, but to the people who have made that technology their own.

> Speak, all the same. . . . . You touch me all over at the same time. In all senses. (Irigaray, 1985: 209)

References

Barthes, R. 1981. *Camera Lucida*, trans. R. Howard, New York: Hill.

Bergson, Henri 1978. *Matter and Memory*, New York: Humanities Press, Inc.

Fudpucker, Orville 1992. 'PC Magnet', *PC Magazine*, 14: 557.

Gallop, Jane 1988. *Thinking Through the Body*, New York: Columbia University Press.

Game, Ann 1991. *Undoing the Social*. Toronto: University of Toronto Press.

Irigaray, Luce 1985. *This Sex Which Is Not One*. New York: Cornell University Press.

Petrek, Melissa and St Jude 1992. 'Putting It On The Line', *Mondo 2000*, 6: 113–15.

Rice, Donald E. and Love, Gail 1987. 'Electronic Emotion', *Communication Research*, 14: 85–108.

Sdorow, Lester 1990. *Psychology*. Iowa: Wm. C. Brown Publishers.

Shields, R. 1992. 'Truant proximity: presence and absence in the space of modernity', in *Environment and Planning D: Society and Space*, 10(2): 181–98.

5

A Geography of the Eye: The Technologies of Virtual Reality

Ken Hillis

Prologue

The current wave of interest in the phenomenon of cyberspace is heightened by promoters describing it as a new frontier, one open to exploration as well as colonization. Within the academy, and often just barely removed from the commercial hype, it has been conceived as 'a globally networked, computer-sustained, computer-accessed, multi-dimensional, artificial or "virtual" reality' (Benedikt 1992: 122). To date, no single technology or machine circumscribes this emerging technology/ medium of virtual reality (VR) – a term confusingly interchanged with cyberspace but here understood as the technical means of access to the 'parallel', disembodied and increasingly networked visual 'world' named cyberspace. An increasing variety of virtual technologies offers windows on to this cyberspatial environment that also has been defined as one in which the user feels *present* (Biocca 1992a: 6), yet where things have no physical form and are composed of electronic data bits and particles of light.

Do cyberspace and VR have a *moment* of invention, do they represent a decisive break that sets them apart from TV and telephony from which they are partly cobbled, imagined and extended? Where might an account of the cultural trajectory informing the electro-mechanics of VR arbitrarily begin, given that much of the 'buzz' surrounding it is concerned with asserting its novelty, thereby to author and secure its future, rather than acknowledging a past? Much interesting writing about cyberspace and VR assumes the technology as a given. However it is useful to examine the human agency that makes this technology possible. What follows is an attempt to do so, a narrative informed by three assumptions, first, that the technology represents an instance of an ongoing (Western) motivation to alter conceptions of space; second, that its development is inflected by a desire on the part of a disembodied, alienated subjectivity for transcendence

The author would like to thank Bob Sack, Paul Couillard, and Rob Shields, editor, for their valuable comments on earlier drafts, and to acknowledge the support of the Social Sciences and Humanities Research Council of Canada (SSHRC).

of bodily limits; and third, that this cybernetically achieved transcendence – as reflected in the 1980s cyberpunk desire to leave the body or 'meat' behind and float as pure data in cyberspace – is also a vehicle for merging a hyper-individuated modern consciousness into a larger whole.[1]

My decision to treat VR as a machine to realize such desires for bodily transcendence (see note 12) is not intended to promote any particular metaphysics, though I do believe that many current materialist analyses of the technology miss the mark in failing to address the importance of metaphysics to virtual consumers. Though military advantage, followed closely by global financial and data services, drives VR's invention, appeals to metaphysics, however subtle, remain important in promoting the technology. Such appeals would fail if they did not tap a pervasive cultural longing. Key VR inventors themselves evince various aspects of this yearning – often cloaked in a belief in progress. Geographer Eric Sheppard (1993: 4, 12) finds that no single path determines technological develop-ment; information technologies are composed not only of machinery but also of the institutional and intellectual infrastructures that invent, deliver and package them. What follows tries to keep Sheppard's caveat in mind. I offer a necessarily selective and critical review. I agree with David Depew (1985) that history is criticism. A narrative history of VR is somewhat ironic given the technology's tendency to foreclose narrative/time in favour of spectacle/space, a consideration taken up in the discussion of science fiction below.

The roots of yearning for a virtual world are anchored by an ongoing Western belief in vision as the most noble organ and sensual metaphor for *extending* understanding. This belief has helped set the stage for an emblematic virtual world of visual language that promises 'transcendence' and affectivity in images, something denied us to date by our physical embodiment. Imaginary transcendence is made more desirable by a rational/empirical system of belief and knowledge organization that denies holism between mind and body, one in which mind centres meaning, and partitions itself from the body, which is then judged an artifact, hence worth superseding. At least since Descartes this dynamic has operated on an imaginative level. VR extends this in suggesting that surpassing bodily limits might now incorporate a spatial dimension.

The late medieval crisis of confidence and faith experienced by 'Euro-peans' following the débâcle of the Crusades helped ferment an intellectual re-evaluation of certain fundamental attitudes undergirding medieval Christian belief. Whereas if 'in the beginning was the Word', Samuel Edgerton (1975) suggests that a shift towards the privileging of vision as a metaphor for understanding/truth arose during this era, along with a demand for the development of a more powerful science of explanation and conquest of nature. As artifacts such as the Hereford and Ebstorf *Mappaemundi* (maps of the world) reveal, medievals possessed adequate vision, though it was arguably a more 'synaesthetic' or place-inflected one than is the case today (see Barfield 1977; Ong 1977). The purer form of vision based on Euclidean geometric principles that Roger Bacon, for example, proposed, was intended to provide a less sensually cluttered access to Divine inspiration in face of loss by Crusaders to the Infidel, one interpreted by Christian thinkers as resulting from a failure of devotional technique and the subsequent 'faulty access' to God's instruction and command. Roger Bacon's *Opus Majus*, written during the 1260s, entreats papal authority to redirect intelligent Christian inquiry/entreaty in accord with a *visionary perspective*. Placing vision directly on an axis of truth, Bacon recommends elevating the status of geometry as a means of accessing

> the *ineffable* beauty of the divine wisdom . . . [so that] after the restoration of the New Jerusalem we should enter a larger house decorated with a fuller glory. Surely the mere vision perceptible to our sense would be . . . more beautiful since we should see in our presence the form of our truth, but most beautiful since aroused by the visible instruments we should rejoice in contemplating the spiritual and literal meaning of Scripture. (Edgerton 1975: 18; emphasis mine)

If Divine wisdom – the Word – was unspeakable, then perhaps mortals instead might elevate the status of Logos' *depiction*. Bacon seeks to meld geometry with vision. In a sense, the history of vision in western culture is a history of how sight has been colonized by mathematics and number. Geometry is a visual language. Bacon wishes to enhance vision with geometry to make it more Divine, but what he really is doing is breaking vision down into mathematics. Depicting God's Word more purely through use of representational geometric 'picture language' is an abstract activity inheriting much from a disembodying Platonic correspondence theory of truth. Only when seekers of knowledge emerge from Plato's Cave freed of their 'corporeal shackles' can they attain the lucid and ideal realm of 'active thought'. Then they may experience clear vision of real things only present to the 'mind's eye' (Heim 1993: 88).

Bacon was not the first to recognize the power of vision, as the exit from Plato's metaphoric Cave makes clear. In his *Metaphysics*, Aristotle had argued that '[Seeing], most of all the senses, makes us know and bring to light many differences between things' (Brenneman *et al.* 1982: 79). Ptolemy's *Geographia* – a culmination of this early (and quite modern) geographer's efforts to represent a systematized relationship between the different features of the earth – is evidence of a second-century AD optical understanding of the world, as are Al-Kindi's and Al-Hazen's theories of optics from the eighth and ninth centuries AD (see Lindberg 1976).

More recently, Heidegger notes that the propensity of visual perception is *curiosity* – a state of desiring inquisitiveness that may be contrasted to the more meditative state of *wonder*, and a trait of immense value, one becoming to the analytical, logical Western science that Bacon may be seen to call for, and one that later techniques such as Renaissance perspective painting appear to engage with and build upon, and which even today helps direct the 'shape' of virtual vision. Heidegger notes that, depending on emphasis in translation, *theoria* means either vision and/or truth, as in a watching over truth (1977: 163–4). As VR theorist Frank Biocca makes clear, as a technology, VR,

> is being refined so that it comes closer and closer to optimally matching the parameters needed for powerful perceptual illusions in each sensory channel . . . [w]e live in a visual culture...when we want information, we '*look* into it' . . . it is not surprising that a significant part of virtual reality development has tried to create better illusions for our eyes. (1992b: 30–1)

Linguist Benjamin Whorf speaks directly to Roger Bacon's argument. 'It is as though European speech tries to make time and feelings visible, to constrain them to possess spatial dimensions that can be pointed to, if not measured' (Whorf 1952 cited in Tuan 1977: 393). Seeing is relatively objective. It does not involve the emotions deeply (Tuan 1974). One sees as an onlooker. Visual perception is more abstracted than the other senses. A conception of space, though not entirely reliant on the eye (one may imagine an acoustical space or the intimate environment of touch) nevertheless, in the West, is tied to vision. As Tuan notes, visual space is bounded and static, a frame or matrix for objects. Visual space is the farthest removed from our bodily sense and covers the largest 'area' experienced by any sense (Tuan 1977: 399). 'In particular, attendance to the purely visual region in the distance excludes awareness of the affective region [closer to the body]' (ibid.: 400). We gaze into a distant and open future. 'What is ahead is what is not yet – and beckons' (ibid.). This 'forward' direction of vision Tuan also detects in the 'space' of progress – a conceptual destination that, I would suggest, was sought by Bacon both in his need to put the Crusades débâcle 'behind' him and in his need for renewed spiritual 'direction'.

Bacon's papal correspondence is a call for what VR theorist and promoter Howard Rheingold (1991: 69) labels the age-old quest for 'intellectual augmentation'. However conceived, this enduring wish has called upon a variety of communications practices in its quest to take on greater meaning and form. Today this means telematics or information technology (IT) – the synthesis of telephony and digital computation. It can be argued that VR, by blending visual communication with mechanisms that allow human gestures to be read by machines, is part of this will towards intellectual augmentation, which in the West has been defined as a *good* since at least the time of Bacon, if not Plato. But if for Bacon, the beauty of Divine wisdom remained ineffable (and it should not be assumed he ever meant this beauty to be approximated in speech), VR proposes that the 'ambiguity of invisible meanings that attends audio speech [will be] replaced by the unambiguous topology of meanings beheld, [that] we will truly *see* what we mean' (McKenna 1991: 232). Reduction, McKenna seems to say, is revelation. Extrapolating from Heidegger's etymological distinction noted above, VR extends visual theory in the sense of extending the purview of truth-as-vision.

Bacon's thirteenth-century papal entreaty offers an arbitrary departure point for the progressive elevation of vision's status in the 'West' – an elevation that sets the stage for the visually-referent communications technologies that follow.[2] At first these are print-based, alphabetic support for an individualized narrative of progressive selves. Yet in the (re)turn towards more iconic visual languages for the depiction of information, there is an echo of a pre-Baconian, medieval way of grasping reality. Both print-based and more purely visual 'languages' or 'picture writing' in which messages *seem* detached from words (see Bolter 1991: 46) depend on optics and the eye, yet picture writing's telematic manifestation may mark something of a return to a less linear, hence apparently more synaesthetic grasping of experiential reality. In order to achieve 'intellectual augmentation' virtually, VR proposes we merge with the object of our gaze that until now has kept us as modern subjects at its beck and call, alternatively enraging us to conquer it as an object or to worship it as God.

Early flight simulation and computation devices

Almost as soon as World War II began, the US government funded development of flight simulators. The research was difficult and time consuming, yielding truly successful results only in 1960, in time for the American space programme. Yet by 1940 it had already been more than a generation since the first major air accident had occurred in 1908 during a trial flight for the American War Department. Flight's power and danger made a training machine to safely simulate it desirable, and designs had been patented as early as 1910 (Woolley 1992: 42). In 1930 Edwin Link patented the Link trainer. In this early version, the pilot entered a mock-up cockpit equipped with controls through which a plane's pitch, roll and yaw could be mimicked. Link's machine, with its pneumatic devices and early hydraulic servomechanisms, was sufficiently evolved to imitate movements experienced in flight, as well as the sensation or force transmitted through physical contact with the joystick.

As Woolley recounts, during the 1930s the breakthrough research of Vannevar Bush had permitted the mechanization of differential equations that were to allow the mathematical modelling of flight. During World War II Link and others worked to physically reproduce Bush's mathematical model, and to marry the promise of Bush's differential analyser (an early analogue computer) to the basic physics of simulation. As applied to flight simulation, the initial challenge they addressed can be expressed as how the 'north–south' movement of the joystick could be integrated with its 'east–west' movement in such a way that moving the stick between any two compass directions would afford the trainee an adequate simulation of the resistance experienced by performing the actual motion in the air.

During this same period, designers improved the illusion of what a pilot might see from the 'cockpit's' windscreen. However, it required invention of the digital computer, born of the war's logic of necessity, with its ability to process the complex algorithms upon which the 'mechanics' of simulation rest, and at previously unimaginable speeds, to realize adequate simulation. ENIAC (Electronic Numerical Integrator and Computer), unveiled in 1946, had been developed at the University of Pennsylvania to process the complex ballistic tables required to predict missile and bomb trajectories. It was soon grasped that ENIAC might provide the advanced computation necessary for simulating flight – that digital computers might exemplify what mathematician Alan Turing called *universal machines*, ones where it would be 'unnecessary to design various new machines to do various computing processes' (Turing 1950: 441).

Vannevar Bush also theorized the personal computer but as a hyper-textual extension of the individual self, and with a choice of words strikingly similar to the contemporary description of the human/machine interface called the cyborg. Bush's machine infects and enhances the body, and is predicated on the non-mechanical electrical dynamics of the body for its functionality. In a discussion entitled 'Memex instead of Index', Bush, director of Roosevelt's Office of Scientific Research and Development (Nelson 1972: 440), writes:

> Consider a future device for individual use, which is a sort of mechanized private file and library. *It needs a name*, and, to coin one at random, 'memex' will do. A memex is a device in which an individual stores all his books, records, and communications, and which is mechanized so that it may be consulted with exceeding speed and flexibility. *It is an enlarged intimate supplement to his memory* . . .
>   In the outside world, all forms of intelligence, whether of sound or sight, have been reduced to the form of varying currents in an electric current in order that they may be transmitted. Inside the human frame exactly the same sorts of processes occur. *Must we always transform to mechanical movements in order to proceed from one electrical phenomenon to another?* (1946: 32, emphases added)

In 1944 researchers at MIT's Servomechanisms Lab, using digital equipment similar to ENIAC, successfully demonstrated that a light-sensitive, hand-held wand-like detector, when pointed at a television-like screen adapted from radar technology, could select or 'highlight' individual bouncing dots pre-programmed to move like bouncing balls across this early version of a monitor. By applying the language of mathematics, these researchers had simulated people interacting with concrete things, thereby also blurring the distinctions between symbol and fact. The experiment had also demonstrated that human interactions with simulations were a possibility worth further investigation. The work of other researchers at this time (Bush 1946; Weiner 1948; Turing 1950) served to strengthen the idea that such human/machine interactivity creates 'an ambiguous boundary between humans and interactive "intelligent" machines' (Biocca 1992a: 8).

Inventions and cultural forces

VR theorist Myron Krueger remarks that the rapid evolution of the computer *vis-à-vis* earlier technologies – when contrasted with the *lack* of evolution of the human form – led him to theorize 'that the ultimate interface between the computer and people would be to the human body and human sense' (1991: 19).

However, as alluded to above, the almost exponential enhancement in computing capacity from the early 1950s onwards – a key factor in making VR conceivable today – must be understood as part of a 'package' of ongoing cultural and technological changes. The manufacture of the stereoscopic display is a necessary development. Rheingold (1991: 64–6) suggests that Wheatstone's 1833 stereoscope forms the first link in a chain leading directly to today's head-mounted VR display units. The stereo-scope and its modern entertainment and informational descendants such as the Viewmaster and stereoscopic photography are based on separate dual images, each depicting 'the same scene from slightly different perspectives corresponding to human interocular distance' (Rheingold 1991: 65). When these are presented separately to each eye, our visual sense merges the two views into a single 3-D scene.

Edwin Land's pioneering work with light-polarized lenses advanced the apparent cohesion of stereo images, and was necessary for the creation of colour 3-D film. Mid-1950s Hollywood features such as *Dial M for Murder* required viewers to don special lenses to perceive the hallucinatory effects provided in the Hitchcock film in which a pair of scissors that Ray Milland uses to threaten Grace Kelly seem to fly out from the screen to menace the audience too, disrupting the 'traditional' spatio-emotional relationship between viewer and screen. Though these experiments in three-dimensionality were cumbersome, and abandoned following the financially successful 1954 launch of wide-screen Cinemascope, the manner they conceive to technically manipulate the apparent spatial relationship between image representation and human perception in order to involve audiences more directly with the images before them is a direct conceptual progenitor of the computer-driven 'ultimate interface' Krueger describes.

During the same period, experiments in stimulating the nervous system with three-dimensional images, binaural sound and odour were conducted by entrepreneur inventor Morton Heilig. His 1956 'Sensorama Simulator', conceived as an entertainment (Krueger 1991: 66), and influenced by the heightened cinematic effects of the Cinerama process (an even more *wrap-around* competitor of Cinemascope, and which may be imagined as an individualistic precursor of the IMAX and IMAX/OMNIMAX instal-lations at science parks and museums), offered the sensation of real experience through the multi-mediated use of 3-D images, sound and scent. In 1953 Heilig had suggested that:

> The screen will not fill only 5% of your visual field as the local movie screen does . . . or the 25% of Cinerama – but 100%. The screen will curve past the spectator's ears on both sides and beyond his sphere of vision above and below. In all the praise about the marvels of 'peripheral vision', no one has paused to state that the human eye has a vertical span of 150 degrees as well as a horizontal

one of 180 degrees. . . . Glasses . . . will not be necessary. Electronic and optical means will be devised to create illusory depth without them. (Heilig 1992: 283)

Heilig anticipates cultural critic Mark Dery's observation that 'in virtual reality, the television swallows the viewer, headfirst' (1993: 6). He continued work on his concept, in 1960 patenting his 'Stereoscopic Television Apparatus for Individual Use', a 'head-mounted display that a person could wear like a pair of exceptionally bulky sunglasses' (Rheingold 1991: 58). Heilig's work in sensory immersion remained marginalized, in part because it was located within an entertainment milieu, in part because of lack of funds. VR theorist Brenda Laurel (1993) writes of the conceptual breakthrough realized by researchers at MIT's Media Lab, who in the late 1970s and early 1980s became aware of the qualitative difference induced when an individual sensorium was *surrounded* rather than, as with film/TV/video, facing a screen at a distance. She finds the vanishing *interface* that this implies, 'broke new ground in bringing our attention to the nature of the effects that immersion could induce' (1993: 204). Heilig had already been there. Perhaps unfortunately for him, at the wrong time and place.

Heilig's creativity notwithstanding, it is Ivan Sutherland who is credited with synthesizing directions in which the idea of simulation might lead (Krueger 1991; Woolley 1992; Biocca 1992a). Affiliated variously with MIT, the cybernetics think-tank at the University of Utah, and the federal Advance Research Projects Agency (ARPA) project, Sutherland's 1965 meditation on virtual affectivity – 'The ultimate display' – anticipates and informs subsequent VR research and development.

> A display connected to a digital computer gives us a chance to gain familiarity with concepts not realizable in the physical world. It is a looking glass into a mathematical wonderland. . . . There is no reason why the objects displayed by a computer have to follow the ordinary rules of physical reality. . . . The ultimate display would . . . be a room within which the computer can control the existence of matter. A chair displayed in such a room would be good enough to sit in. Handcuffs displayed in such a room would be confining, and a bullet displayed in such a room would be fatal. With appropriate programming such a display could literally be the Wonderland in which Alice walked. (1965: 506–8)

It would seem that metaphors of violence and transcendence underpin VR from the moment of its conception.

New media are informed first by the technologies and conventions of the past. Sutherland writes that 'the force required to move a joystick could be computer controlled, just as the actuation force on the controls of a Link Trainer are changed to give the feel of a real airplane' (1965: 507). Here the 'father' of simulation models his ultimate display on flight simulation. This is not surprising, for Sutherland also founded Evans & Sutherland, a leading flight simulation company. Neither, given Sutherland's prestigious *vita* of computer science background and Defense Department support, should one be surprised that this publicity-shy individual is now called the 'father' of VR. Heilig's earlier and obscured entertainment-directed research previews the Nintendo-directed escapism of current VR arcade games such as 'Dactyl Nightmare'.[3] Though Sutherland's conceptual genius should in no way be minimized for its contribution to making cyberspace conceivable, military support for his work must be recognized, particularly following the surprise of Sputnik in 1957, and the 1958 American response both in the formation of ARPA, with its mission to synthesize technological superiority and computational abilities (Brand 1987: 162), and in the space agency NASA. Heilig's self-funded work had inverted the 'commonsense' temporally determined hierarchy often thought to exist between military-industrial invention and later socially diverting entertainment spin-offs.

Sutherland's 1968 paper 'A head-mounted three dimensional display' accompanied the 3-D head-mounted computer graphics display he constructed at the MIT Draper Lab in Cambridge MA (Stone 1992a: 95), 'that allowed a person to look around in a graphic room by simply turning their head. Two small CRTs (cathode-ray tubes) driven by vector graphics generators provided the appropriate stereo view for each eye' (Krueger 1991: 19). Financed by ARPA, the Office of Naval Research and Bell Labs, the display marked a step in realizing the vision Sutherland had expressed in the 1965 paper 'The ultimate display'. 'Our objective . . . has been to surround the user with displayed three-dimensional information . . . objects displayed appear to hang in the space all around the user' (Sutherland 1968: 757).

In resorting to a head-mounted display Sutherland and Heilig sought to overcome human perceptual awareness of certain technical limitations of conventional film and TV that necessitate retention of distance between these technologies and viewers. The two men build on earlier stereoscopic research designed to foster an illusion of three-dimensionality. Without stereoscopy, each eye would see the same scene, which would appear flat, like a painting, instead of reflecting our more 'curved' sense of vision made available via the slightly different perspective 'take' that we receive through each eye from the ambient world around us. As well, when we move our bodies in the physical world, our point of view alters. As of yet, this is restricted within these virtual media. Biocca notes, 'we are not inside the space of the video image, only the camera is. We are spectators, not actors' (1992b: 32). It should be noted that Biocca's distinction ironically parallels the distinction made by human geographers between the 'inside' position of an individual experientially 'in place' and an 'outsider' who consumes/views a landscape composed by its frame (Cosgrove 1984). Extrapolating from Biocca, only the camera as metaphor for the eye freed from the body is at home *in* the image. Yet Biocca fails to address what happens imaginatively when the 'space of distance' between viewer and technology is collapsed. Though the conceptual world of cameras and images remains empirically distinct from the viewer's perception of same, the literal collapsing of space between the viewer and immersive technology may also facilitate a key goal of VR: the merger of spectator/camera and actor/viewer.

The introduction of head-mounted displays altered the perceptually defined relationship Biocca notes between spectators and image/scene (or landscape). By means of a tracking device connected to a computer, binocular vision and motion cues now could be generated and continually adjusted to provide the sense of parallax that is one of the sensed 'truths' or biases of our vision. Still, because of the physical weight of its auxiliary technologies, Sutherland's original display had to be suspended from above (Biocca 1992b: 37). Neither could it yet provide a truly emotionally real sense of the *surround environment* which was its inventor's main goal. Two tiny TV screens covered each eye of the participant donning the display and offered the viewer a stereoscopic computer-generated picture. Tracking sensors monitored individual position and movement in a kind of reverse application on to the body of flight simulation technology's replications. Sutherland's intention was to make the objects in the computer-generated space accessed via the TV screens not only visible but tangible. He reasoned that the application of geometrical laws to reproduce size and shape could be extended to the application of physical laws to reproduce qualities such as mass and texture (Sutherland 1968; Woolley 1992: 55). The programming that lay behind the sense of resistance experienced through manipulation of a flight simulator's joystick could be applied to simulate the sensation of pushing and weight; in other words, the rudiments of touch.

Other than flight simulation and momentary stimulation and novelty, how were subsequent plausible uses for this proto-technology first conceived? A slight digression permits making a link between Turing's (computing) 'universal machine', how Turing's machine is applied, and Sutherland's 'ultimate display'. The latter exemplifies an aspect of Turing's 'machine' – a concept depending on deductive, Aristotelian logic to solve mathematical problems (Sheppard 1993: 3), and originating in a philosophy of mathematics associated with the symbolic logic advanced by Alfred North Whitehead and Bertrand Russell (see Bolter 1984: ch.5).[4] Turing's abstract, immaterial machine is 'a machine that can be lots of different machines' (Woolley 1992: 67). When personal computers were first developed in the early 1970s their eventual poly-utility, except for certain thinkers such as Sutherland and Ted Nelson (1973), was unsuspected, Bush's and Turing's prescient remarks notwithstanding or forgotten. Many 'machines' reside within the PC, itself devolved from the more powerful forms of computation it has subsequently absorbed and displaced. Today the machine that processed the words you read on this page might, in another setting, have helped design a building, provided access to geographically distant information, or maintained the files and financial accounts of a commercial establishment. Such a comment is now commonplace. The personal computer can exist on its own or as networked into a communications matrix. But the PC can also be understood as an aspect of an abstract process of mind that has found physical expression. Bolter defines a Turing machine in this way: '[b]y making a machine think as a man, man recreates himself, defines himself as a machine' (1984: 13).

Computers are intended to be virtual machines in this manner. My screen simulates the thoughts I set down, but in its logic predicated on abstract mathematics, there is no necessary reason, as Sutherland grasped early on, why it need only simulate the actual or the real.

Turing's 'universal machine' – a machine that can be many different machines, or 'none of the above' – is a first step in conceptualizing the electro-mechanical simulation of our selves, and one, I suggest, that is empowered by a Western belief that to take the measure of all things is to be all things. Representation supersedes reality because to achieve widespread recognition it must imply the universally coded standards and legal measures that also reliably undergird stable political organisms. Yet in the very naming of these devices and concepts – *ultimate* display, *universal* machine – a metaphysics suggests somehow having come to an end or an irreducible element. The stability of a particular form of social relations is naturalized or accorded timeless universality.

As early as 1962 Sutherland had developed 'Sketchpad', an interactive program that allowed a user holding a lightpen to make designs on a screen that then could be stored, retrieved and superimposed atop one another (Sutherland 1963; Rheingold 1991: 90). Sketchpad demonstrated that computers could be used for more than swift number crunching. It suggested they could introduce a new form of what might be called by some a 'truth situation', by others a 'power situation'. The lightpen 'drew'/ transmitted the circle its holder first described with the arc of his or her bodily motion, and the computer simulated this action as a circular line onscreen. In a sense, the lightpen guided the human hand into (a conceptual integration with) the computer technology. If 'the ultimate display' was a prototype of VR hardware, the earlier Sketchpad provisionally inaugurated a conceptual pathway for inscribing what later would be seen on the stereoscopic TV sets within the 'display'. It did so by reading human motion. No substantive training was demanded of the user. Of Sutherland's contributions in this regard, pioneer computer and virtuality theorist Ted Nelson writes:

> You could draw a picture on the screen with the lightpen – and then file the picture away in the . . . memory . . . magnify and shrink the picture to a spectacular degree . . . Sketchpad . . . allowed room for human vagueness and judgement. . . . You could rearrange till you got what you wanted, no matter for what reason you wanted it . . . a new way of working and seeing was possible. The techniques of the computer screen are general and applicable to everything – but only if you can adapt your mind to thinking in terms of computer screens. (Nelson 1977: 120–3 as quoted in Rheingold 1991: 91)

Nelson notes that 'a new way of working and seeing was possible'. The claim of novelty can be partially challenged by noting that Sketchpad (or the mouse–screen–hand interface of a Macintosh computer) is only a sophisticated way to sketch and erase – what anyone reasonably skilled at drawing would do on paper. What does seem novel, as people who use graphics technologies with whom I have spoken attest, is that they allow/

facilitate a disavowal/displacement of authorship/artisanship. Stated otherwise, users feel less anxiety about drawing on computer, as though one is not committing in the same way as one does on paper. The claim of novelty cannot be organized only around the technological mechanics of drawing (media as environment) – though the medium is different – but also around the process and relationships it engenders (media as language) that also may be thought of as effecting a shift away from a set of moral attitudes towards creativity partly reified by print technology. As N. Katherine Hayles notes, the body and the book are formed on a 'durable material substrate. Once encoding [on either] has taken place, it cannot easily be changed', and 'electronic media . . . receive and transmit signals but do not permanently store messages, books carry their information in their bodies' (1993: 73). I infer that Hayles makes certain assumptions about the specific materiality of paper, as well as of flesh, in her assertions.

Though innovations ranging from the computer mouse to such text-graphics applications as Hypertext generally are believed to be no older than their 1980s commercialization, it was during the early to mid-1960s that these computational advances were made at Douglas Englebart's ARPA-funded 'Augmentation Research Center' in California. With the mouse, 3-D gestural input becomes a command language for computers. In Hypertext, users perform 'automatic link-jumps' (Nelson 1972: 442) from one document to another by selecting specific icons on the screen. Collapsing and expansion of multiple onscreen cut-and-paste documents is made possible along with the use of text-enhancing graphic imagery. All of these functions imply virtual activity, and are precursive conceptual inventions that permit VR technologies. Ted Nelson has continued to defend and extend Vannevar Bush's original concept of hypertext and personal computing – the Memex – profiled above.

Rheingold notes that the direct manipulation interfaces, developed by Englebart and others at the Xerox Corporation's Palo Alto Research Center (XEROX PARC), remained relatively unutilized until Steve Jobs, Apple Computer's whiz-kid, toured this facility. If one seeks proof that Turing's 'ultimate machine' lies waiting to be discovered within the imagination, Jobs's popularization of computing through marrying algorithmic power to graphic interfaces offers fair example. Since the first Apples were marketed in 1984, applications have proliferated. These software packages are instances of the machine within a machine. They trade on the power released in the merge between computation and the graphics programs computation makes possible.

The cluster of scientists working at XEROX PARC exemplifies a partial shift from military to civilian-business research that had resulted from the Mansfield amendment drafted during the Vietnam war. This legislation sought to limit ARPA funding to weapons-related research, yet in causing certain scientists to leave ARPA-funded labs, it stimulated the invention of personal computing on the part of those who disagreed with US foreign policy orientation (Rheingold 1991: 85).

However, ongoing R&D within the academy by others willing to accept the restrictions placed on ARPA disbursements remains central to this story. During the early 1970s the University of North Carolina (UNC) emerged as a major centre in VR research, specializing in medical and molecular modelling, and architectural walk-through or computer-aided design (CAD). The first graphic manipulator was created there. When its user moved a mechanical manipulator in the lab, a graphic manipulator onscreen also moved. If this onscreen image was used to 'pick up' another object represented on screen, the user felt its weight and resistance as well (Krueger 1991: 19). In the late 1980s the Human Interface Technology Lab was started at the University of Washington in Seattle (UW-S). The connection with Boeing serves to underscore VR's continuing links with flight simulation.

Contemporary VR research occurs within a complex and intertwined hybrid of profit-driven private consortia such as Autodesk or Apple; entrepreneurial activity that circulates between quasi-military facilities such as NASA's Ames Human Factors Research Division at Mountain View, California; and schools such as MIT, Carnegie-Mellon, Stanford, USC, UC Berkeley, UNC and UW-S. The move away from military applications in the 1970s is relevant, but NASA remains the engine of much research initiated by radicalized scientists who withdrew from the military orbit during the 1960s. The contemporary space programme has clear military implications. In passing, it is worth noting that NASA's mission has always assumed a taking leave of the earth. Accessing cyberspace – a 'place' no less predicated on conceptually leaving the 'space' of this earth than 'cosmic' space flight – seems poetically congruent with NASA's broader 'mission'.

Inter-bureaucratic rivalry also plays a role. Since the late 1970s, it has been the US Air Force, specifically the Wright-Patterson Base near Dayton, Ohio, that has spearheaded head-mounted display design. Directed by Tom Furness, a series of heavily funded projects into human perception and optics led to the development of visual displays far more sophisticated than any currently in commercial usage (Krueger 1991: xiv) and which form the basis for the VR guidance systems used in the American air war upon Iraq.[5] Wright-Patterson's placing of a million-dollar price tag as the cost of one of these displays in response to a request from NASA's Ames facility for a share in the technology spurred the less financially endowed Ames operation to devise its own display from existing technologies such as flat-screen CRTs. But NASA since has gone much further than duplicating a head-mounted display on the cheap. The DataGlove™ – originally acquired from the private company VPL (Virtual Products Limited) which subsequently re-engineered its usage for video games (Krueger 1991: xvi) – and full-body input devices developed by a consortium of Ames and its subcontractors more fully integrate the human form into virtual space than the earlier airforce head-mounted displays. The sophisticated precision of the virtual war games technology the airforce has since developed, one that has borrowed heavily from NASA's lead, illustrates the continuing synergistic effects generated by this tax-funded competition between state agencies, healthy or otherwise.

Visual perception theorist James Gibson (*The Perception of the Visual World*, 1950; *The Senses Considered as Perceptual Systems*, 1966) asserts that how we navigate our 3-D world and handle things within it shapes our vision and how we see the world (in particular, Gibson 1966: ch.13). Scientists at Ames were intrigued by his cognitive theories, and sought applications. The DataGlove™ that manipulated a virtual object in cyberspace simulated Gibson's belief that we literally grab on to our world and make it part of our experience. The extension of the user's virtual arm and hand into cyberspace was theorized as allowing for a kind of mapping of the dimensions of the virtual world on to internal human perception structuring processes. Such a connection forms the basis of *telepresence* – 'experience of presence in an environment by means of a communications medium' (Steuer 1992: 76) – which is computational power in abundance that allows the robot or hand (the virtual body and/or its parts in cyberspace is sometimes called a *puppet*) to serve as the servo-body of the person wearing the wrap-around sensing mechanisms. The link between the human body and the robot is informational; remote control is at hand. The entertaining and transcendent possibilities of telepresence notwith-standing, this emerging technology is thought to be central to the engineering of a space station constructed by semi-autonomous robots (ibid. 1991). But perhaps something more important is also at work here. This is the coming to be of a view that the body itself is only informational – a kind of reduction implied in Michael Heim's description of cyberspace as Platonism as a working product, one where 'the dream of perfect FORMS becomes the dream of inFORMation' (1993: 89). I would note that *information* is a series of rules and routines useful insofar as capable of being acted *upon*. Body-as-information equates with a formula by which contingency and surprise, wisdom and judgement have all been explained away.

Writing about the links between text, body and VR, N. Katherine Hayles notes that people 'have something to lose if they are regarded solely as informational patterns, namely the resistant materiality that . . . has marked the experience of living as embodied creatures' (1993: 73). Though she notes the potential for loss, she also observes that the interactions between people and these machines increasingly are based on exactly this kind of reductive patterning that would have bodies materially correspond to sets of signals.

'Functionality' is a term used by virtual reality technologists to describe the communication modes that are active in a computer–human interface. If the user wears a DataGlove, for example, hand motions constitute one functionality. . . . Functionalities work in both directions . . . they both describe the computer's capabilities and also indicate how the user's sensory-motor apparatus is being

trained to accommodate the computer's responses. Working with a VR simulation, the user learns to move her hand in stylized gestures that the computer can
accommodate. In the process, changes take place in the neural configuration of
the user's brain, some of which can be long-lasting. The computer molds the
human even as the human builds the computer. (1993: 73)

Mapping the virtual world on to human perception, and linking text, body
and VR, are two ways of describing what also may be stated otherwise.
Though VR may well afford simulated access to a virtual and digitized
community of representations – arguably a 'global public sphere' achieved
at the loss of embeddedness and context – given the individuated manner
in which the technology is being developed and will be accessed, the
conflation between the conception it affords the user and this user's own
perceptivity needs to be acknowledged and theorized. Extending Heilig's
Sensorama in surrounding the user's vision, the frame of earlier visual
technologies, from landscape painting to TV, recedes from view and with it
a degree of awareness of our separation from the machine. Positioning the
machine and user in close spatial proximity allows the latter's active
perception to collapse into the active conceptions contained within the
technology. Part of an emerging 'informational imperialism', immersive
technology suggests that the conceptions it proposes are at one with the
user's perception, thereby suggesting that the subject's independence is a
fiction.

Like a braided desert stream whose channels rejoin downslope, it is at
NASA that the majority of the developments and institutional players
noted above are brought together. Unlike many universities, NASA
thrives on a kind of backdoor publicity (Rheingold 1991; Stone 1992a) and
many of the writers most involved in popularizing VR were permitted their
first glimpse of cyberspace after hours or via a friend at Ames.[6] Not only
has beleaguered NASA taken care to make known in a way beneficial to its
interests the cutting edge of its research, it has done so in a way that
encourages the use of VR by medical and educational professionals.
NASA's relatively open sharing of intellectual property (compared to the
airforce) is asserted to be for everyone's benefit.[7] A recent example will
suffice. Time lag remains a problem for VR. Overcoming its effects
virtually, as with film, depends on presenting framed snippets of reality at
such a speed that they blend into the illusion of realistic motion. But within
VR the coordinates of the depicted space have to be recomputed each time
a frame is changed, every thirtieth of a second. The demands of reality
create a bottleneck for VR. NASA's cooperation with freelancers and
other industry players has meant that even what appear to be the most
farfetched experimental computer architectures receive support from
NASA, for perhaps it will be an employee at a small software design
company, for example, who will make the significant conceptual breakthrough in computational logic. Current international private sector
research on transputers, much of it British, partly sponsored by NASA,

may succeed in refining such computer architectures, so that they become capable of juggling the vast ocean of data bits required to synthesize eye–hand real-time coordination in cyberspace at sufficient speeds to overcome the disorienting and reflexivity-inducing perception of time lag, an experience within which the user's ironic subjectivity may still be found.

The space of science fiction

The advances in computation noted above form a pool of techniques from which VR technologies can draw, select, refine and redeploy. What of the so-called entertainment dimension of virtual technologies? In its ties with the Western quest for transcendence, whether this be an out-of-body or off-the-planet experience, this facet equally sustains the will to develop VR, and is set forth most eloquently in the pages of science fiction (SF). It might seem ironic that much of the impetus for popularizing virtuality originates in print form. But it might equally be argued that, in a spatial fashion, the novel also echoes Turing's ultimate machine;[8] it remains a virtual form until we give it meaning and intentionality.

In his fascinating study of the interplay of the production of SF, postmodern academic theory and virtual technologies, Scott Bukatman (1993) has coined the term Terminal Identity to refer to the birth of a new subjectivity at the interface of the body and the TV/computer screen. Within technology's increasing pervasion of concepts of the self, Bukatman identifies a growing belief that (hyper) individualism can merge with virtual technologies yet current notions of humanity somehow be retained. Bukatman asserts that narrative form now gives way to spatialized concerns that engage our fixation with the distances, and proximities between embodied humanity and the electronic machines invented to facilitate an interpenetration of individuated subjectivity and global capital flows.

SF addresses how these technologies inflect our being in the world, constructing 'a space of accommodation to an intensely technological existence' (Bukatman 1993: 10). Replacing modernist visionaries such as Vannevar Bush, SF is now the prescient mind that has first plausibly imagined the virtual world now under contract to be built. As the Holodeck on the starship Enterprise in *Star Trek – The Next Generation* discloses, as a cultural technology SF fosters the belief that technology might now offer humanity a 'wrap-around' alternative space to the present reality of embodied existence. SF has always been an ideological narrative or 'discourse'. Its constructed visions and overt use of metaphors of space in its descriptions of power relationships are segues into the contemporary 'geographic imagination' and part of the apparatus facilitating technology's social acceptance.

Both Bukatman and Hayles argue that contemporary SF has turned away from an earlier interest in utopian futures and antipathy towards technology as the 'other'. They also note its discarding of narrative in advancing the history of any one protagonist from one place within the novel to the next. Narrative histories are set aside in a turning to techniques that feature description of the merger of people and their technologized worlds.[9] As Hayles writes, the new science fiction is so successful because it is honest to its thematic. The novels 'embody within their techniques the assumptions expressed explicitly in [their] themes' (1993: 84). Such an authorial move could only be possible when '[t]he posthuman is experienced as an everyday lived reality as well as an intellectual proposition' (ibid.).

Heidegger's extended essay on the development of 'World Picture' (1977) traces a Western belief that the world is best understood as if it were a picture. A picture such as a landscape painting relies on the technique of a bounded representative space closed to what our lived world might disclose. In accepting technique as a defining metaphor for the world we are reduced to being only agents – Men at Work – oblivious to our surroundings and what they might tell us. However plausible SF might seem, it is a variation of 'world picture', a construct. To choose to model VR on SF is to conceptualize a concept based on an earlier concept. This may well be imaginative and creative but also implies a feedback loop shut to exterior influence. The merger of people with their technologies is a merger of people into concept. The 'posthuman' has dispensed with the non-formulaic body in favour of codes, languages and cultural productions – a contemporary and less hopeful reformulation of the story of Exodus as a flight from the 'oppressive limits' of the body, and redemptive deliverance into the promised 'land' of dataspace – or its more unworldly eventuality that the body would have died and gone to heaven, the self remembering, in this extended return, that in the beginning was the WORD.

In the case of William Gibson's *Neuromancer* (1984), a sci-fi vision revealed in text format offered researchers following in the footsteps of Sutherland *et al.* a framework for further imagining the virtual world gridded within the 'ultimate display'. Peter Fitting writes that, 'Gibson's cyberspace is an image of a way of making the abstract and unseen comprehensible, a visualization of the notion of cognitive mapping' (1991: 311). It is hard to overstate the impact of this book. Scarcely a thing written about VR neglects to pay it homage. Allucquere Rosanne Stone, one of the most considered of academic theorists writing about VR, argues that this novel demarcates the boundary between an information technology epoch extending from the 1960s until the book's publication, and the virtual reality and cyberspace epoch that ensues (1992a: 95). She believes this one novel

> reached the technologically literate and socially disaffected who were searching for social forms that could transform the fragmented anomie that characterized life in Silicon Valley and all electronic industrial ghettos. In a single stroke, Gibson's powerful vision provided for them the imaginal public sphere and

refigured discursive community that established the grounding for a new kind of social interaction. (1992a: 95)

Earlier I noted the movement and fluidity of personnel within the field of VR research. Stone argues that the widespread background anxiety this had promoted within the VR research community created a need that *Neuromancer* filled. In delivering to this spatially fragmented community – defined as much by e-mail, bulletin board services (BBSs), and the Internet as by any face-to-face geography[10] – a plausible future, based on the dynamics within which researchers themselves were located, the novel gave voice to a virtual community identity which was in turn to suggest broad new avenues of research.

> The critical importance of Gibson's book was partly due to the way that it triggered a conceptual revolution among the scattered workers who had been doing virtual reality research for years: As task groups coalesced and dissolved, as the fortunes of companies and projects and laboratories rose and fell, the existence of Gibson's novel and the technological and social imaginary that it articulated enabled the researchers in virtual reality – or, under the new dispensation, cyberspace – to recognize and organize themselves as a community. (Stone 1992a: 99)

Hayles's identification of two literary innovations deployed in *Neuromancer* can be read against Stone's thesis about the novel's appeal to spatially isolated hackers. Hayles finds these innovations, 'allow subjectivity . . . to be articulated together with abstract data' (1993: 82). The first – 'pov' for point of view – is the mechanism by which individual consciousness, in the novel, 'moves *through* the screen to become the pov, leaving behind the body as an unoccupied shell. In cyberspace point of view does not emanate from the character; rather the pov literally *is* the character' (ibid.: 83). Cyberspace is the data landscape in which the pov can take place. Awareness is joined to data, the latter are thereby humanized, subjectivity computerized, 'allowing them to join in a symbiotic union' (ibid.: 84).

The alteration of spatial relationships between viewers and what they see reflects parallel changes in technology. With live theatre the viewer remains at a distance from the action on stage, a distance traditionally reinforced by the proscenium. She places or situates herself imaginatively within one of the characters performing, yet a critical distance of subjectivity is maintained within this temporary spatial relationship. Cinema effects a more extensive projection of subjectivity and augments a subjective narcissism in suggesting that our self-interest may more fully lie elsewhere than the body's spatial coordinates.[11] With VR the vestige of distance is collapsed into the emblematic and representational space occupied by the pov, a space that is both landscape and subjectivity. The *frisson* of transcendence and pleasure of virtual control over a pre-defined world notwithstanding, an entirely informational, hence commodifiable representation of the self is made available for corporate and individual *use*. Along the way the self has become 'other' even to itself.

Earlier in this chapter, I critiqued Terence McKenna's reduction of sensual experience to the visual. The Californian sage of psychedelics and virtuality offers a most succinct and ahistoric understanding of the move from narrative to virtual spectacle and its potential impact on the modern subject.

> A world of visible language is a world where the individual doesn't really exist in the same way that the print-created world sanctions what we call 'point of view.' That's really what an ego is: it's a consistently defined point of view within a context of narrative. Well, if you replace the idea that life is a narrative with the idea that life is a vision, then you displace the linear progression of events. I think this is technically within reach. (cited in Rushkoff 1994: 58)

It is in *Neuromancer* that 'cyberspace' – the novel's second innovation, according to Hayles, and the immaterial space that sets the stage for the places within which the vision McKenna seeks would be played out – is first depicted. The novel also debuts Gibson's now-famous 'consensual hallucination' (1984: 51) as one aspect of highly mediated social relations taking place in an intensely corporatized world predicated upon overwhelming inequality and punctuated by a series of altercations among humans, human-machines and machines that occur in material and virtual reality. The most cursory scan of writings on VR makes clear that this concept has been latched on to with an astonishing, almost feverish tenacity, and that within the American VR community at least, that consensuality has come to be equated summarily with equality. It is intriguing that so widely excerpted a concept has been so wrenched from the context in which it was located, for though the term is indeed employed, it refers to some kind of polymorphous freedom not for individuals but for *data*: 'cyberspace . . . a consensual hallucination experienced daily by billions of legitimate operators . . . by children being taught mathematical concepts . . . a graphic representation of data abstracted from the banks of every computer in the human system' (ibid. 1984: 51). For Fitting (1991: 302–3), consensual hallucination is the novel's most striking concept, and it is here that the disappearance of direct, unmediated experience is, as Hayles suggests, demonstrated, even darkly celebrated. For a consensual hallucination is always a mediated one, never ethically experienced face to face. It is also one where the tension between positive and negative uses of technology has dissolved, along with the meaning of distinguishing between human and non-human – a duality already threatened in 1962 with respect to human/computer interactions following the unveiling of Sutherland's Sketchpad.

There is also a larger-scale dissolution of distinctions at play here and it touches on the already noted shift from narrative to spectacle under way in SF. Narrative has been a requisite artifact in the construction of the modern nation-state (Hobsbawm 1990; Anderson 1991). In a post-national infomatics, narrative gets in the way of data, and cyberspace becomes both the new spatial metaphor and actual location of global power – one for which any isolated junkie might consider giving up their body in exchange for wired, fibre-optical entry and communion 'therein'.

Suggesting that science can inform fiction, as well as the other way around, Benjamin Woolley argues that Gibson extended Sutherland's 'looking glass into a mathematical wonderland' to the entirety of information. 'With cyberspace as I describe it you can literally wrap yourself in media and not have to see what's really going on around you' (W. Gibson, cited in Woolley 1992: 122).

It is intriguing that although this novel has been taken up as a kind of holy grail justifying the bionic makeover of people into cyborgs – machine/human syntheses – there is a general (though not complete) failure to note a broader thematic at work. While the premise of the text has been interpreted as a radically dystopian consumerist future where 'perception and experience are similarly contaminated' and paralleled with 'remarkable new technologies and commodities [that] exist alongside the shabby and outmoded products they have replaced' (Fitting 1991: 301–3), I find that it is Gibson's detailing of the exponential mutation of two giant corporate AIs (Artificial Intelligences) into Gods which centres the real action. In traditional humanist sci-fi such a change always is associated with a monster (technology = evil other), based I would suggest on a dynamic similar to Bruce Mazlish's (1967) understanding of Frankenstein's monster as technology spurned. It then comes to pass that the humans must fight it and whether they win or lose, the battle between self and other is the primary moral locus that occludes any possibility of interchangeability between the two. Similarly, earlier research on Artificial Intelligence was predicated on *replacing* human faculties, a concept now largely superseded by what Heim (1993) identifies as a cultural theorizing of (personal) computers as *components* of our identity – a notion entirely consonant with the now trendy cyborg.

In *Neuromancer*, the 'heroes', dimly aware that they play and live within a society where embodied human integrity and history are *passé*, battle against establishment forces in order to allow this mutation to take place. The eventual fusion of the two AIs is a meta-joining of both sides of a capitalist cybernetic brain by an evolved fibre-optic *corpus callosum*. Technology may be seen to use its creators here to attain the state of union only it has been existentially capable of imagining, thereby to achieve a kind of returning. But this time the God is not the imaginary and therefore absolute and naturalized technology of older religious belief, but a systematic technology that humans have loved and set free. Paul Virilio (1994) points to this in noting that all technologies converge towards a *deux ex machina*. '[T]echnologies have negated the transcendental God in order to invent the machine-God. However, these two gods raise similar questions.'

Gibson's AIs mutate into something unintended – 'a vast mind engulfing the whole of the Matrix. A god for Cyberspace' (Grant 1990: 47). If there is merit to Larry McCaffery's assertion that postmodernism is a condition that 'derives its unique status above all from technological change' (1991: 3), then as Grant argues, '[i]f technology is to be our method of transcendence, Gibson seems to be saying, we should not be surprised to discover that our technology might have a greater potentiality for transcendence than we do' (1990: 47).

A less charitable, more materially-rooted understanding of the human–machine relations influenced by Western physics and technology is offered by Lewis Mumford. 'Machines – and machines alone – completely met the requirements of the new scientific method and *point of view*: they fulfilled the definition of "reality" far more perfectly than living organisms' (1934: 51; emphasis mine).

Neuromancer suggests that transcendence is to be achieved by machinic and virtual means. This argument is given weight by the novel's assumption that the human body is 'meat' – 'obsolete, as soon as consciousness itself can be uploaded into the network' (Stone 1992a: 113). In the aftermath of the novel's impact, Gibson has seemed less than comfortable with his creation. In 'Academy leader' he has written:

> Assembled word *cyberspace* from small and readily available components of language . . . preceded any concept whatever. Slick and hollow – awaiting received meaning.
>   All I did: folded words as taught. Now other words accrete in the interstices.
>   . . . These are dreams of commerce. Above them rise intricate barrios, zones of more private fantasy. (1992: 27–8)

As accurate a critique of the ambition wedded to mathematical creativity within the VR community as this may be, by 1992 cyberspace was no longer a concept awaiting meaning. The company Autodesk, for example, was founded by members of the community Stone identifies above who had been excited to build aspects of what they had first gleaned from the novel's pages. The discourse of cyberspace has been taken up by others, academics included, and reflects in part a 'widespread desire to come to grips with the cultural implications of new electronic technologies' (Biocca 1992a: 17), Gibson's caveat aside.

Neuromancer is book one of a trilogy that includes *Count Zero* (1986) and *Mona Lisa Overdrive* (1988). Though *Neuromancer* has been the focus of academic interest and virtual imagining to the degree that there is now a 'received truth' that the later novels cannot compare to the first's *tour de force*, it is the third novel, incorporating Gibson's awareness of the cultural processes *Neuromancer* has helped set in motion, that offers a more mature version of his VR futureview. Arguably, the possibility of entering a cyberspatial *aleph* is the most entrancing concept *Mona Lisa Overdrive* details. Seeming to 'sample' from both Jorge Luis Borges's aleph, and German mathematician Georg Cantor's definition of transfinite numbers and theory of infinity, the *aleph* is 'an approximation of everything' (Gibson 1988: 128), a place that is not a place, yet a complete synthesis of experience that feels as though it is. Cantor's work on set theory led him to posit that the cardinal number of a set of real numbers is larger than the aleph-null; in other words the possibility exists for exponentially expanding worlds of mathematical numbers to exist or nest within even larger such worlds, an approximation not dissimilar to Turing's machines within machines, or PCs and software. But Cantor was able to deduce from this what he called the power of the continuum, one that, 'is not denumerable, not algebraic, hence transcendental' (Reese 1980: 79). In *Mona Lisa Overdrive*, past fiction – allusions to Borges's magic realism – and the mathematics informing cybernetic theory coalesce. Two passages from *Mona Lisa Overdrive* are reproduced to provide a glimpse of the vision that the virtual research community has found so arresting. They suggest the ability of virtual technologies to fill a vacuum in meaning left by the explanation, and hence denigration, of the old Christian God. In the novel's suggestion that virtual technology might fill this vacuum, an opening is offered to inventors and programmers who might themselves share in the power of creation, and achieve a heady antidote to their alienated sensibilities. The first passage traces a future 'history' of virtual environments and might be read as a research agenda, or a comforting myth to virtual researchers that their endeavours will surely succeed, the 'death' of narrative notwithstanding.

> There's no *there, there*. They taught that to children, explaining cyberspace. She remembered a smiling tutor's lecture in the arcology's executive creche, images shifting on a screen: pilots in enormous helmets and clumsy-looking gloves, the neuroelectronically primitive 'virtual world' technology linking them more effectively with their planes, pairs of miniature video terminals pumping them a computer-generated flood of combat data, the vibrotactile feedback gloves providing a touch-world of studs and triggers. . . . As the technology evolved, the helmets shrank, the video terminals atrophied. (1988: 40)

Terminals which atrophy have already learned from their human inventors. The cyborg dynamic infects and inflects the machine and the human equally.

The second passage is a didactic exchange between one of the 'fractured selves' contained within the cybernetic/alephic god and a human 'construct' seeking her cyborg origin and basis for identity. It can be read as a contradictory blend of moral cautionary tale and tantalization of the VR research community Gibson has helped identify. The god speaks first.

> 'the mythform is usually encountered in one of two modes. One mode assumes that the cyberspace matrix is inhabited, or perhaps visited, by entities whose characteristics correspond with the primary mythform of a "hidden people". The other involves assumptions of omniscience, omnipotence, and incomprehensibility on the part of the matrix itself.'
> 'That the matrix is God?'
> 'In a manner of speaking, although it would be more accurate in terms of the mythform, to say that the matrix *has* a God, since this being's omniscience and omnipotence are assured to be limited to the matrix.'
> 'If it has limits, it isn't omnipotent.'
> 'Exactly. Notice that the mythform doesn't credit the being with immortality, as would ordinarily be the case in belief systems positing a supreme being, at least in terms of your particular culture. Cyberspace exists, insofar as it can be said to exist, by virtue of human agency.'
> 'Like you.'

'Yes. . . .'
'If there were such a being,? she said, you'd be a part of it, wouldn't you?'
'Yes.'
'Wouldn't you know?'
'Not necessarily.'
'*Do* you know?'
'No.'
'Do you rule out the possibility?'
'No.' (1988: 107)

Altered States

Several strands now synthesize a virtual world. One is hard/soft/wetware –
computer technology and technical ingenuity. A second falls under the
'cultural software' umbrella of 'arts and entertainment'. Both appear
equally important to the genesis of any extant VR commodity or intellectual
property now before us. A third strand touches directly on the notion of
transcendence implied at various points above. The turn to VR by
prominent individuals involved in the promotion of psychedelic drugs
speaks to a larger shift in interest from illegal to legal commodities as forms
of release from material reality (as well as the progressive commoditization
of experience), but also to a continuing cultural interest in the juncture
between meaning and identity such as these intersect with transcendence,
magic and their symbolic/desirable forms. Such a focus has broadened
interest in VR away from its more purely military and entertainment
applications, and also nudges a research agenda which in engineering a
space for what is arguably either a disembodied subjectivity or a newly
emerging quasi-material cyborg, partly following Gibson, fosters and
foresees a utopian moment when the material body will be forgotten.
Psychedelia meets the Gulf War head on at this juncture in cyberspace.
Gibson's not-quite-dystopian future is as addiction prone as the present. A
mind-numbing array of legal and not-so-legal substances are indiscriminately
consumed by all manner of people residing this side of the interface in
equal measure to the amount of time large portions of the population
spend jacked-in to a VE Gibson calls Stims. Stims offer a brave new television in which users experience somatic merger with the emotions and
memories of cybernetically reconfigured media celebrities courtesy of
electrodes implanted at the base of their skulls. In the (very near) future,
Gibson suggests, celebrity status will be Divine, a potential eventuality that
extends and complements terrain explored by John Fiske (1993) in his
study of Elvis, celebrity status, and the popular grasp of science.

In arguing the connection between the will to VR and psychedelia,
Terence McKenna notes that 'technology has already proven that it is the
drug most palatable to the Western mind' (1991: 233). In a society of
addiction, he wonders if VR will be judged by administrators as a safe and
harmless substitute for drugs, but on a level more germane to this review
he notes that the synaesthesia facilitated by VR echoes the hallucinogenic

reality where vocal performances are experienced visually and tactilely; further, that like the quality of a drug, the altered consciousness implicated by VR will be no better than the *quality of the codes* – the underlying software or language upon which it will depend and through which it will be conveyed.

Rheingold investigates the mainstream media interest that has conflated VR to an electronic LSD, suggesting that such concerns override more real applications of the technology such as modelling radiation therapy for cancer patients, or walk-through CAD architectures (1991: 354). Such mainstream interest, Rheingold suggests, stems from a more general problem in American society about how to handle ecstasy, as in *ex-stasis*. In this, I find he supports a claim that transcendent imagining, wishing to enter a dream state, is one of the key drivers of this technology. He raises the possibility that people will use cyberspace to get out of not only their bodies but also their minds, and argues as to the good of this, by comparing VR favourably to the inappropriate contexts within which real-time addiction takes place in contemporary society. Kelly's (1994) 'hive-mind' – his belief that the Internet's exponential growth discloses a yearning for 'one planetary soul' – speaks to the continuing need for community once met by an earlier religion supplanted by Virilio's 'machine-God'. In all of this there is no space for the body. This is *ex-stasis* – out of the body's stance and into the visibilized world of language, fibre-optics and trance.

Epilogue

In his discussion of the relationship between GIS (Geographic Information Systems) and social theory Eric Sheppard observes that:

> A critical history of the possibilities opened up by GIS requires an investigation of the *silences* in GIS technology; of the many things that it has not been developed to do, of the alternative paths that were not pursued, and why. . . . The proper question is not whether the technology is better now than before, but whether it is better than it could have been if other paths had been pursued. (1993: 5)

Sheppard's caveat might well be appended to Frank Biocca's observation that 'a developmental logic' – a set of goals for the medium's future – already exists to circumscribe the various versions of cyberspace under development (1992b: 25). The need for limits, standards and conventions will condition the spectacle of cyberspace equally as the editorial decisions forced by the narrative form of this chapter. If anything is implicit in the present paper, it is that ideologies or developmental logics that underlie the intention behind technologies then get built into the technologies themselves. The limitations of each technical form constrain and empower what they do. Here lies a difficulty in a shift from metaphoric understanding based on narrative to one based on images and living in visions. The importance of a temporal dimension that is implied in narrative is set aside in a programmed illusion of a potentially infinite, spatialized present. If, for example, *Neuromancer* gave voice to a virtual community, it did so in a print format arguably closer to orality than the VR 'picture writing' which is part of its fascination.

It is worth recalling the connection between voice and orality and by implication that people may only really come into a fuller knowledge of things when they physically speak to each other about them. 'Giving voice to' admits that it takes time for someone first to have spoken, others to listen, later to rebut, reply and circulate. To give voice implies a discursive community different from the politically neutralizing isolation that telematics, however extensive of the self, may well imply.

Yet to date resistance to unwanted political use of technologies most often has been theorized around an implicitly unitary individual situated at a remove from the (misused) technology under review. VR as a transcendence machine that delivers the overly atomized modern individual into a merger of subjectivity and landscape, a scene in which he or she potentially may communicate with other disembodied selves gathered in a virtual room but situated anywhere around the globe, challenges traditional notions such as that of Gramsci's organic intellectual – concretely positioned in relation to both allies and enemies – with respect to how opposition of a technology's undesirable implications might be constructed.[12]

While virtual social organization might take on a more collective organization, not unlike some of the more progressive understandings advanced by the cyberpunk counterculture, this *form* of resistance would depend on mediated standards and hence a central power. Such an ambiguous eventuality might demand a painful and lengthy reconsideration of the modern distinctions erected between humans and their technology, even between existence and communication. Are they worth retaining within what, politically, might become an extended struggle over codes? Do 'we' value the space of individual subjectivity, or has the weight of responsibility placed upon it become such that certain individuals would gladly give it over to an electronic hive-mind based on the 'truth' of propositional logic – one wherein the 'correspondent' representation has become more real than the real?

Finally, just who is this 'we'? Who is so eager to give up their subjectivity to the hive-mind planetary soul? Would this be an illegal Latina maid working under the table in Westside, LA? Would it be a gay Colombian man who cannot claim refugee status lest he be deported back to Cali death squads? I think not. Most of the world still struggles to attain the space to practise a subjectivity a certain Western male bourgeoisie would discard as an outmoded Enlightenment commodity, content instead to face itself online, and tell itself collectively that it subsumes the larger totality, that its cartoon-like representation of the human and spatialization of social relations are aesthetically complete.

Notes

1. Kevin Kelly, promoting his vision of society modelled on the collective intelligence of the beehive – as HiveMind – writes that 'a recurring vision swirls in the shared mind of the Net, a vision that nearly every member glimpses, if only momentarily: of wiring human and artificial minds into one planetary soul' (1994: 24). In passing I note the similarity to Durkheim's *conscience collective*, defined in *The Division of Labour* as 'a set of beliefs and sentiments common to the average members of a single society [which] forms a determinate system that has its own life' (in Lukes 1972:4). Like the emerging (post)modern forms of IT, networked communications sytems/VR, the *conscience collective* is only realized through individuals yet is distinct from individual conscience. It inheres in a 'psychic type of society', is 'diffused throughout the whole' of that society, is 'indpendent of the particular conditions in which individuals are placed' and 'results from fusion of individual impressions' (Lukes 1972: 4). Durkheim's critics disliked the metaphysical nature of the concept (see Gane 1988), pointing out that it blurred distinctions between the moral, the religious and the cognitive. In this it anticipates the 'electronic sublime' (Carey and Quirk 1970) which telematics achieves in its marriage of computation to telephony. The networked conflation of morality, religion and cognition parallels the collapse of, and helps set up a need to rethink the categories of culture and information, between culture both as a commodity and a form of life that thereby resists the reduction implied by commodity.

2. I would note the Renaissance invention of camera obscura, the period's rediscovery of Ptolemaic perspective, the codification and application of perspective techniques by Alberti, da Vinci and others, the development of cartographic mapping and the landscape idea which depend on enframement and visual techniques to extend the spatial power of the user/subject, and, over time, magic lanterns, the camera, cinema, television and video as precursors of newer fibre-optical technologies which further extend the power of the eye.

3. 'Within' the space of this game, pterodactyls swoop down through an illusion of three-dimensional space to snatch unwary players engaged in killing one another, and who are then carried 'high' into the air to be dropped to their 'death' on the cartographic chessboard surface 'below', but who then experience immediate 'resurrection' so that the virtual killing may resume.

4. Turing (1950) asserted that 'at the end of the century the use of words and general educated opinion will have altered so much that one will be able to speak of machines thinking without expecting to be contradicted' (1950: 442). A machine that imitates human intelligence may provide little or no useful service (Bolter 1984); there are already plenty of humans to do human tasks. Instead (shades of Marx) the 'Turing machine' has come to be seen by subsequent inventors and assorted 'technotopians' as a kind of defining technology (metaphor) of the age, one that reorganizes the way humankind relates to nature. Humans become 'information processors', nature 'information to be processed'. Within the 'world' of the 'Turing machine', computation is 'nothing more than *to replace discrete symbols one at a time according to a finite set of rules*' (Bolter 1984: 47 – synopsis drawn, in part, from Bolter 1984: 10–14, 43–7).

5. For a chilling account of these applications in action see Sterling (1993).

6. Though with personnel movement from NASA to educational institutions this may now begin to change, as exemplified by Hayles's testimony: 'From my experience with the virtual reality simulations at the Human Interface Technology Laboratory [at the University of Washington – Seattle] and elsewhere, I can attest to the disorienting, exhilarating effect of feeling that subjectivity is dispersed throughout the cybernetic circuit' (1993: 72).

7. Politicized social relations renders NASA keen to construct and preserve legitimacy in the taxpaying public's eye. More so than in the case of the US Air Force, there are regular Congressional movements to dismantle, downsize or restructure the agency. It behoves NASA to air its successes widely, given concerns with industrial espionage and national security.

8. When Turing's cybernetically influenced model of reality is applied in this way a certain impoverishment of vision inherent in it is revealed. As Pagels notes (1988: 94), mathematics formalizes objects in space; human perception always functionally relates objects to their roles – a difference I take as similar to that between geographic conceptions of absolute and relational space.

9. Though within this earlier formula, traditional SF managed to comment on social relations. This passage from Heinlein's *Beyond This Horizon* (1942), a description of a computer, is strikingly descriptive of today's global cyberspatial data flows: '[t]he manifold constituted a dynamic abstracted structural picture of the economic flow of a hemisphere' (cited in Kurland, 1984: 200).

10. This 'community' corresponds to an alternative definition of cyberspace offered by Heim (1993: 32): 'the broad electronic net in which virtual realities are spun'.

11. In 'Visual pleasure and narrative cinema', Laura Mulvey invokes the Freudian 'scopophilic' pleasure of looking and being looked at to locate her argument that a fascination with film is reinforced by pre-existing fascinations already at work within the individual subject (1975: 6). Though she thereby acknowledges a certain historic specificity, it is restricted to the individual level by her psychoanalytical take. VR and other 'psychotechnologies' also trade at this level. Mulvey relies on a Freudian conception of narcissism as fascination with the human form wherein (self) identity ironically is located in an act of self-recognition with a corresponding image. VR and IT promote self-extension. All communication promotes this within an understanding of what it is to be human. However, following McLuhan (1964: 51) who argued that the West's cultural bias is evident in its misinterpretation of the Narcissus myth as meaning only an injunction against a false self-love achieved through reflection and image, I want to note the *nar*cotic in *nar*cissism, and the numbness that results from an unwise over-extension of the self into exteriorized image, such as body-as-information. In identifying self-interest with the screen, the cinema is also an anodyne for an overtaxed subjectivity perhaps too closely identified with reproducing the demanded stability which is a precondition of the state's existence (see Deleuze and Guatarri 1987). In a post-national culture such stability seems increasingly less central to global selves.

12. At the outset I named VR as a machine to realize desires for transcendence. Deleuze and Guattari (1987) and Raulet (1991) write of 'desiring machines' – at the very least as a subset of a 'collective assemblage of enunciation, a machinic assemblage of desire' (Deleuze and Guattari 1987: 23) that would allow us to 'arrive at the magic formula we all seek – PLURALISM = MONISM – via the dualisms that are the enemy, an entirely necessary enemy, the furniture we are forever rearranging' (1987: 20–21). These passages echo Durkheim's *conscience collective* discussed in note 1. They also well describe the merger with a collectivity the modern Western(ized) self may seek within VR. Access is individuated. 'We' are all together online, yet home alone via the 'dualism' of binary logic, the 'furniture' of mathematical codes which permit the constant 'rearranging' of picture language within VR's representation and emblematic 'space'. Yet a 'desiring machine' already has swallowed the subject that Deleuze and Guatarri also identify as representationally coeval to the state. Even an intermediate stage of political agency such as the man-machine cyborg seems unavailable to their approach for those who would choose not to cede subjectivity to the machine at this historical juncture, given the appetite implicit in 'desiring machines'. Raulet grasps that desiring machines efface locality within a seamless web of *network* – the rhizomal structure Deleuze and Guattari privilege. Desiring machines, ironically, are an anthropomorphisis that occludes humanity, let alone a reconsideration of the political complicity of subject re: the state. Though rhizomes are an ideal metaphor for the content/form of modern IT and telematics, rhizomes-as-metaphor reproduces the power of representation Deleuze and Guattari seek to undermine. I argue that although representative forms are essential to communication, their excessive use is worth resisting and that VR's current developmental trajectory manifests many aspects of such excess. Machines *for* transcendence intends to skirt the metaphysics that swirls around these issues by suggesting a relationship *between* human agents and technology equally as I acknowledge that technology now inflects human *existence*.

References

Anderson, B. 1991. *Imagined Communities: Reflections on the Origin and Spread of Nationalism*, revised edn, New York: Verso.

Barfield, O. 1977. *The Rediscovery of Meaning and Other Essays*. Middleton: Wesleyan University Press.

Benedikt, M. 1992. 'Cyberspace: some proposals', in M. Benedikt (ed.), *Cyberspace, First Steps*, Cambridge, MA: MIT Press.

Biocca, F. 1992a. 'Virtual reality technology: a tutorial', *Journal of Communications*, 42(4).

Biocca, F. 1992b. 'Communication within virtual reality: creating a space for research', *Journal of Communications*, 42(4).

Bolter, J.D. 1984. *Turing's Man: Western Culture in the Computer Age*, Chapel Hill: University of North Carolina Press.

Bolter, J.D. 1991. *Writing Space: The Computer, Hypertext, and the History of Writing*, Hillsdale, NJ: Lawrence Erlbaum.

Brand, S. 1987. *The Media Lab: Inventing the Future at MIT*, New York: Viking Penguin.

Brenneman, W.L. Jr., Yarian, S. and Olson, A. 1982. *The Seeing Eye: Hermeneutical Phenomenology in the Study of Religion*, University Park: Pennsylvania State University Press.

Bukatman, S. 1993. *Terminal Identity: The Virtual Subject in Post-Modern Science Fiction*, Durham, NC: Duke University Press.

Bush, V. 1946. *Endless Horizons*, Washington, DC: Public Affairs Press.

Carey, J. and Quirk, J.J. 1970. 'The mythos of the electronic revolution', *American Scholar*, Winter.

Cosgrove, D. 1984. *Social Formation and Symbolic Landscape*, London: Croom Helm.

Deleuze, G. and Guattari, F. 1987. *A Thousand Plateaus: Capitalism and Schizophrenia*, trans. B. Massumi, Minneapolis: University of Minnesota Press.

Depew, D.J. 1985. 'Narrativism, cosmopolitanism, and historical epistemology', *Clio*, 14(4).

Dery, M. 1993. *Culture Jamming: Hacking, Slashing, and Sniping in the Empire of Signs*, Westfield: Open Media.

Edgerton S.Y. Jr. 1975. *The Renaissance Rediscovery of Linear Perspective*, New York: Basic Books.

Fiske, J. 1993. *Power Plays, Power Works*. New York: Verso.

Fitting, P. 1991. 'The lessons of cyberpunk', in C. Penley and A. Ross (eds), *Technoculture*, Minneapolis: University of Minnesota Press.

Gane, M. 1988. *On Durkheim's Rules of Sociological Method*, London: Routledge.

Gibson, J.J. 1950. *The Perception of the Visual World*, Boston: Houghton Mifflin.

Gibson, J.J. 1966. *The Senses Considered as Perceptual Systems*, Boston: Houghton Mifflin.

Gibson, W. 1984. *Neuromancer*, New York: Ace Books.

Gibson, W. 1986. *Count Zero*, New York: Ace Books.

Gibson, W. 1988. *Mona Lisa Overdrive*, New York: Bantam Books.

Gibson, W. 1992. 'Academy leader', in M. Benedikt (ed.), *Cyberspace, First Steps*, Cambridge, MA: MIT Press.

Grant, G. 1990. 'Transcendence through detournement in William Gibson's *Neuromancer*', *Science-fiction Studies*, 17(5).

Hayles, N. K. 1993. 'Virtual bodies and flickering signifiers', *October 66*, Fall.

Heidegger, M. 1977. *The Question concerning Technology and Other Essays*, trans. W. Lovitt, New York: Garland.

Heilig, M.L. 1992. 'El Cine del Futuro: the cinema of the future', trans. U. Feldman, *Presence*, 1(3).

Heim, M. 1993. *The Metaphysics of Virtual Reality*, New York: Oxford.

Hobsbawm, E.J. 1990. *Nations and Nationalism since 1780: Programme, Myth, Reality*, Cambridge: Cambridge University Press.

Kelly, K. 1994. 'The electronic hive: embrace it', *Harper's*, 288: 1728.

Krueger, M. 1991. *Artificial Reality II*, Reading, MA: Addison-Wesley.

Kurland, M. 1984. 'Of God, humans and machines', in S. Ditlea (ed.), *Digitaldeli*, New York: Workman Publishing.

Laurel, B. 1993. *Computers as Theatre*, Reading, MA: Addison-Wesley.

Lindberg, D.C. 1976. *Theories of Vision from Al-kindi to Kepler*, Chicago: University of Chicago Press.

Lukes, S. 1972. *Emile Durkheim: His Life and Work*, New York: Harper & Row.

McCaffery, L. 1991. 'Introduction: the desert of the real', in L. McCaffery (ed.), *Storming the Reality Studio*, Durham, NC: Duke University Press.

McKenna, T. 1991. *The Archaic Revival*, New York: HarperCollins.

McLuhan, M. 1964. *Understanding Media*, New York: McGraw Hill.

Mazlish, B. 1967. 'The fourth discontinuity', *Technology and Culture*, 8(1).

Mulvey, L. 1975. 'Visual pleasure and narrative cinema', *Screen* 16(3).

Mumford, L. 1934. *Technics and Civilization*, New York: Harcourt Brace.

Nelson, T.H. 1972. 'As we will think', in *International Conference on Online Interactive Computing, ONLINE 72 Conference Proceedings*. Uxbridge, UK: Brunel University.

Nelson, T.H. 1973. 'A conceptual framework for man–machine everything', *AFIPS Conference Proceedings*, 42, Washington, DC: Thompson Book Co.

Nelson, T. 1977. *The Home Computer Revolution*, self-published.

Ong, W.J. 1977. *Interfaces of the Word*, Ithaca, NY: Cornell University Press.

Pagels, H.R. 1988. *The Dreams of Reason: The Computer and the Rise of the Sciences of Complexity*, New York: Bantam.

Raulet, G. 1991. 'The new utopia: communication technologies', *Telos*, 24(1).

Reese, W.L. 1980. *Dictionary of Philosophy and Religion*, Atlantic Highlands, NJ: Humanities Press.

Rheingold H. 1991. *Virtual Reality*, New York: Simon & Schuster.

Rushkoff, D. 1994. *Cyberia: Life in the Trenches of Hyperspace*, San Francisco: Harper-Collins.

Sheppard, E. 1993. 'GIS and society: ideal and reality', position paper for NCGIA conference on Geographical Information Systems and Society, Friday Harbor WA, 11 November.

Steuer, J. 1992. 'Defining virtual reality: dimensions determining telepresence', *Journal of Communications*, 42(4).

Sterling, B. 1993. 'War is virtual hell', *Wired*, 1(1).

Stone, A.R. 1992a. 'Will the real body please stand up?: boundary stories about virtual cultures', in M. Benedikt (ed.), *Cyberspace, First Steps*, Cambridge, MA: MIT Press.

Stone, A.R. 1992b. 'Virtual systems', in J. Crary and S. Kwinter (eds), *Incorporations*, New York: Zone.

Sutherland, I. 1963. 'Sketchpad: a man–machine graphical communication system', *AFIPS Conference Proceedings*, 28, Washington, DC: Thompson Book Co.

Sutherland, I. 1965. 'The ultimate display', *Proceedings of the International Federation of Information Processing Congress*, 2, Amsterdam: North Holland.

Sutherland, I. 1968. 'A head-mounted three dimensional display', *AFIPS Conference Proceedings*, 33(1).

Tuan, Y.F. 1974. *Topophilia: A Study of Environmental Perception, Attitudes, and Values*, Englewood Cliffs, NJ: Prentice-Hall.

Tuan, Y.F. 1977. *Space and Place: The Perspective of Experience*, Minneapolis: University of Minnesota Press.

Turing, A. 1950. 'Computing machinery and intelligence', *Mind*, 59: 236.

Virilio, P. 1994. 'Cyberwar, God and television' (interviewer L. Wilson, trans. G. Illien), *CTHEORY* 21 October (c.theory@concordia.ca).

Weiner, N. 1948. *Cybernetics; or Control and Communication in the Animal and the Machine*, New York: John Wiley.

Whorf, B. 1952. *Collected Papers on Metalinguistics*, Washington, DC: Foreign Service Institute, Department of State.

Woolley, B. 1992. *Virtual Worlds: A Journey in Hype and Hyperreality*, Oxford: Blackwell.

6

The Coming of Cyberspacetime and the End of the Polity

Dan Thu Nguyen and Jon Alexander

In addition to the conditions under which life is given to man on earth, and partly out of them, men constantly create their own, self-made conditions, which, their human origin and their variability notwithstanding, possess the same conditioning power as natural things.

Hannah Arendt, *The Human Condition* (1958: 9)

Cyberspace and virtual reality are compelling ideas. Here literary fantasies and technological feats meet to project whole universes at the human–machine interface. However, they have so far proven unsatisfying for critical political analysis. The field of study has no recognizable boundaries or parameters within which social scientists could use traditional approaches to formulate criteria for analysis. A manic frenzy characterizes changes in the electronic world, and thus analysis often reduces to piecemeal descriptions of segregated facets of the whole. This phenomenon's components operate in ways that render obsolescent all previously analysable and easily understandable relationships. In particular, relationships one has with the self – the technology of the self or self-construction – and social relationships between people, and relations between humans and their tools, all become in new ways problematic. We need to understand the choices people are making *de facto* every day in living 'wired' lives and sharing a universal discursive space. We are equipping our world with a social nervous system similar to those in our own bodies. What then is becoming of us, individually and collectively? As we shall see, on the Internet, boundaries – temporal, spatial, associative and identity-forming – all dissolve.

We have achieved the human dream of transcending materiality at an unforeseen cost. Our civilization's goal of wisdom (perfect knowledge) has warped into a deluge of information. While valid knowledge is inescapably human because it resides tacitly and actually in bodies, machine-readable information is technical. Technology abstracts us from our existence as physical beings in the world. We ignore the boundedness of experience that leads to knowledge. Without limits, we have just information and data. This alters the old relationship between knowledge and power. Without knowledge, what happens to power? Without body-centred knowledge and power, how can we act? Activities replace action. Operations replace power. This change, we will argue, dissolves our political communities, our polities.

All technologies appear magical at first. Retired farmer Levitt Burris never had a telephone. He never even used one. Years ago, Jon Alexander asked him why. Levitt said:

> Ah jest don' trust 'em, tha's why. Look at 'er this way. Most ever time, Ah'm sure, they're perfectly OK. But say Mama Bell has sent yer voice out long distance. S'pose the power te the phone suddenly goes out. How're yuh gonna be sure yuh'll get yer voice back?

We may smile at Levitt's naivety, but are we today any more sophisticated about how to understand cyberspace, virtual reality and the Internet? In 1994 the *Star Trek* command personnel repeatedly experienced problems similar to what Levitt feared. Software flaws in the *Enterprise*'s holodeck continually endangered Federation staffers' return from cyberspace to the starship's bridge. Like Levitt, they and we still lack an adequate frame of reference with which to ground our too changeable existence.

The basis for reframing critical analysis will require certain prerequisites. We need a fresh delimitation and definition of the field under study. We also must construct new analytical tools. In other words, ultimately we must choose some concepts and research materials over others, and seek an Archimedean point from which we can begin to review the field. In this chapter, though, we only propose a few detours across the terrain of cyberspacetime. These may help inform some pertinent questions on our elusive electronic domain.

The social realm goes online

Must we restrict cyberspace to the realm inhabited by users of Internet and the other 'nets'? Is it a freemasonry-type universe reserved only for those electronically linked to others? Or is cyberspace a more diverse and polymorphous reality, in which computer technology mediates practically every human action, speech, even thought? Cyberspacetime is much larger than the Internet and the other nets. Do we not enter cyberspacetime whenever we plan a holiday, buy a package tour or book an airline flight? Many mundane activities are engagements in cyberspacetime. One goes there by visiting an automatic teller machine, buying by credit card, or paying bills via touch-tone phone. The simple act of calling overseas hurls one into cyberspacetime. Now we can also watch simulated virtual reality (VR) and its first cousin telepresence (TP) on TV.

Strictly speaking, virtual reality is a specific technology. It lets us immerse ourselves in, see and touch (even shoot virtual bullets at) computer-generated object-images. For most of us, though, virtual realities have already formed parallel spheres of existence for quite some time. Despite the stubborn resistance of our limited physical bodies, we have long tried to explore, and set up as real, domains beyond our immediate senses. As a civilization, we have learned to live with many virtual realities. Think of the molecules and atoms of our physical and chemical structure. Think of the virtual reality of this pulsating universe measured in light-years and sprinkled with black holes and supernovas. We have learned to find compelling the virtual reality of other people's suffering across oceans and time zones. Our TV screens display every day the contemporaneity of all possible human experiences. We sample a chaotic jumble of peace and war, prosperity and starvation, laughter and grief. We have so entrenched ourselves in a kaleidoscope of virtual realities that this jumble no longer jars us.

In 1994, cyberspace, VR/TP firmly caught the public's imagination. Mass media began to use them to channel the public will to fantasize. Desmond Morris's British TP documentary on the biology of love reached a new level of daring (*Nightlife* 1994). It features live microcamera coverage of the human orgasm from perspectives inside the vagina and atop the penis. This spectacle gives viewers carnal information culled from some sixty copulations. A San Francisco couple exchanged their marriage vows in 1994 inside a VR ceremony on the lost continent of Atlantis (*Southern Illinoisan* 1994). Swedish photographer Lennart Nilsson made a new TP film that follows life from a perspective inside the uterus. One sees life's every phase from conception to birth (*Health* 1994). This is truly a womb with a view.

Children were not being left out. Sales by electronic game producers Sega and Nintendo alone were out-grossing the motion picture industry (Berg 1994). Also, in fall 1994 the solitude between the schools and the media began to break down. A magical VR-TP school bus chugged on to PBS television (*Newsweek* 1994):

> Ms. Frizzle's bus can fly, shrink, submerge and turn itself into a time machine, her class gets to explore the solar system, the inside of a volcano, sound waves, weather fronts, anthills and a classmate's entire digestive system. . . . Commands Ms. Frizzle as they enter the large intestine: 'Two by two, class.'

As Marshall McLuhan taught, any new medium forms an environment that casts deep cultural shadows. Major technologies qualify as media if they provide extensions of biological abilities. Radar, sonar and aircraft extend animal capabilities. Clothes and houses extend the skin. Wheels extend the legs, radio the voice and ears, cameras the eye, tape recorders and computers the brain. Money stores human energy. Because such technologies do what bodies once did, they produce cultural mutation. A culture is partly an order of sensory practices and preferences. An environment is an accustomed, unnoticed set of conditions that limits an organism's world at any given moment. Once we notice an environment, this transforms it into an 'old environment'. The old environment becomes content for the currently operative one, of which we remain oblivious. Each medium-environment controls how people who use it will think and act. Each alters how people use their five senses. Each affects how people react to what they perceive. The new environment helps decide what we and our societies will become. McLuhan says (1962: 22–3):

> Those who experience the first onset of a new technology, whether it be alphabet or radio, respond most emphatically because the new sense ratios set up at once by the technological dilation of eye or ear, present men with a surprising new world, which evokes a vigorous new 'closure', or novel pattern of interplay, among all of the senses together. But the initial shock gradually dissipates as the entire community absorbs the new habit of perception into all of its areas of work and association. But the real revolution is in this later and prolonged phase of 'adjustment' of all personal and social life to the new model of perception set up by the new technology.

We are scarcely past the first onset of this new technology-environment. In world history, no new medium has diffused so quickly as cyberspacetime is doing, or required such rapid adjustment. Obviously something highly addictive has been happening. By February 1995 only 13 per cent of adult Americans had already gone 'online', but the number of modems had doubled since the previous May (Fineman 1995:30). Analysts expected that half of American homes would have modems within the next five years (Alter 1995:34). We need to understand why this is happening, to glimpse what it means. Why, for example, is the freewheeling culture of cyberspace so addictive?

The non-place of cyberspacetime contains innumerable networks resting on logical lattices abstracted from unthinkably complex data fields that unfold across an endless virtual void. Somehow we get there without physical movement. 'Cybernauts' connect through their modem-equipped computers or 'decks' by 'jacking in' to the 'matrix' of cyberspace to access some data. The cardinal points and life's materiality disappear into the weightlessness of cyberspacetime. One initially experiences a bodiless exultation that may shortly settle into the armature of addiction. Going online 'flatlines' a person. That is, it immobilizes the body and suspends normal everyday consciousness. One remains at once wholly engaged in and yet set apart from the information nexus. Cyberspacetime technologically extends and partly replaces consciousness. As with drugs, we can speak of going into an altered state, experiencing alternating eddies of need, frustration and gratification. We may get an endomorphic high when jacked into a deck that projects our disembodied consciousness into the 'consensual hallucination' that is the VR-TP cyberspace matrix (Gibson 1984). This is like the out-of-body experiences long-distance runners enjoy and people who have nearly died sometimes recall. While we immerse ourselves in cyberspacetime, physical limitations and boundaries collapse or disappear.

Internet users recognize others by their online aliases or 'handles'. Ottawa Freenet director Chris Bradshaw (1994) explains the net's power of attraction as people getting hooked on anonymity. He calls MUDs a good example. On the Internet, collective utopian fantasies have produced enchanting virtual reality games called MUDs or multi-user dungeons. These are cyberplaces where hordes of people 'go' every day – and from which many do not return for days on end. People mainly jack into the MUDs to fight without anger, gain experience points and virtual capabilities, and become like gods. There, they may also pursue nihilistic 'techno-fetishes'. They may share fantasies about being cuddly, furry animals with unlimited subjective dimensions. Although university students regularly become Net habitués in ways that improve their grades (Bailey 1994), they often drop their studies entirely because courses take too much time away from their MUD existence.

DungeonMaster Lambda [Pavel Curtis] created a MUD called LambdaMOO (Quittner 1994: 95). 'It is clear to me,' he says, 'that MUDs are sufficiently attractive that many people get themselves in self-control trouble with them. They are certainly addictive to an amazing number of people.' Cyberspace MUDs are captivating because people get an intense thrill from the shock of networked communication. They find their new global yet intimate connections exhilarating. Feeling like a combined rush of adrenalin and whole blood serotonin, this experience is genuinely sensational. In cyberspacetime one can live out any fantasy. Everything goes or is at least possible. In the LambdaMOO MUD, for instance, players adopt any one – or more – of three sexes. The cyberhip call this 'identity hacking' (see the discussion of MUDs in Chapter 9).

The online experience

Themes of the end of modernity, and of a castelike society that squashes opportunities for youth run starkly, Chris Bradshaw says, through the cyberpunk literature of William Gibson and his followers. So does the theme of unrelenting anonymity. In Gibson's 1993 book *Virtual Light*, a subtheme is that everywhere there are signs of closure, of opportunities thwarted due to increasingly rigid social stratification. Against this closure stands a key element in role playing: anonymity. It lets us become any animal, mineral, vegetable or disembodied intelligence we could ever wish. Cyberspacetime devotees among the younger generation do face less real-world employment opportunity than their parents enjoyed. This alone would make the curent younger generation especially escapist. Its members see vertical and hierarchical relationships controlling and putting stress on older people. The younger generation gets stress relief by escaping from a hierarchical world that lacks a place for them – into electronic fantasy games or data surfing.

Jacked into the matrix, they find a lateral world of people cooperatively connecting to play roles, share ideas and experiences, and live fantasies. Common courtesy is much in evidence on the Internet. When structures are falling, common courtesy is a strong form of order-seeking behaviour. The chaotic flux of cyberspacetime makes common courtesy an essential navigating tool. What they do in the matrix every day is making the denizens of cyberspace seemingly more literate and articulate. At the same time, they become more and more detached from any common frame of reference. In simultaneously bringing back lost arts of chatting and letter writing, the Internet is fusing the oral and the written. People must judge you solely based on the words you write. However, because 'identity hackers' abound, people know too that you may not be telling the truth. Pamela Kane (1994: 204) makes a common point: 'Unless you choose to disclose it, no one else knows whether you are male, female, tall, short, a redhead or blond, black, white, Asian, Latino, in a wheelchair or not.'

Observers often conclude from this phenomenon merely that computer-mediated communications are highly susceptible to deception. This is a serious understatement. Something much deeper is going on. As McLuhan and Fiore (1967: 94–5) tell us: 'Electric circuitry is orientalizing the Western legacy. The contained, the distinct, the separate – are being replaced by the flowing, the unified, the fused.' Under power's endless refraction within the new electronic dispensation, old assumptions about the nature of identity have quietly vanished. Our individual concreteness dissolves in favour of the fluid, the homogeneous and the universal. Once the palpable particularity of individual identity is lost, we become relational feedback units among endless arrays of refracted power.

Language that is no longer checked and verified by physical reality loses its very grounding. Eventually it may well cease to maintain its *raison d'être* as a tool for human communication. Without the materiality of lived existence how can one sustain responsibility for one's words, written or oral? How can people say what they mean and mean what they say? In short, to what does language refer? Internet commentators speak in mistakenly reassuring ways only about a 'narrow bandwidth' effect. This 'effect' has apparently led throngs of people concerned about their differences, disabilities, defects, diseases and dreads to swarm online. There they get virtual equal treatment, an experience they find empowering. That could only happen once language began to transcend physical being. Within the structure of the sign, signifiers do not just split off from that which they signify. That occurs in modernity. Also the sign is cut off from the referent. This is a postmodern phenomenon.

Having a large measure of control over the information given out does make people in some senses more sociable and friendlier than they would otherwise have been. Chris Bradshaw (1994) says this is like going from the society of urban apartment living to something more like rural seclusion within single-family homes. People are more sociable under conditions in which they can better control the presentation of self in everyday life. This is why architects tear out walls to increase office efficiency. Richard Sennett (1976: 15) explains:

> When everyone has each other under surveillance, sociability decreases, silence being the only form of protection. . . . People are more sociable, the more they have some tangible barriers between them, just as they need specific places in public whose sole purpose is to bring them together. . . . Human beings need to have some distance from intimate observation by others in order to feel sociable.

This helps explain the gregariousness some introverted people display online. It is why both utilitarian professional and purely social virtual communities are suddenly so popular.

Under these conditions, the social activity we must investigate is complex and elusive. What can one say of the actors or agents who move through it? Is it still possible to speak of rational subjects or actors? Habermas (1987: 362–3) describes a new form of domination and de-politicization, the 'colonization of the life world'. This means that governments and private agencies increasingly subject clients and consumers to meshes of micro-authority. In so doing they define for the client or consumer the form and meaning of the needs the institutions aim to meet. Has the once dominant conceptual category of the 'individual' now reconstructed itself into a universal 'user'? What can one say of a political discourse carried out between users? Because cyberspace forms an extension of everyone's nervous system, it forms a seamless web that pushes toward a convergent yet conflictual unity.

Heim (1993: 73) proposes to replace the notion of user with that of 'monad' to capture the essence of the human–computer bond. A monad is a person and work station viewed together. Heim suggests that within each monad the collectivity exists in its entirety. Every monad can display a virtually complete range of perspectives based on the range of softwares and databases at its disposal. The Internet is diffusing in large part by virtue of making mountains of software available. It is there for the taking through the anonymous file transfer protocol (ftp) that permits free downloading. This treasure trove provides a wide range of adoptable perspectives. These prostheses add to each monad's anonymity. The last requirement of a common ground remains the compatibility of hardware, but, even then, hardware provides no absolute. It, too, is subject to obsolescence. We see here a radical reformulation of human agency to adapt to the fact of computer technology.

Further, the transformation of human agency into usership or monadism is a particularly Western phenomenon. The language of cyberspace is English and cyberspacetime itself is a Western, post-industrial and specifically American creation. For most people on the planet, this reconstruction of reality is far from being of paramount importance or relevance. It remains to be seen what effects this reality gap will have on relations between the West and the Rest, and on humanity's ability to deal with the very real problem of earthly scarcity and limitations: resources, population, pollution.

People connect because of shared interests, not physical location. Any number can play. It matters not how many participate. Once one gets online, cyberspace is spacious. There is little sense of crowding. This depends on the massive amount of parallel computer processing always going on. The Net is a moving frontier in that anyone feeling crowded can move on to form a new Usenet discussion group. The number of computers hooked up on the Internet is more than doubling every year. Up to 50 million people now use e-mail (Leslie 1994: 42). The computer networks are fast becoming the world's principal medium for imparting and exchanging information (Barlow 1994: 86).

The globalization of time

Predictably, a warping of our arrow of time accompanies the blurring of boundaries within our discursive space. The abstraction from spatial materiality has allowed not only the unbounded creation of identity – identity hacking – but also the escape from temporal parameters. The once-immutable natural boundaries of our existence in time, by which we ordered individual and collective life, have quietly crumbled. There is no longer a clear demarcation between daytime, our time for action, speech and thought, and night-time, our time for sleep and rest, peace and quiet.

J.T. Fraser (1987: 314) calls this phenomenon the greying of the calendar, evident in a time-compact globe. He writes: 'we witness in our age a revolutionary recasting of the calendar: profound, silent, irreversible. It is done without governmental action or fanfare or even much public attention.' The greying of the calendar is the smoothing out of differences between day and night. It is also the disappearance of distinction among the days of the week and among the seasons of the year. To see this clearly, let us examine what everyday life is like for someone working at the information frontier's forefront.

Bob Cameron (1994) and his wife Peggy run a global cottage business out of their home in Brentwood, Tennessee, a suburb of Nashville. They teach about, develop and sell the coming generation of digital telephone technology or ISDN technology, which will form the infrastructure for low-cost, accessible video telephones. These videophones will eventually replace both modems and conventional phones – and thus give people the broader bandwidth so many have begun to crave.

Bob has formed a virtual corporation with a Taiwan high-tech company called Lodestar Technology. He does 'beta testing', trying out new ISDN telephone products and checking them for software flaws, as they come straight from the design labs. For system integration and sales, Bob may get his first call from the US Eastern standard time zone about 7.30 a.m. Calls from the Pacific time zone come as late as 6.30 p.m. Most of the work, though, is eight to five – unless there is really good sailing weather. In beta testing, the defects mainly show up at customer sites, so he must see these customers during their business day. People call to say they cannot do this or that, or something else does not work. On site, Bob figures out whether the problem lies with the equipment or with the phone company's service. Once he gets a defect isolated to his equipment, he changes the equipment to prove it is not a hardware problem. If a defect remains, he documents it so his Taiwanese co-workers can fix the software.

For the first two or three months of a new product, Bob typically requests software 'fixes' every day or two. Taiwan and Nashville are twelve hours apart. When Bob finds a flaw, he sends an e-mail or fax. His Taiwan partners read it when they get to work. While Bob sleeps, they fix the problem. They issue a new software release by uploading the amended program to the CompuServe network. ISDN phones let the software program traverse cyberspace almost instantly, immune to customs or tariff barriers. Then, while the Taiwanese sleep, colleagues in Seattle download the software and burn it into read-only memory chips. These they send by courier to Bob – who makes them available to customers the same day. The work continues nonstop around the ever greyer clock.

Bob argues that people's biological clocks prevent them from working well through night shifts. Typically, one gets only two-thirds to three-quarters of a standard day's performance from people on the midnight shift. Such workers also call in sick more often. A corporation with people spread across the time zones will have a 24-hour-a-day labour force with everyone working normal hours. At closing time, employees will hand off work electronically. Colleagues in the next time zone can pick it up and carry the work forward in a temporal relay race. This is a definitive, technology-driven standard, melding cyberspace with cybertime.

In Bob's virtual corporation, one Taiwanese engineer carries all the ISDN software on his laptop's hard disk. He can work at home, as can the Americans. Thus, cyberspacetime permits a virtual corporation to operate with low overhead. It needs no office towers, mainframe computers or other infrastructure that will help make a company unprofitable. This is the extreme in work efficiency. It therefore defines the standard form that global corporations must now begin to take. The virtual corporation's global conquest of cyberspacetime gives it a competitive advantage by speeding up the product development cycle. To compete successfully, corporations must get themselves wired in ways that let them take full advantage of the time-compact globe.

The breakdown of modernity

We must try to distinguish here two separate but parallel developments. Net play is addictive; Net work is hegemonic. Both are disordering our primordial frame of reference – human subjectivity within spacetime. Together, these network-generated operations conclusively undermine political discourses centred on notions such as agency, action, territory, progress and development. Usership, operation, non-linearity, recursivity and chaos appear as traits of computer technology and of cyberspacetime itself. These are characteristics of the breakdown of modernity itself. Peter Emberley (1988: 50) claims:

> [T]he old vocabulary of forces, pressures, bodies, plane surfaces, densities of mass, uniform motions, action-reaction – in short, the language where cogs, wheels, and springs compose a thing in uniform space and time classified by a detached observer – has been relinquished. In its place we have the organic

metaphors of process, feedback, biopower, waste disposal, data-environment patterns, and entropy. Or the metaphors of field theory – displacement, circuits, differential equations of motion, exchanges, and relations. Thus our electronic media-data come to be nothing but an extension of our central nervous system.

The old economy of production, of industrial policy, of state initiative, of discrete and singular actors and audiences, of centers and margins, form and contents, in brief, the great order of referential finalities where the world was compartmentalized, taxonomically ordered, and prescriptive – all this is over.

William Tolhurst *et al.* (1994: 61) write that the Internet forms a tangled web of assorted machines in different networks with different users: 'One way to describe the amorphous physical structure of the Internet is as a "cloud" of computers, with the corresponding image of continuous melding and shifting over time.' Our desire to reconstruct ourselves and our environment electronically has led us to a critical threshold. Behind us lies the historical reality of well-defined boundaries. On the other side lie clouds. We must learn to look at everyday life from both sides now.

The old boundaries framed an order in which people thought of time as flowing relentlessly forward, unidimensionally and irreversibly. Within that order, one could effectively enclose and control space. Within that frame of reference, states organized human affairs accordingly. They could segregate peoples within geographical borders. States could hand down political judgements based on arbitrary criteria selected out of the 'progress' of their own discrete civilizations. Can nations still protect the integrity of international borders when bits flow across them with total freedom, and governments can neither tax their value nor limit their content?

The old definition of spacetime on which our nation-based order rested is quickly becoming in McLuhan's terms our 'old environment', mere content for the new one. Now the single-minded can find each other with the speed of light. In the old nation-state people met face to face and compromised on the basis of shared everyday lives. In cyberspace each precinct is virtual, and people only 'meet' in it to talk about one specific thing. The old mass media were unifying media; they assembled and sustained nations with real-time theatre. In cyberspace, there is no centre stage; however immense, cyberspacetime is intensely decentralizing. The proliferation of means of communications has surpassed governmental control capabilities. Computers linked to the Internet are so numerous and so broadly diffused (30 million subscribers in 92 countries) that they are virtually impossible for any nation to control. The Communist regimes were dissolved or weakened gradually by radio and television signals. West German programmes affected East Germany, and Hong Kong broadcasts fed the appetite for reform in mainland China. Even Chinese dissidents now use e-mail. News about Chinese repression in Tibet comes regularly through cyberspace from the London-based Tibet Information Network. According to *Newsweek* (1995: 37):

> In the Soviet Union, the Internet played a small but vital role in defeating the attempted coup by Communist hard-liners in 1991. Soviet computer scientists

had hooked up to the Internet only a few months before. When Boris Yeltsin and his reformists holed up in the White House, the Russian republic's Parliament, someone inside the building started sending bulletins, including Yeltsin's edicts, on the Internet. They were picked up by the Voice of America (VOA), which broadcast them back to the Soviet Union by radio, helping to rally public support for Yeltsin.

By connecting dissidents with each other and with supporters outside the country, long-distance telephone service also helped to undermine the Soviet Union's very existence. Thus national truth was the first element of the polity to go. Although nations still exist, their polities and political elites are progressively losing control over their people.

Political science textbooks treat 'gatekeeping' as a key element of political power. A related development now subverting steeply hierarchical political power within organizations is the rapid automation of the gatekeeping function. As Tolhurst *et al.* (1994: 248) explain: 'with network technology, people can bypass gatekeepers (people who hold the key to information access) and get information directly'. This is a major shift in the nature of embodied power, an erosion of the attachment to specific central individuals who used to 'hold' power. Information technology is randomly but effectively undermining whole categories of political power bases. The centre no longer holds.

Applying social science analysis to this technological tapestry can be misleading. As many traditional conceptual boundaries are suddenly obsolescent, one cannot realistically say one circumstance or event 'causes' another in an electronic field (Deutsch 1966: 13).[1] Everything depends on the current yet changing system state, so everything happens simultaneously. Moreover, societies are losing earlier clear-cut lines of demarcation that so recently let people specify what was acceptable political discourse. Can we still maintain that politics and relations of power characterize the public sphere? Can we still distinguish the public sphere from the private or personal sphere?

Hannah Arendt tells how this distinction arose. She writes (1958: 28):

> The distinction between a private and a public sphere of life corresponds to the household and the political realms, which have existed as distinct, separate entities at least since the rise of the ancient city-state; but the emergence of the social realm, which is neither private nor public, strictly speaking, is a relatively new phenomenon.

Now the wildly proliferating fields of cyberspacetime are in this sense not only extremely social, they are also profoundly apolitical. In cyberspacetime, the social realm is engulfing and overwhelming the political realm. The 'social' is decomposing the body politic. Decay of politics is proceeding as quickly as the matrix is growing.

Time (1994) claims the US government is expanding its use of 'Clipper Chips' to help the FBI *et al.* eavesdrop on computerized messages. Reportedly the FBI is also investigating increased use of 'sniffer' programs that steal passwords and access to 'privacy protected' Internet data. Such behaviour stands well within the old paradigm, blithely oblivious to the fact that the environment has become new. All Internet books properly caution readers to navigate and behave on the assumption that for individuals nothing on the matrix is private. Struggles between data encryptors and hackers remain important, but note that the roles have suddenly transposed. Self-styled computer 'nerds' at *Wired, Mondo 2000* and the other countercultural 'zines are now the champions of encryption, while the state adopts the old criminal hackers' role. Reactionary official hacking cannot hold back the shrivelling of the polity. The forces impelling political atrophy are far too strong.

Is the social engulfing the political? In such a circumstance, politics could scarcely be the monopolization of the means of power that mainstream political scientists conventionally presume. They view power as centrally residing within the state. Yet the state is barely able to deal with social and technological developments. Mainstream political science becomes ever less applicable to reality, virtual or 'straight up'. The rise of the social and the atrophy of the political through the Internet are making Michel Foucault's writings increasingly true. To understand why we must take a detour through Alvin Toffler's concept of demassification, and several related postmodern developments.

As society becomes more differentiated and complex, it comes to require more widely distributed internal communications capabilities. As this need became apparent, businesses rushed to produce such means. This dynamic produced an information revolution. The breakup of mass production and mass marketing continue to feed this revolution. The breakup of the old industrial polity and economy are proceeding apace. Rising social diversity is riding on the back of economic demassification and the shift from goods production to information processing. Demassification and fragmentation are occurring in production, consumption, energy use and family structure as well as in communications. Socially, we see ever greater diversity evolving in areas as remote as technology and ethnicity.

From the centre, government and big companies once effectively controlled the most powerful industrial age communications media, the mass media. Political and corporate elites used forceful vertical or top-down communications processes of mass advertising and propaganda. Now, however, existing communications channels and media have become saturated. Technological innovation responded with egalitarian, demassifying information media.

The more mass society fractures, the more (and the more broadly distributed) information the social system requires. Such high information requirements force societal steering mechanisms to become equally widely distributed. The Xerox machine, tape and disk players, computers, dot matrix and laser printers, and now the computer networks helped turn the industrial polity into a McLuhanesque old environment. This is a polity-destroying development. Products, values and attitudes become more heterogeneous. Such a system requires so much more information that political information loses much of its coherent and cohesive value. The information outpouring produces widely distributed but highly positive feedback loops. Diversity now feeds on itself, continually raising the system's required information levels (Toffler 1983: 24–5, 42, 115–20). Because change is diversity in time, the faster the world changes, the more information we need to cope with change itself. The system is experiencing an extended transformational crisis. Now information has a peculiar nature. If you use it, so can I. If we both use it, chances go up that we will produce more information. However powerfully it acts to break up and tear down the industrial age polity, information is nonetheless a generative force.

Sitting before a PC has different consequences from sitting before a TV. On the Internet, the notion of office disappears. People do what they know how to, not their assigned roles. This is an enormously liberating force working against hierarchies of all kinds. This is the democracy citizens in advanced nations always dreamed of. What people are creating on the Internet is a conversational, demassified, non-representational democracy that transcends the nation-state.

As the breakdown of modernity and the mass industrial age polity proceed, we must ask another basic question. What is the relationship between information and knowledge, and how do they contribute to the identification and analysis of power? In other words, is political discourse still political in the old sense when technology comes to mediate it so transparently yet so thoroughly? What happens to power when there is only technologically produced bodiless information? Dan Nimmo and James Combs's 1990 work *Mediated Political Realities* (2nd edn) does not even mention the Internet. It remains caught in the problematique of centralized, top-down informational power. Thus, much of what we thought we knew about mediated political realities is quickly becoming wrong. Today, even the truth-value of logic, as traditionally conceived, has begun to dissolve.

The Worldwide Web ('the Web') is a set of databases that ignores formal logic or conventional library classifications. Its information lacks the straitjacketing of data paths imposed by the logic of classifying conventions. In such a database, the more general term still includes the more particular, but the opposite is now also true. One may jump either way, or laterally instead. More important, one treks through such a database without regard for formal classifications. The Web's basic design principle is its underlying architecture of hypertext. Increasingly user-friendly databases such as the Web contains have led many observers to confuse the avalanche of information with the attainment of what they persist in calling some form of knowledge. Gary Wolf writes (1994: 118):

> In the world of the Web, knowledge is not something you produce, but something you participate in. A document isn't a self-sufficient individual creation, but a perspective, or collection of perspectives, on the entire Web. . . .

All the documents in the Web are within reach. What path will you take to get to them? What path will you mark for others to take?

It is not convincing that any true 'participation in knowledge' is actually taking place, as the anonymity of users precludes responsibility, and any claim to responsible action reduces to endless activity. In this instance, power based on knowledge, as exercised by subjects, may have transformed itself into operations based on information, exercised by monads.

The Web and, by extension, the Internet represent a historically unprecedented diffusion of activity beyond the scope of conventional power relations. This activity threatens to overshadow real-world action. It nonetheless has potent real-world effects. Should it become decisive, then much of the political science literature will be wrong. If this is so, then the relationship between power, knowledge and information will change still more. Traditional analyses of power relations based on criteria of interests, classes, monopoly of force etc. remain nostalgically comforting. However, they give less and less insight into our electronically saturated world. For example, online, one must appear uninterested in steering or governing. Directive behaviour quickly leads to 'flaming' attacks from other participants. There is of course a hidden elite that keeps the Internet running. However, it shrewdly labels the basic protocols or rules of interaction merely 'Requests for Comments'. One Usenet newsgroup (discussion group) moderator found an apt metaphor (Bradshaw 1994), saying that doing the job of moderator is like herding cats. To learn how to herd cats we must now turn away from mainstream social science.

Transcending the body

Natural and human-constructed boundaries in space and time have become harder to differentiate. Electronics mediate most human interactions. These facts reflect significant changes in how self and collective identity occur. For David Bolter, electronic technology is our age's best defining technology. He writes (1984: 12): 'By promising (or threatening) to replace man, the computer is giving a new definition of man, as an "information processor," and of nature as "information to process."' Has man's relationship to nature changed from a stance of domination and mastery to one of processing? To what extent is this a qualitative shift? A logical continuity remains between a notion of nature as resource to exploit and one of nature as information to exploit. In both, nature remains external to man. Man can and therefore must use, transform and rationalize such a commodified world. Nonetheless, the world as information also underlies our return to non-industrial society. As civilization fractures, its replacement takes the form of clouds of intentional communities. Thus does the tool as computer present new characteristics.

The mechanisms of computer operations are hidden works, always beyond human sensory perception. McLuhan said every new technology changes how our sense organs operate to perceive reality, and it may be that computer technology changes not only our perception of reality but also our very selves. Electronic pulses permeate our daily lives. The extent of demand for greater and greater interdependency in human–computer interaction compels us to consider the computer as more than just an instrument or machine. It is a constructive medium. It has become an 'evocative object', a medium through which we project and realize our thoughts and undertakings. It is a constructive medium.

In studying computer culture Sherry Turkle (1984: 3) focuses on the 'subjective computer'. It shares our social lives and as such engages in psychological development. A product of our minds, it 'affects the way we think, especially the way we think about ourselves'. Computer technology comes eerily close to our humanity's core. This is the one machine that can manipulate symbols. 'The new machine that stands behind the flashing digital signal, unlike the clock, the telescope, or the train, is a machine that "thinks". It challenges our notions not only of time and distance, but also of mind.' Thus does the computer exceed the metaphorical role we usually assign to an age's traditional defining technologies. People do use computer jargon freely in association with psychological states or human anatomy (hardware/software, 'wetware', programming, accessing, etc.). People have proven oddly willing to 'interface' with a computer as opposed to interacting directly with others, to constitute ourselves and our world.

More than any previous defining technology, computer technology has forced us to rethink technology as practice instead of mere technique. The holding power of computing can create a twilight zone of electronic time and space and lived time. We cannot avoid living through the computer even if we never turn one on. This is why we must come to question this latest extension of our being. It is our consciousness and nervous system. We need to re-question the uniqueness of that which is human, and to redefine differences between human and animal, human and machine. This is, in a sense, the age-old investigation into the nature of mind and body, reason and intelligence.

In its extreme and perhaps most corrupt articulation, wherein reasoning is equated with calculation, man-the-rational-animal may at first look like computer-the-rational-machine. However, closely observing sophisticated computer manipulation of abstract symbols and logical operations shows us their respective limits. Human intelligence encompasses more than just logic and calculation. This is most salient in artificial intelligence (AI) research, where questions of computer 'mind' have made us rethink the nature of human reason and intelligence.

In the 1970s, at the University of California's Berkeley campus, computer scientists, linguists and philosophers held a series of informal discussions about the nature of language and mind. This happening suggests that computer technology had already affected traditional concep-tions of body, mind, reason and intelligence. Hubert Dreyfus called AI researchers 'the last metaphysicians'. They proved able to 'bypass brain and body, and arrive, all the more surely, at the essence of rationality'. This led Dreyfus to take up the challenge AI research posed by rethinking the nature of human reason and human 'worldliness'. He wrote (1972: xxvi): 'What we learn about the limits of intelligence in computers will tell us something about the character and extent of human intelligence. What is required is nothing less than a critique of artificial reason.' AI research in such diverse areas as game playing, language translating, problem solving and pattern recognition follows a recurring trajectory, marked by early success followed by inextricable difficulties. This pattern reveals the power of computers to simulate only certain very specific aspects of the human mind. Beyond this threshold, the computer inevitably falters. Dreyfus concluded (1972: 216):

> We can then view recent work in artificial intelligence as a crucial experiment disconfirming the traditional assumption that human reason can be analyzed into rule-governed operations on situation-free discrete elements – the most important disconfirmation of this metaphysical demand that has ever been produced. This technique of turning our philosophical assumptions into technology until they reveal their limits suggests new areas for basic research.

Having to look at one's reflection in the mirror of computer logic led to a sharp existential (and phenomenological) return to the worldly body's safe confines. For Dreyfus and for other AI critics, the argument based on the worldly body provides the crucial distance between man and machine. Dreyfus viewed the body and the situation as the two basic elements that elide computer mind. He claimed: 'what distinguishes persons from machines . . . is not a detached, universal, immaterial soul but an involved, self-moving, material body'. Moreover, 'the situation is organized from the start in terms of human needs and propensities which give the facts meaning, make the facts what they are, so that there is never a question of storing and sorting through an enormous list of meaningless, isolated data' (1972: 148, 174).

William Barrett's argument concerning the body (1986: 160) also echoes this critique of the computer's disembodied mind. 'How much of our consciousness', he asks, 'is embedded in and inseparable from this fleshy envelope that we are?' Barrett says a computer cannot learn because it does not have temporal life. 'Properly speaking, indeed, a machine cannot mature, for it is not an organic body, growing and ripening through time.' Contemporary mainstream concern with the lived body as a site for reality grounding, evident in existential phenomenology and humanist AI critiques, coincides with feminism's theorizing from the body, with postmodern philosophies of difference, and with radical pluralism. Information-based technological disruptions have thus shaken the foundations of traditional hegemonic Western subjectivity to the point where the discourses of feminism and postmodernity become a matter of necessity as well as choice.

The return to the body as *terra firma* of our human-ness nevertheless presents difficulties. Continuing his inquiries into human technological self-construction, Michael Heim echoes Dreyfus's challenge. Heim poses metaphysical questions within the electronic world. For him (1993: 59), 'cyberspace is a metaphysical laboratory, a tool for examining our very sense of reality'. Heim has little concern for the mental competition between human and machine and focuses instead on the human drive to absorb ever increasing forms of computer technology into daily life. This fascination transcends practical and utilitarian applications and reaches deeply into humanity's more inarticulate needs. Heim claims: 'Our fascination with computers is more erotic than sensuous, more deeply spiritual than utilitarian' (1993: 59).

Our love of and hunger for information in cyberspace are a logical extension of an erotic love of a sensationless world of pure ideas. This is the pursuit of the Platonic Forms themselves, made concrete by computer hardware. The impossibility of achieving wisdom, that is, divine and perfect Knowledge, does not deter us from striving to touch its beauty. The drive compelling us toward this peak is an erotic one, which should not be confused with physical love and desire. For Heim (1993: 63), Eros 'inspires humans to outrun the drag of the "meat" – the flesh – by attaching human attention to what formally attracts the mind'. Thus does Eros guide us to Logos, to thought and speech. The love of beautiful bodies and beautiful objects is but a first step toward greater and purer loves. These are the love of beautiful thoughts and knowledge. Finally, there is the love of Beauty itself. Heim thus refers aptly to Diotima's speech in Plato's *Symposium*. It forms a manifesto of Western culture's renunciation of the body. Listen to Plato (1956: 105–6):

> For let me tell you, the right way to approach the things of love, or to be led there by another, is this: beginning from these beautiful things, to mount for that beauty's sake ever upward, as by a flight of steps, from one to two, and from two to all beautiful bodies, and from beautiful bodies to beautiful pursuits and practices, and from practices to beautiful learnings, so that from learnings he may come at last to that perfect learning which is the learning solely of that beauty itself, and may know at last that which is is the perfection of beauty. There in life and there alone, my dear Socrates . . . is life worth living for man, while he contemplates Beauty itself.

This negation of the body has proved difficult. No learning or strategy could assure, or even ease, the leap from physical embodiment in space and time to the world of pure Forms, eternal and unchanging. The arrival of the information deluge provides for the moment a halfway point between Body and Form. As Heim notes (1993: 64), 'computerized representation of knowledge . . . is not the direct mental insight fostered by Platonism. The computer clothes the details of empirical knowledge so that they seem to share the ideality of stable knowledge of the Forms.' Heim's concern is with the illusion of knowledge that the information avalanche prompts (Heim 1993: 65): 'With an electronic infrastructure, the dream of perfect FORMS becomes the dream of inFORMation.'

Heim also shows what perversions inhere in trying to negate embodiment. He calls these paradoxes. They operate within cyberspace's cultural terrain. As cyberspace erases the boundaries of time and space, it also erases the materiality of our bodily boundaries. Online, we seem to break free from the limitations of bodily existence. Jacking into the matrix appears to give us (Heim 1993: 73), 'an unrestricted freedom of expression and personal contact, with far less hierarchy and formality than is found in the primary social world'. However, this godsend exacts its price. Physical presence is simulated and re-presented in a virtual world of like-represented personae. Cyberspace therefore diminishes the range and quality of human encounters, for, as deliberate and selective creations of ourselves, these re-presentations lack the responsibility of an actual bodily commitment. This remains a fundamental characteristic of human action, of direct human-to-human association.

In Toronto, for example, Telepersonals Ltd. will happily wire you up. Anyone can listen to ads or record an ad free. Men pay 55 cents a minute to send and retrieve messages. Women pay nothing – except perhaps their souls. Addiction sets in rapidly. The urge to call in to get one's messages becomes compelling. Jennifer Cowan is 28, 5 foot 10, 135 pounds, has brown hair, green eyes, and finds herself attracted to men who are intelligent and funny. She became almost instantly addicted while researching an article. In trying to explain her abrupt addiction, Ms Cowan mused (1994: 63):

> I realized I didn't want to meet people as much as to talk to them, explore who was out there and what they were thinking. I was addicted to covert communication. How else do you rationalize sitting naked in bed with the phone tucked up to your shoulder, pen and notebook in hand, until three in the morning? If on some level I wanted a man in my bed, the phone had become my placebo.

Jennifer found herself compulsively reaching out to touch someone, and then someone else, and someone else. . . . Like the cyberpunk literature (see Bukatman 1994) this reflects a new problem. Residents of the information age are proving perilously willing to play tiddlywinks with their personal identities. Millions of people have made drifting in and out of digital realities a significant part of their everyday lives. This is a global retreat from our now empty public lives, from roles we once acted out in a real-life political realm. It is a retreat from nations, from nationalism and from politics itself. This is a retreat from civilization. It places millions in a tribalized fantasy culture, a theatre of the bizarre and the absurd. Fantasy culture becomes universal by making all the world a proliferation of cyberstages, an inauthentic virtual simulation of Shakespeare's old *theatrum mundi*.

In other chapters virtual sex is discussed. Online discussions can be drily academic or viciously aggressive as well as bawdy. We hear on good authority though that cybersex chat does effect the transmission of the old message well enough to evoke physical orgasms. *Boardwatch* magazine's Jack Richard estimates that 50,000 people now engage daily in cybersex using up to 700 real-time chat lines (Kane 1994: 21). The main problem they face is not being able to type quickly enough, especially with one hand. Countless others practise more leisurely cybersex with e-mail postings; the body's most erotic organ remains the mind.

Participation in the illusion of an eternal and immaterial electronic world has other, more sinister effects. Because we have a new power to flit about the universe, we let our communities grow ever more fragile, airy and ephemeral. We are more equal because online, stand-in bodies are costless. Bodily contact is either impossible or purely optional. One never needs to stand face to face with other virtual community members. Soon we forget that our stand-in bodies lack our primary identity's vulnerability and fragility (Heim 1993: 74). 'The more we mistake the cyberbodies for ourselves, the more the machine twists our selves into the prostheses we are wearing.' Our faces are our 'display devices', our eyes the windows that set up a neighbourhood of trust. Without face-to-face, personal and private communication, our very 'ethical awareness' based on lived experiences 'shrinks and rudeness enters' (1993: 76).

The paradoxes that lurk within cyberspace gradually translate into cultural perversions and social-political distortions. The body's suppression leads to a tendency to create fetishes. It has led to commodification and reification of much human experience. There is little wonder that pornography has found a fertile field on the matrix. Destructive stances and discourses, which would demand and provoke resistances in the bounded political 'real' world, remain largely unopposed. Note the brutality, violence and enslavement that flourish in virtual worlds, especially in the MUDs. Note the prevalence of narcissism, alienation, cynicism and anomie. Here we see extremes of human behaviour and discourse at both the individual and collective levels. Given our available bandwidth, computer-mediated interactions between people must simply lose much essential meaning. Virtual worlds, distorted by disembodiment dreams, drain their inhabitants of commitment, responsibility and, ultimately, purpose. Online, Logos reduces to increasingly nihilistic play. The erotic drive that forces us to transcend our flesh may have, therefore, found its most dangerous accomplice in computer technology.

Our virtual life in cyberspace paralyses our bodies. Cyberspacetime promises us liberation from the constraints of space, time and materiality. However, without the experiences of our bodies, our thoughts, our ideas, our ethics and polities must all suffer. We know ourselves and our world mainly because we live and move in the world through our bodies. Merleau-Ponty wrote (1945: 97, our trans.): 'The body is the vehicle of being in the world. To have a body is, for a living being, to join itself to a certain environment, to involve itself with certain projects and therein to engage itself continuously.' The unfolding of the world's phenomena forms the basis of our knowledges – precisely because human-ness imposes limits. We must continually engage the world to locate ourselves compared with others and the non-human environment. To put oneself within borders is a prerequisite for ethical considerations of any kind. Merleau-Ponty continues: 'My body is the axis of the world: I know that there are many sides to objects because I can go around them, and, in this sense, I am conscious of the world by means of the body' (ibid.). In cyberspace, we no longer need to stand physically in the world to see all different sides of situations. What then becomes of our faculty to learn and to acquire knowledge, as opposed to our technical ability to gather information? In cyberspace we no longer need to face and live with the presence of others. What then becomes of our ethical and political consciousness?

The body of power

The body's arrest by the electronic promise of perfect information may be a substitute for perfect knowledge, yet it remains a voluntary subjection. As such, it is hard to subsume it under traditional conceptual strategies or understandings of power structures. We see a massive turning away from knowledge of the world that our lived bodies gathered so painfully. Replacing this knowledge is information stored in burgeoning data banks. This trading of knowledge for information brings with it an end to human action itself. In particular, it aborts political action.

In this age of the Western world's global conquest on behalf of capitalism, it may no longer be possible to make sense of or to speak sensibly about politics. Whatever is political staunchly demands a recognition of boundaries. These include the encircling walls of the polis, the segregation of governmental powers, and political sovereignty. Without boundaries, the political atrophies and becomes quietly obsolescent. In the long sweep of human history, this shift to an apolitical Western world is a sudden departure. This is one reason our subject proves so hard to analyse. Our very ease within the electronic world should, however, eventually direct us toward new lines of inquiry and unconventional conceptual categories if we are to start understanding ourselves anew. To this end, let us listen to mad prophets who speak of 'polymorphous techniques of power' (Foucault 1976: 20).

Jean Baudrillard has written an astute and extended critique of Michel Foucault's works, focusing particularly on his notion of the polymorphous techniques of power. Baudrillard attributes the appeal of these writings to their uncanny resemblance to the very power mechanisms Foucault seeks to describe. Baudrillard claims Foucault's discourse stands as a mirror image of power relations. His medium is his message (1977: 9–10, our trans.):

> The writing of Foucault is perfect in that the very movement of the text is an admirable account of that which he is proposing. This generative spiral of power is not a despotic architecture, but an ever deepening relationship, a coil, a strophe without beginning (but without climax either). It spreads ever further out and ever more rigorously. Then there is this interstitial fluidity of power which floods the entire porous network of the social, the mental, and of bodies. This is an infinitesimal modulation of the technologies of power, where relations

of power and of seduction are inextricably intertwined. All of this one can read directly in Foucault's discourse (which is also a power discourse): it flows, it empowers, and it saturates all the spaces it opens up.

While Baudrillard argues that Foucault's discourse is too seductive to sustain its claim to truth, he nevertheless correctly spotlights (Shields 1995: 24) the 'miniaturization' of power relations. This becomes evident in such notions as the 'micro-desire of power' and the 'micro-politics of desire'. Here may lie a new set of analytical tools. Rob Shields (1995) writes:

> For Foucault, institutions of legitimated politics and the statistical social sciences that buttress them are mere window dressings. They hide the real exercise of power. Power occurs precisely outside the glare of official rhetoric and rational debate. It operates at the level of individual discipline. The body's own unconscious reflexes learn to yield to power.

Perhaps we can use Foucault's toolkit to confront our electronic world.

In speaking of the 'polymorphous techniques of power', Foucault has sought to indicate the present impossibility of determining precisely the boundaries of both the field of power relations and power's techniques and strategies. Modern power operates through a 'démultiplication' or gearing down. This term covers both the proliferation of politically pertinent areas and power's breaking down into finer and finer specific practices. Power technics have framed and supported every truth claim uttered throughout history. Now, however, one carves out power relations through social engineering, say in designing the architecture of buildings. Power also inscribes itself on to the sexual body. Power has spread and broadly diffused. It has escaped the confines of the state. It is everywhere. Thus, as we lose our defining boundaries, power comes to reside precisely nowhere. It becomes far more polymorphous than earlier scholars thought. Today, we find that the centre and with it the polity are quickly dissolving.

The detailed histories Foucault selected to study are particular social domains. In each, the play of power and discourse deploys in virtually anonymous ways. His descriptions of the strategies and techniques of power lead unerringly to the formulation of a theory. This theory holds that power is elusive. The subject and object of power are themselves elusive in the sense that both are continually shifting – like clouds. When Foucault tries to address the dynamics of power beyond mere description, he can only speak of counter-power's evasive and resistant dynamics.

In this sense we can no longer understand power as having an 'essence'. Nor may we continue to view it simplistically as an attribute of those who have or hold it (Deleuze 1986: 35). It is a precariously shifting relationship between dominant and dominated, the knower and the known. It does exceed their singularities. As it spins and twirls, it produces one human turning point after another. Eventually, it always transforms the people it catches up, their relationships, their contexts – and itself. It continually produces an ever new matrix of discourses, of bodies, of strategies, and of techniques. Power's nature is no longer essential. Just as the new form of the subject is the user or monad, the new forms of power are operational.

We may therefore speak of the techniques of power, or of a technology of power. One can carry out the functional micro-analysis of such power across the terrain of human bodies. Operating on their social and personal relationships and associations, work and leisure spacetime, education and training, etc., it gives form to everyday life. The new topography of power, understood as a technology both of the self and of the collective, may then become an appropriate virtual map to guide us through the world's electronic nervous system. Knowledge, Truth and Power have become as shadowy and elusive as the virtual bodies and subjectivities that claim membership in cyberspacetime.

Conclusion

We conclude that the demassification and atrophy of the polity, the diffusion of mass powers of creation, and our loss of contact with the real world of time and space are together producing conditions for outbreaks of chaos. Our weakened polities may prove unable to contain these outbreaks. There is a basic conflict between the coming society of which the Internet is the leading edge and the democratic institutions we inherited from the industrial era.

Liberal democracy as we have known it these last three hundred years rested upon the reasoning individual representing people residing in geographical areas as its lever for progressive change. Representative democracy requires that citizens who live in local geographical communities freely choose people to represent them for strictly limited time spans in larger political arenas. The assumption is that individuals have concrete identities and interests. These must be essentially grounded in the here and now, in corporeal bodies and in geographical communities. The national democratic aggregation of interests is the finding of common ground for mass collective action between and across discrete geographical regions. Democracy is as bounded in time as it is rooted in space.

As Bob Cameron's everyday life shows, time has escaped the confines of locality. As the everyday experience of life on the Net shows, cyberspacetime is the escape from geographical rootedness into an endlessly seductive, addictive and hallucinogenic data matrix. Within the environment created by our new cyberspace media, people form virtual communities on the basis of the functional representation of narrow interests, not the geographical representation of whole living persons. These functional interests rapidly come to be increasingly limited and specialized. The oncoming society may therefore be at fundamental odds with the most basic requirements of liberal democracy.

Most social scientists did not look favourably on Foucault's reformulation of the locus and operations of power. American political science has long defined itself pragmatically, as the study of the state, its polity and very little else. Traditional and mainstream scholars have stubbornly resisted acknowledging the apparent obsolescence of their still young discipline. They doggedly try to paste old blueprints back on the collapsing walls of an imploding, spiralling, looping and recursive world. This resistance is unfortunate. It helps prevent the creation of new spirals of discourses, through which and by which we might again articulate our human-ness.

Recent entrants to the scholarly discursive community have had a different experience. They suddenly found themselves effortlessly liberated from the old boundaries, segregations, exclusions and oppressions. Para-doxically, in the same spacetime, they found themselves deprived of any chance to construct new, solid identities and subjectivities. Identity formation had become problematic. The recovery of the material body has become a central theme and a focal point for feminism, as it has been for mainstream philosophy in its encounter with disembodied computer mind. These are strategies of counter-power against the anonymity and weight-lessness of cyberspacetime. According to Allucquere Stone (1991: 1–13): 'Forgetting about the body is an old Cartesian trick, one that has unpleasant consequences for those bodies whose speech is silenced by the act of our forgetting; that is to say, those upon whose labour the act of forgetting the body is founded – usually women and minorities.' It is a deep paradox in this apolitical age that political minorities are precisely those who have most frequently found themselves being drawn on to the Net.

Yet the revival of the material body as a weapon against the techniques of a polymorphous power may be a doomed strategy. The physical body has already proved itself a fertile terrain for the deployment of technological discourses and practices. The material body has already undergone its own 'démultiplication' into fields of operation, imbued with 'power' and wired into cyberspace. Démultiplied categories include the reproductive body, the criminal body, the diseased body, the athletic body, even the dead body. Bodies can no longer serve as the last outpost of a vanishing world of finite spacetime and bounded order. Perhaps cyberspace's very 'order' will make us learn to embrace both order and disorder, linearity and recursivity, power and resistance, within our reflections on the world.

The West finds itself caught in indecision and uncertainty. So does the rest of the world that aspires to become developed and Western. In a global economic regime structured by linear production and consumption patterns, we nevertheless seek to practise recycling. Ecological concerns demand recognition of cyclical change patterns. Although electronic and satellite technologies have reduced the world's time to a single instant, we still pass budgets in our legislatures and plan our social schedules based on the conception of progressive time. Western social scientists long hoped the former colonies would develop liberally, along democratic lines. These worthies remain dumbfounded by the chaos that reigns in the so-called Third World. Current theory (and pursuit) of progressive linearity must derive from an inadequate paradigm within which scholars try to under-stand change processes. Progressive linearity has less and less to do with either the real or the virtual world. Foucauldians and the postmodernists might smile if they see mainstream theorists thus paralysed by the fear that they may already have lost their own voices. This would vindicate farmer Levitt Burris's concerns. Just when mainstreamers had sent their voices out long distance, the polity's power failure naturally began among the weakest polities – in the Third World – and this has left conventional social scientists speechless.

As societal demassification and fragmentation proceed, it is natural that the equation of the average with the normal and the good should have come under increasing attack (e.g. Canguilhem 1991). For this, the Net bears a strong responsibility. Philosophical banners of European continental 'différance', democratic pluralism, and North American rights discourse have also encouraged ever narrower minorities to make vocal demands and 'act up'. Such social groups are demanding acknowledgement and respect for their distinct and un-averageable characteristics. In cyberspace we encounter a lot of single parents, gays and lesbians, visible ethnic minorities, AIDS victims, alcoholics, drug addicts and the physically challenged. The matrix also abounds with the mentally, socially and morally challenged (Companion Disk 1993). All of these, among others, are clamouring for the satisfaction of their own particular needs.

To meet all such demands would require cancelling any notions of linear progress or a 'normal' path of human development, because normality arises only in massified social settings. Normality depends upon highly uniform social expectations. It is not accidental that the Net is well on its apolitical way toward enforcing such a cancellation. The loss of the normal destroys the possibility of collective action based on the democratic aggregation of interests. No doubt we will always call whatever is replacing liberal democracy a form of democracy, perhaps democratic corporatism. Nonetheless, the old liberal democracy rooted in human everyday life, based upon the geographical representation of persons and constrained within the earth's compass points, is withering. It will soon remain only as a withered stump, as happened with the monarchy. Before the nihilistic forces we have unleashed upon ourselves, our democratic polities are sand castles. We need not wax nostalgic for the hierarchically controlled mass society of the old industrial order. That is shattering into its innumerable separate parts. Yet let us, like Levitt Burris, confess our fears. The new society crashing in upon us is terrifying.

Modern physical science has had to embrace uncertainty, randomness and unpredictability as ordering ideas with which to understand the physical world. So perhaps must social science also unleash a new imagination into the unbounded world of cyberspacetime. We must make desperate efforts to reach some consensus on the direction and manifestations human life is taking in the exotic data fields exploding all across the grey void of cyberspace. The present state of upheaval may already have been anticipated by Nietzsche when he wrote:

> Alas! The time is coming when man will no more shoot the arrow of his longing out over mankind, and the string of his bow will have forgotten to twang!

I tell you: one must have chaos in one, to give birth to a dancing star. I tell you: you still have chaos in you. (1972: 4–6)

Notes

A grant from the Social Sciences and Humanities Research Council of Canada supported research for this chapter. Parts of this chapter first appeared in Dan Thu Nguyen, 1991. 'The measurement of time and the measure of man'. PhD dissertation, University of Toronto, Political Science Department.

1. Long ago, R.M. MacIver (1942) pointed out the pitfalls of the concept of causality in the social sciences.

References

Alter, Jonathan 1995. 'The couch potato vote', *Newsweek*, 27 February: 30.

Arendt, Hannah 1958. *The Human Condition*, Chicago: University of Chicago Press.

Bailey, Martha 1994. 'USENET discussion groups in political science courses', Paper presented to the American Political Science Association's annual meeting (New York, 1–4 September).

Barlow, John Perry 1994. 'The economy of ideas: a framework for rethinking patents and copyright in the digital age', *Wired*, 2(3): 84–90, 126–9.

Barrett, William 1986. *Death of the Soul: From Descartes to the Computer*, Garden City, NY: Anchor Press.

Baudrillard, Jean 1977. *Oublier-Foucault*, Paris: Editions Galilée.

Berg, Jeff 1994. 'Not content with content', *Wired*, 2(3): 99.

Bolter, David J. 1984. *Turing's Man: Western Culture in the Computer Age*, Chapel Hill: University of North Carolina Press.

Bradshaw, Chris 1994. Interview (October).

Bukatman, Scott 1994. *Terminal Identity: The Virtual Subject in Postmodern Science Fiction*, Durham, NC: Duke University Press.

Cameron, Bob 1994. Interview (August).

Canguilhem, Georges 1991. *The Normal and the Pathological*, New York: Zone Books.

Companion Disk 1993. 'Using the Internet, special edition, companion disk', Indianapolis: Que Corporation.

Cowan, Jennifer 1994. 'Press "2" for a Lover', *Wired*, 2(10): 58–66.

Deleuze, Gilles 1986. *Foucault*, Paris: Editions de Minuit.

Deutsch, Karl 1966. *Nerves of Government: Models of Political Communication and Control*, New York: Free Press.

Dreyfus, Hubert L. 1972. *What Computers Can't Do: A Critique of Artificial Reason*, New York: Harper & Row.

Emberley, Peter 1988. 'Technology, values and nihilism', *Science, Technology & Politics*, 3(1): 41–58.

Fineman, Howard 1995. 'The brave new world of cybertribes', *Newsweek*, 27 February: 30–33.

Foucault, Michel 1976. *Histoire de la sexualité: 1) La volonté de savoir*, Paris: Editions Gallimard.

Fraser, J.T. 1987. *Time, the Familiar Stranger*, Redmond, WA: Tempus Books.

Gibson, William 1984. *Neuromancer*, New York: Ace Books.

Gibson, William 1993. *Virtual Light*, New York: Bantam Books.

Habermas, Jürgen 1987. *The Theory of Communicative Action*, vol. 2. Boston: Beacon.

Health 1994. 'The man who first photographed life before birth', *Health*, May–June: 17.

Heim, Michael 1993. 'The erotic ontology of cyberspace', in Michael Benedikt (ed.), *Cyberspace: First Steps*, Cambridge, MA: MIT Press. pp. 59–80.

Kane, Pamela 1994. *Hitchhiker's Guide to the Electronic Highway*, New York: MIS Press.

Leslie, Jacques 1994. 'Mail bonding: e-mail is creating a new oral culture', *Wired*, 2(3): 42–8.

MacIver, R. M. 1942. *Social Causation*, Boston: Ginn.

McLuhan, Marshall 1962. *The Gutenberg Galaxy: the Making of Typographic Man*, Toronto: University of Toronto Press.

McLuhan, Marshall and Fiore, Quentin 1967. *The Medium is the Massage*, New York: Random House.

Merleau-Ponty, Maurice 1945. *Phénoménologie de la perception*, Paris: Editions Gallimard.

Newsweek 1993. 'Live wires', *Newsweek*, 6 September: 43–7.

Newsweek 1994. 'Ms. Frizzle explains all', *Newsweek*, 26 September: 59.

Newsweek 1995. 'When words are the best weapon', *Newsweek*, 27 February: 36–40.

Nietzsche, Friedrich 1972. *Thus Spoke Zarathustra*, trans. R.J. Hollingdale, Harmondsworth: Penguin Books.

Nightlife 1994. 'News of the weird: lead story', *Nightlife*, 15–22 September: 22.

Nimmo, Dan and Combs, James E. 1990. *Mediated Political Realities*, 2nd edn, New York: Longman.

Plato 1956. *Great Dialogues of Plato*, trans. W.H.D. Rouse, New York: New American Library.

Quittner, Josh 1994. 'Johnny Manhattan meets the furrymuckers', *Wired*, 2(3): 92–7.

Sennett, Richard 1976. *The Fall of Public Man: On the Social Psychology of Capitalism*, New York: Vintage Books.

Shields, Rob 1995. 'Foucault's microtechnics as sociotechnics?', in Adam Podgórecki, Jon Alexander and Rob Shields (eds), *Social Engineering*, Ottawa: Carleton University Press.

Southern Illinoisan 1994. 'San Francisco couple weds in cyberspace', *Southern Illinoisan*, 22 August: 2A.

Stone, Allucquere Rosanne 1991. 'Will the real body please stand up?: boundary stories about virtual cultures', in Michael Benedikt (ed.), *Cyberspace: First Steps*, Cambridge, MA: MIT Press. pp. 81–118.

Time 1994. 'Big brother chips?', *Time*, 14 February: 18.

Toffler, Alvin 1983. *Previews and Premises*, Toronto: Bantam Books.

Tolhurst, William A. *et al.* 1994. *Using the Internet*, special edn, Indianapolis: Que Corporation.

Turkle, Sherry 1984. *The Second Self: Computers and the Human Spirit*, London: Granada.

Wolf, Gary 1994. 'The (second phase of the) revolution has begun', *Wired*, 2(10): 116–21.

7

Contradictions in Cyberspace: Collective Response

*Interrogate the Internet**

Access as emancipation: the Enlightenment ethos and underdevelopment

We see Internet as an expression of, and even the saviour of high modernism. Its development is consistent with the logic of late capitalism. It, above all else, promises the possibility of achieving the ends of the Enlightenment: a sense of mastery and escape from the limits of the frailties of incarnation. As the product of a prolonged period of incubation, meditation and scientific development, it represents not only the culmination of more than fifty years of computer design, but the scientific solution to the death of God. However, like any other Enlightenment enterprise, the Internet contains the contradictions of its age.

While every technology has dual impulses toward both liberation and domination, questions about the potential of the Internet have been inadequately understood as primarily a function of access to information. On this account, access has been seen as in and of itself emancipatory. But of what value and validity is information? And how does one access it in a usable form? What is the meaning of authorship and fact in virtual reality? The Net makes a type of equation:

data = information = knowledge = wisdom = truth = freedom

But a high level of industrial and economic development are requisite before access to the Internet or to e-mail can be at all meaningful.** More

---

* Interrogate the Internet is an interdisciplinary working group that meets on a bi-weekly basis to critically examine and discuss the impact and implications of cyberspace. Participants come from a diversity of backgrounds and include students, system operators, professors and computer consultants. If there is a recurring theme that runs through our response and the meetings of our group more generally, it is that the contradictions which characterize late modernity are made manifest in cyberspace itself. Our contribution maps the sites of such contradiction using the Internet imagery of a series of discursive threads. We are: Heather Bromberg, Marco Campana, Wade Deisman, Reby Lee, Rob MacLeod, Thomas Pardoe and Marc Tyrell.

** The limits of such a simplistic approach become clear in the case of Jamaica (see Chapter 3). When access is achieved in situations of severe underdevelopment, where living standards are abominably low, the contradiction becomes clear. Access to the Internet is not really for everyone. If the supercomputer is next to a shanty town bereft of running

information does not automatically lead to problem solving. Moreover, the idea that the Internet is full of *knowledge* as opposed to information is false. Knowledge taken out of context is really just noise. As a globalizing strategy for the Third World, the imperative to go virtual, to get on the Net, may in fact contribute to the colonization rather than the emancipation of locals. Discussions about bringing the Internet to the Third World seldom acknowledge the extent to which global underdevelopment issues are inseparable from the operation of the Internet itself.

The language of the Internet, and not just its structure, is specific to the Western world. The question of teleliteracy, therefore, which is often asked in general ways, is actually not one which could be answered in the abstract. For example, are those who are online from countries with peripheral economies most likely to be (but are not always) local elites who have an overseas education and/or maintain a high standard of living?*

Diversity or the replication of uniformity

The hyper-construction of cyberspace as the 'new' frontier and a 'place' premised on democratic diversity needs to be fundamentally rethought. A clearer case can be made for the claim that as a populist media, the Net is a microcosm of social reality and that Net relations imitate and intimate real life. Clearly the Net blurs the boundaries between 'reality' and 'virtuality', but rather than revelling in the idea of ratiocination, we suggest that ontogeny recapitulates phylogeny: on the Net one may try to do things differently, but too often we end up plugging in the same old attitudes. Instead of seeing this as a failure of creative consciousness, it is more appropriate to see it as 'home-making': we get imprinted by our geographically proximate communities and transfer our patterns of perception and reception in the virtual community. Similarly, with respect to Usenet content, it is clear that the Internet poses a challenge to the broadcast media, precisely because it is interactive and thus allows for a great deal of diversity.

Still, Usenet groups (such as the **alt**. hierarchy of groups) do not

---

water, no amount of access to e-mail will remedy the problem: no knowledge will be emancipatory (poor and homeless people in First World countries face a similar situation, as access to unlimited information is unlikely to improve their lot in life).

* There is good reason to question whether the Internet, with its English-language emphasis, does not subordinate specific linguistic groups. Even though foreign-language alt. groups flourish, and foreign-character interfaces are available to professionals and at a price, the command structure and logic of Internet and its operating protocols are strongly anchored in an English-language and Western-experience-based idea of what constitutes common sense. Furthermore, it is not simply a matter of English having a linguistic hegemony on the Net, but that facility with English is often exclusive of others. It freqeuntly consists of a kind of interminable word play, irony, double meanings, subtle denigration and slippery insinuation (consider the flame). thus, a full set of communicative capacities, in English, are privileged for participation on the Internet.

represent a radical break with such traditional media. Rather, the traditional content reappears in a sort of pastiche wherein new media refer to old, and vice versa. Rather than a radical break, then, there is a continuous loop of influence. The structure of the technology and the content are altogether indissociable from the broader cultural context. Thus the alt.fan groups refer to performers, television stars, rock and roll bands and game shows. In this sense, the Net paradoxically works both to reproduce and reinforce existing 'hegemonic' structures as well as enabling new forms of inter-activity. Virtual communities display a structural attachment to mass culture. Here MUD and MOO citizens demonstrate acquisitive behaviour, display forms of conspicuous consumption, and engage in the tribalism and warlike behaviour typical of feudal fiefdoms. Although these 'alter egos' reflect the frame of fantasy and mythos, one wonders whether the feeling of familiarity that often characterizes such role playing does not reflect the limits of the contemporary imaginary[1] – an imaginary formed in the crucible of modernity.

Usenet Groups, MUDs and MOOs all create the illusion of the heterodox: they give the impression of thousands of participants and suggest a great deal of diversity. This impression of multiplicity and multivocality may in fact conceal a more fundamental homogeneity. The vast majority of Internet access is via computers and occurs in North America (*Time* 1995: 78–9). Access itself, however, is not the only limit to diversity. Consider for example that the latest 'Net metrics' show that approximately 73 per cent of users in the Internet are men.[2] Why the sex/gender split?

As witnessed earlier, there are quite significant structural barriers that keep many voices from being heard. The level of multivocality, diversity and difference engendered by the Net is also a function of technological socialization and training. In newly developing areas like the more graphical version of Internet, the World Wide Web, few know how to make a 'Web Home Page'. Not only access but technical knowledge determines the 'metaphysics of presence'. The consequence is that only certain, technical, voices are present to be noted. Thus, while the promise of the Net is its ability to spread knowledge, its paradox consists in the fact that the speed of change sometimes precludes the possibility of full participation. Beyond the democratic ideal of diversity, then, the Internet enforces uniformity.

Cybernetic capitalism, colonization and commercialization

The Net is ostensibly free from unabashed solicitation and advertising. Yet it was, and to some extent still is, the purposeful project of the capitalist military-industrial complex. This is the contradiction. The 'invisible hands' of the blind economy continue to control the alphanumeric freeway – or do they?

The most recent migration of Fortune 500 companies and the instant erection, all along the electronic 'roadside', of virtual shopping malls foretells a new era of supra-cybernetic capitalism. The Net is quickly being constructed as the ultimate site of both production and consumption. The hanging question, however, is in what ways will the Internet instigate a fundamental transformation in wage-labour relations? We posit the advent of a third, and fundamentally ambivalent class relationship to the mode of production under supra-cybernetic capitalism that is neither ownership nor subservience.

Rather, as a result of this new class position, a *balance of terror* comes to exist between the entrepreneurial capitalists and the techno-anarchists. Internet users relate to the Internet both as the producers and consumers of content. Capital and technicians, a 'technoclass', are in control of the structure. This structure is essentially contested. The rise of the technicians as a social class needs to be distinguished from the rise of the 'virtual class' (Kroker 1995). In the post-industrial age, the technoclass status is analogous to the pre-modern artisan. The virtual volition of the technoclass distinguishes it from the more general user class: techno-artisans master the electronic environment, using the technology to achieve their own extropian* ends. This struggle over control through knowledge has definite religious precedents. The secular restriction of esoteric and occulted knowledges purposefully limited to the hands of a few acolytes under medieval Christianity directly parallels the current composition and constriction of Net knowledge in the hands of a few. These technicians, sys-ops and consultants make up the 'virtual' class hierarchy and act in the name of the masses whose minds, bodies and souls are 'saved' and 'structured' with or without their consent.

We thus suggest that the new technological relations be thought of as occurring between a virtual class and a 'virtual vanguard'. The essentially contested question is what kind of ontological reconversion is achieved within the new 'Net-ontology'. The Marxist-utopian dream of socialized labour is not only dead, it is *displaced* by the technotopic promise of a post-scarcity society premised on full mechanization. A new technopian dream emerges out of the obscurity (Habermas 1989).

The role of capitalism in and of itself becomes difficult to identify in this context, but the question of capitalist power persists as an important one. In order to argue that there is a fundamental redistribution of power relations in the post-industrial society, one would have to make the case that the technicians (or the virtual class) have substantive power.**

---

* In this context extropianism represents a transhumanist philosophy which attempts to redefine the nature of ontology by seeking an expansion of intelligence and wisdom. Online it is made manifest in attempts to redefine our relationship with technology and particularly the commitment to the organic forms or regulation. For more information about extropianism see http://www.c2org.arkuat.extropy.html.

** This is not clear, as suggested by the Kevin Mitnick fiasco. Mitnick's power online never translated into power in the real world: he was unable to significantly 'profit' from his

The power outside the Net is still greater than the power inside, but the balance of power is probably changing. Online and off-line, the degree to which one is determined by prevailing forces of supra-cyber-telekinetic technocapitalism is quite clearly a function of one's level of technological prowess. Thus, the degrees of economic determinism enacted in the post-industrial society may decline while the degree of technology determinism and technoliteracy determinism may increase.

Oppression and resistance

The principal paradigm of the Net is not control but dissemination. Not 'them against us', not the zero sum scenario as in the old mass media models, but rather the win-win technology of the Web. At the same time there are limits. The initial impulse of technology is to spread information, but then the regulatory and disciplinary efforts emerge. Refusing to get on the Net is still conceivable, although like everything else, there will be consequences. What happens to techno-illiterates in the long run? How long can the technophobes resist? Or, following Haraway (1991), is there any point in resisting? The trend toward computerization cannot conceivably be resisted in the context of automated bank teller machines, 'smart' health care cards, workplace networks and digitization. Computers are not an indispensable part of the educational apparatus. Yet much of the future hopes for Canadian society are being pinned on computer literacy. Thus, in the long term, the bio-politics of the nation-state may be managed from cybernetic silicon towers while their terminus is tele-inscribed on every individual. In short, the benevolent goal is to create and maintain the population, but a cyborg population promises the best tax base.

The critical question is whether these developments presage a new electronic Panopticon.* The Net may well be simply another extension of social control through the control of information. It is important to deploy Gramsci in this context, since the hegemony of our relations with technology both exists apart from our experiences online and also dictates the kinds of things that take place online.[3] The question of resistance cannot be put in the abstract, but rather must be understood as a function of reflexivity and communication. We invoke Trotsky in our supposition that the level of oppression must reach a level of intolerability before collective action is conceivable. However, Net neighbourhoods are not collections of cultural dopes but retain some semblance of critical con-

---

exploits even hacking credit card numbers. Moreover, it was good old-fashioned police 'legwork' that resulted in his apprehension. A similar argument can be made in the case of 'Pengo' and the Chaos Computer Club in Berlin.

* It is certainly possible, following Foucault, to argue that the Internet is the electronic epitome of the penal panopticon and, moreover, that it is a technology designed to produce docile bodies. For an extended discussion of both of these concepts see Foucault's *Discipline and Punish* (1979).

sciousness. In support of this position we cite the recent activities of the Electronic Frontier Foundation (EFF)* and the Whole Earth Electronic Link (WELL)** in opposition to the American Wire Tap Bill.

Radical forms of resistance have arisen not only with respect to governmentality but also to commerce. Swift and certain reprisals have followed actions wherein entrepreneurs attempt to take their services beyond the bailiwick of the 'e-malls'. Advertising is still generally seen as sacrilege by believers in democratic discussion. We see this dual focus of resistance as an essential element of the extropian ethos that characterizes not only much of the virtual vanguard, but the Net user population more generally. Some of the more mediagenic exemplars of this ethos are discussed in the special cyberspace issue of the e-zine **Bad Subjects**† and exhibited by the more populist print magazine *Wired*.

Virtual reality and cyberspace: sending 'selves' through

Virtual realities and virtual communities are important ways of re-enacting myth and as important forms of storytelling. These virtual environments redefine our notions of deception and duplicity, as the fundamental imperatives of self identity, self-disclosure and authentic interaction are abandoned for the sake of experimentation and play. Nonetheless, there is often a high degree of attachment to the narrative and to the electronic persona in cyberspace. That people hold their MUD/MOO/IRC characters close to themselves suggests a high degree of identification. It is, however, important to problematize and analyse virtuality as *mode of being* where the forms of identification with your virtual persona are in fact variable. We refer to Bruckman's work on identity in order to investigate the relationship between virtual characters and real life.[4]

Virtual encounters have real-life effects: they are transformative of consciousness. People carry their virtual memories into the real world in significant ways. That there are real effects of virtual encounters suggests that these events are, in fact, experienced as full social encounters wherein people can have a full range of feelings: acceptance and esteem as well as rejection and denial. In this context, MUDs and MOOs have an intensity that is unlike other kinds of role playing. MUDs and MOOs as communicative environments can be contrasted with the Internet-Relay-Chat (IRC) system which is also a synchronous system of communication, but the communication does not occur in a virtual background.

The quality of virtual life on the Net is not yet indistinguishable from the 'real' thing, but while cyberspace is not yet hyper-real, there is a progressive process of conditioning involved where individuals 'learn' to

---

* Now available at a new Web site at WWW.eff.org.
** Access is via Telnet. The command is thus: Telnet well.sf.ca.us
† See http://english-www.hss.edu/bs/

identify their online experiences as real. The naturalization of the Net is thus the first operation in ensuring its efficacy as a medium that 'represents' reality. Only by understanding this process of training is the claim that the body is left behind intelligible, for the body is left behind and becomes 'data trash' only by virtue of a certain selective inattention that is the product of socialization.* The myth of incorporeality is just another way that the naturalized Net conceals the ideological implications of terminal-bound docile bodies. The corporeal body may be left behind, but the lived body is carried through the interface in people's discursive constructions of themselves and the world.

Closing comment

The old, albeit hackneyed, computer expression 'GIGO' – Garbage In, Garbage Out – has been removed from vocabulary and rhetoric at a time when it seems most needed. The hype about the Internet has in fact created a *new enchantment* in Western societies. Dealing with the realities of 'virtual reality', however, will be a process of progressive disenchantment wherein the limits of communication and information as the essence of emancipation become clear. The Net, then, has attained a status much like God . . . before rationalization.

Notes

1. See Chapter 4.
2. Estimate of the Fall Netrics Report, 1994 Internet Association semi-annual meeting.
3. In other words, the intractability of such relations makes a war of manoeuvre appropriate and essential. At the same time, the war of position online is ongoing. For an in-depth discussion of this distinction (see Gramsci, 1992: 243–5).
4. Cited in 'Constructions and reconstructions of self in virtual reality' by Sherry Turkle, archived at the MIT Media Lab Site.

References

Burchell, Graham, Gordon, Colin and Miller, Peter (eds) 1991. *The Foucault Effect: Studies in Governmentality*, Chicago: University of Chicago Press.
Cornwall, Hugo 1987. *Data Theft*, London: Heinemann.
Cornwall, Hugo 1988. *The Hacker's Handbook*, 3rd edn, London: Century.
Elmer-DeWitt, Phillip 1988. 'Invasion of the body snatchers', *Time*, 26 September.
Finlay, Markie 1987. *Powermatics: A Discursive Critique of New Technology*, London: Routledge & Kegan Paul.
Foucault, Michel 1979. *Discipline and Punish*, New York, Vintage Books.

---

* The reference is to Arthur Kroker and Michel A. Weinstein's *Data Trash: The Theory of the Virtual Class* (1994). We think that Kroker and Weinstein don't adequately interrogate the discursive formations that are the precondition for the possibility of the body becoming data trash.

Foucault, Michel 1980. *Power/Knowledge*, ed. Colin Gordon, New York: Pantheon.

Frankel, Boris 1987. *The Post-Industrial Utopians*, Oxford: Basil Blackwell.

Gramsci, A. 1992. *Prison Notebooks*, New York: Columbia University Press.

Habermas, J. 1989. 'The new obscurity', in *The New Conservatism*, Cambridge, MA: MIT Press.

Hackers in Jail 1989. *2600: The Hacker's Quarterly*, 6(1): 22–3.

Haraway, D. 1991. 'A cyborg manifesto: science, technology, and socialist feminism in the late twentieth century', in *Simians, Cyborgs, and Women: The Reinvention of Nature*, New York: Routledge.

Hayes, Dennis 1989. *Behind the Silicon Curtain: The Seductions of Work in a Lonely Era*, Boston, South End Press.

Kroker, A. and Weinstein, M. 1994. *Data Trash: The Theory of the Virtual Class*, Montreal: New World Perspectives.

Landreth, Bill 1989. *Out of the Inner Circle: The True Story of a Computer Intruder Capable of Cracking the Nation's Most Secure Computer Systems*, Redmond, WA: Tempus, Microsoft.

Lundell, Allan 1989. *Virus! The Secret World of Computer Invaders That Breed and Destroy*, Chicago: Contemporary Books.

Mosco, Vincent and Wasko, Janet 1988. *The Political Economy of Information*, Madison: University of Wisconsin Press.

Time 1995. 'Welcome to cyberspace', Special issue (Spring): 78–9.

Turkle, S. 1994. 'Constructions and reconstructions of self in virtual reality'. Archived at the MIT Media Lab Site.

Wilson, Kevin 1988. *Technologies of Control: The New Interactive Media for the Home*, Madison: University of Wisconsin Press.

8

Life after Death

Katie Argyle

Every day the mailbox in my computer account fills up. E-mail continuously flows to my 'home' address from four mailing lists that I subscribe
to. Every day I am challenged by the volume of mail these lists generate. If
I don't attend to them, they are soon unmanageable, multiplying to masses
of 400 and 500 messages awaiting my attention.

Soon all the message headers become familiar, because topics are
constantly recirculated within the lists as 'threads'. It all becomes boring
and tedious. What I forget is that I *feel* bored by the incoming e-mail, and I
feel tired at the thought of constantly cleaning out the mailbox. But I am
still *feeling* something; I am connected to the lists, to the topics and the
mail in my mailbox sent there by others who are on the Net with me.

'Cybermind' is the mailing list I subscribe to which is the primary source
of all this mail.* In over a year of membership of Cybermind, there is a
single event which haunts me. It occurred in July 1994, quietly appearing

---

* In effect, **Cybermind** is a discussion group concerning itself with topics related to Internet
or cyberspace culture. Prospective participants to this list must send a request message to
the home address for **Cybermind**, and they are subscribed to the service. Messages written
by users then begin to appear in your e-mail soon after. To end your participation in the
group, you must request to be unsubscribed. Topics are described in one-line sentences
which allow me to decide which ones I will actually read, which I will delete, and which I
will save for later. These are the very banal maintenance activities of my Internet account.
The Usenet news group called news.lists keeps an accurate, up-to-date record of all mailing
lists available on the Internet. It recommends that you check its postings to obtain the most
recent subscription directions before you send out a request to join a mailing list. It updates
its lists monthly. In March 1995 the **Cybermind** entry was:

Contact: majordomo@jefferson.village.virginia.edu
Purpose: We are all dwelling in cyberspace, coursing through the wires,
becoming cyborg and becoming human. We are subjects of a realm which is totally charted,
and completely unknown. CYBER-MIND is devoted to
an examination of the new subjectivities that have emerged and might
yet emerge in this arena. We are interested in particular in the
philosophical, psychological/psychoanalytic and social issues
engendered, particularly as they concern the user and the social.
To subscribe send a message to
    majordomo@jefferson.village.virginia.edu
and say
    subscribe cybermind
Cybermind has a WWW home page at http://www.uio.no/~mwatz/cybermind/

amidst all the usual postings of cybervamps, unsubscribe messages, and banter about threads of discussion that had been ongoing over several days. Postings and exchanges began to appear about the death of Michael Current. It sometimes happened that Michael Current was a focal point for discussion on Cybermind, but this was talk *of* Michael, not talk *from* Michael. As one of the administrators, Michael Current was extremely active on Cybermind.[1] Every day there were two or three messages written by him as he reached out over the wires to address questions posed to him, or to express his point of view. I was accustomed to seeing letters from him on the list.

Amongst the routine chatter of messages competing for my attention there was a series addressed to the group as death, net.death, and various 'goodbye Michael' combinations. Had he 'really' died, I wondered? I was suspicious that this was an esoteric and metaphorical use of the word death – the kind of semantic wordplay that the Net is filled with (see Chapter 10). Never assume that anything is as it first appears on the Net.[2] But in this case, it was: Michael had died.

I have never encountered this situation before or since. In over five years of online activity this was the first time someone whom I had never met in the flesh, but who was very familiar to me in textual form, had died and would post no more. I thought it wasn't real. I thought it was a hoax, and so did others.*

> pardon my lack of knowledge, who was (is) Michael CUrrent?
> Is he dead?**[3]

> I'm sure, like many, the first notice that came through I
> thought, 'How cruel, this isn't funny. Michael's on this
> list and I am sure he doesn't need to read forged postings
> about his death.' And then the reality sinks in a little
> and I realise how cruel it really is.[4]

And perhaps if I had only read the messages that questioned his death, and maybe one death notice, I would have dismissed it as just talk. I would have assumed that Michael Current just wanted off the Net.

A few times on BBSs in the past, I have witnessed the furious deletion of messages by someone who wants to remove all traces of their existence and past participation. In one case, I was online and logged into a newsgroup when a member known as Quiet erased all writings they had posted.

---

* This situation recently recurred in the case of a person central to pmc-list the online journal of postmodern culture (published in hardcopy by Oxford University Press). An attempt at an online 'funeral' in the multi-user discussion space pmc-moo was disrupted by dubious users posting doubting messages suggesting that the death could be a hoax, leading in turn to outrage on the part of the deceased online friends and co-administrators.

** Often the proper grammatical rules and proper spelling are not adhered to in texts that are written for the Net. For the sake of accuracy, I have quoted that texts as they appeared in the posts. Spelling mistakes and grammatical errors have not been corrected.

Threads of conversations now referred to someone who did not exist. On every level I was disturbed by this action he was taking. I watched my screen as messages disappeared before my eyes.

I paged Quiet over the system.* Did he know he was changing the landscape, re-writing the history of what had been? Yes. He was committing suicide. As a protest gesture, he was killing the persona of Quiet. The deletions were a loss; I wondered at the psychological state of the man-who-was-Quiet. Was the man the next suicide? At other times, I had witnessed the growing boredom, the growing disenchantment with the Net, and the need for users, myself included, to take a break from Net activity

This was not the same situation on the Cybermind list. There was to be no life after Net death here. I became more convinced as the messages piled up. Each one filled with grief. Each one filled with the process of mourning, and the need to stop and adjust to the event. Each one trying to understand what this meant to them. I did not write then. I feel self-conscious writing about it now. This is private: for those not on the Net, who 'weren't there', I can only explain that I am transgressing. Off-line, net.death is a taboo subject. I am speaking about something that is so personal (yet collective), so private (yet public), and so emotionally painful (yet technologized), that it is better left alone. I am digging and disturbing the ground that's been laid to rest, for my own purposes. I am going against the group, and speaking out of turn. The time has passed for this. I had my chance, I missed it. I – and many other recipients with even no sense of membership or loyalty at all – chose to be silent.

It is odd that I feel so personally about the death messages. I didn't *know* Michael Current, yet I will never forget him. His death, rather than an ending, is an event which haunts me. The emotional force of the postings, the emotional impact on Cybermind members, and the willingness to grieve in public, is very striking. For, as concerned as I am about upsetting those who wrote the messages I quote from and dissect, the messages were placed in an extremely public forum. Anyone could have copied them, and they were indeed distributed throughout alt.groups and lists on the Net. There were no guarantees that these private lamentations would stay amongst the grievers. I am sure they are archived with the rest of the material Cybermind generates, waiting for someone to read them, when they will again appear in exactly the same format on a screen, as fresh as when they were first composed.

---

* Paging is a method that many communication systems, such as BBSs or bulletin board services, offer their patrons. A 'page' will be sent directly to a designated user which will interrupt whatever activity they are involved in. It opens up a direct chat line between users where they exchange words (text) from different areas of a BBS. In this example, I paged Quiet from a newsgroup while he was erasing his messages in his mailbox. Intrigued by his actions, we arranged to have a conversation over the telephone about what he had done as I was concerned about his actions. He confirmed that he was, "committing suicide" re: the persona Quiet,' and that all traces of Quiet's existence would be removed from the BBS.

The events of that day in July brought into focus how tied I am to the list, the extent to which participants rely on each other for support, even as non-posting list-members, or as silent lurkers, and how willing they are to express this. Western society tells us to grieve quietly. Be brave and stoic in public despite your loss. Don't risk appearing foolish or weak. Cybermind transgressed those rules.

> Oh Alan. Everybody. I am so sad. I watch these letters
> inch by, worm by, and spurt packets of tears. Words don't
> come.[5]

I felt exactly the same. What was going on with me? Why was I so upset? Why did I have to read all of these messages? Why do I still think about it now? I am sure that part of the reason is a basic curiosity and a fascination with my involvement in a situation that I have never encountered before. Also it is the privilege of witnessing raw emotions, of sharing in something with a larger group. A feeling of belonging. I always knew that *I* was this involved with the Net; what I didn't realize was that so many others felt the same way. It was good to know that I was *normal* and my feelings were similar to others who read the announcements and responded without self-censoring their messages. It made me grateful that these ties of sociability were there. Members turned to each other to help them through this crisis:

> Yes, yes to all of it.
> Thanks, thank you all who are never thanked enough,
> or hugged or kissed or silently embraced.
> For everything, forever.
> There is always time for memory.[6]
>
> Can anyone still doubt that we are a
> community?[7]

What I have since concluded is that we were all involved in a process of growth and transformation. The list grieved as one, strengthening the bonds between its members whether they were active 'posters' or not. Others saw this too:

> as i sat here last night, watching in horror as
> cybermind grieved its loss, watching the postings pop up
> one by one, knowing that others sat there with
> me – somewhere.[8]
>
> There is a void where Michael's electricity was, where his
> energy took up this space, made things happen. The quiet of
> the _list_ is eery. What does it mean that we're here, to and
> for eachother; doesn't the presence of even the least of us
> make some difference to the rest of us. Or not![9]
>
> For me the ritual has already begun in the cycling of
> messages repeated and repeated from list to list and I leaf
> through five, six, seven copies of the same awkward anguish,

one copy for each place we haunted together, one current copy,
and one copy bouncing off to mcurrent@picard.*[10]

The talk of ritual, of voids, of spaces, has caused me to think of the Net as a unique place that allows for the transgression of cultural rules, the breaking of taboos, the freedom to express what you need to, when you need to. Often members discuss the subject of a threat to these freedoms through the imposition of outside legislation or authority upon the Net and, therefore, upon the freedom of its users.

This Internet space, of which Cybermind is but one representative piece, has a special character that cannot be found in 'real life'. In many aspects it displays signs of the carnivalesque as described by Mikhail Bakhtin in his books *Rabelais and his World* (1984) and *Speech Genres and Other Late Essays* (1986).[11]

During carnival, all codes of conduct, all rules of behaviour are abandoned. Carnival 'discloses the potentiality of an entirely different world, of another order, another way of life' (Gardiner 1992: 58). When we are in another type of world, where the rules of behaviour are not familiar to us, there is an opportunity to turn such rules upside down as Bakhtin describes in the carnivalesque. As an illustration I think of the 'myth' of the 14-year-old hacker who can take a corporation down with his ability to break into their security systems. In real life, he's just another 'troubled youth' who cannot wield power over corporation heads were he to step into their offices. In cyberspace, the hacker is king.

The potential for the subversion, and the inversion of our societal rules, can cause confusion amongst participants who seek to act 'correctly' but may not know exactly what that is on the Net.

I'm bothered I guess, by the fact that there are no
rituals of loss, mourning, passage . . .[12]

I think some sort of ritual is called for what exactly
its form would take I'm not sure . . .[13]

Never having lost an e-mail friend, I don't know the
protocol for this . . .[14]

The default method for coping on the Net then lies in the choice between writing or lurking. Lurking is participation by watching without revealing your presence to the group. The catch is, others may not know you are there, but you know you are, and so you are as involved as they are. You are still part of the group.

Carnival, in short, 'is "the only feast the people offer themselves," and there is no barrier between actors or performers and those who witness it' (Gardiner 1992: 52). Send your mail, follow your own feelings, and see what others do in response.

The act of writing was the choice many made in the crisis created by Michael Current's death. Others, myself included, participated by reading,

---

* mcurrent@picard was the home Internet address of Michael Current.

and experiencing other users' words. As with quoting,* which uses the
texts of others to speak for us, something that is rampant on the Net and
Cybermind, I and others allowed the group to voice our pain.

This voicing, this continuous dialogue amongst members, whether it
goes on in the written text or in the minds of those reading the text, is an
indicator of heteroglossia. Bakhtin noted that during the carnivalesque
there would be many voices, many forms of speech. One form would not
supersede the other. All voices are allowed to speak, and so a mixing of
voices shares the same space.

> ping, dammit. ping, ping, ping. not in so many words.
> ping.[15]
>
> The desert crying, Carry the Net in your head!
> The desert crying, Your body is imaginary!
> And the desert crying, Your are ghosts!
> And the desert crying, Ghosts, ghosts!
> And the desert crying, All of you are ghosts!
> (Crying, the desert to itself. Crying, the flat plate
> of the sky.)[16]
>
> Or. . . . . Would the memory of the Michael whose shadow I have
> traced through your grief be better served by a vigorous
> examination of the concept of Mortality?[17]

These 'voices' of the Net express human needs and feelings. They are
evidence that humanity is alive on the Net. Here there is room for voices
that are neither those of work, or the workplace, nor that of leisure,
though both of these can be found. This is a further example of the
heteroglossia of the Net which cannot be limited to one style of textual
expression, one topic, or one area of the Internet. Bakhtin wrote that the
carnivalesque, with the 'grotesque body' as an element of it, 'always
supersedes its apparent boundaries' (1992: 49).

Mike Gurstein posted a message on Cybermind that contained no text
written by him. He quoted a message written by 'tommyc'. Tommyc's
message originated on another mailing list called Future Culture. Tommyc
in turn had quoted a message that he saw in a Usenet group called
soc.motss.** This message contained the news of Michael's death, the
circumstances of his death, and a personal reaction to this death.

This particular Cybermind poster did not reveal his own feelings directly
to the group.[18] However, by appropriating the words of others, he used
them to speak for him. The boundaries between individual expression and

---

* Remember that communication programs often allow users to reply to the messages that
  they have just read. Users may choose to post only their opinions on the topic at hand,
  (this is also called continuing a 'thread'), or they may choose to include the text of the
  previous post. The system will prompt them to answer yes or no as to whether they want
  the text 'quoted' in their own letter. Often communication packages will allow the user to
  choose what specific parts of the previous text they would like to quote, giving the user
  editing tools that they can apply to their own textual productions.
** Thus a group on social issues concerning 'members of the same sex' (motss).

the demarcated areas of activity on the Internet as defined by addresses that place you into these areas (freenet@ccs.carleton.ca, alt.hi.are.you.cute, or the scribes' mailing list scribes@ossi.com for example), are easily violated. Text, and its accompanying expressiveness, can be copied and deposited where it can inform any group the user decides to post it in. Outside authorities cannot prevent these acts except by blocking reception of entire groups on their institutions' computers (e.g. alt.bestiality and alt.fan.karla-homolka have suffered this fate in Canada: see Chapter 1).

Even in these situations, users may choose to log into other, geographically, remote systems until they can access the offending groups – not just through long-distance telephone link to some foreign bulletin board, but through a local connection to the Internet itself using programs such as telnet to log on to a foreign computer via Internet connections. Authority extends only so far into the Net. If need be, a user may have their account killed by authorities, but this doesn't preclude them from getting an account with Net access from somewhere else in their community. It is difficult to completely ban an individual from the Net. This leaves individual behaviour on the Net governed entirely by the judgement of the users themselves.*

Bakhtin views the grotesque body as an 'indivisible entity, a collective' and says that 'there can be no strict demarcation between the human body and the sphere of culture' (1992: 49). Free agent?rez addresses this in his letter entitled 'michael current and the meat'. In it he writes,

this is visceral. words words words words meat.[19]

It is visceral. He tells us Michael's death is felt in his body. In his blood and guts; in the viscera. So much for leaving our bodies out of this.

The body is often referred to as the 'meat' in cyberspace. Meat is a collective term for flesh. It does not categorize or differentiate between types of meat. It is just all meat. And the body, meat, is vulgar. This collective, lowest common denominator type of body is exactly what Bakhtin had in mind with his term 'grotesque body' – not beautiful or idealized but above all alive, sensate, feeling and interacting.

One term, one flesh, one group. What is felt in the words is also felt in bodies. Michael Current has died, but his presence remains in Net postings, and in us: he has entered the realm of the meat. His physical death has been transformed from that of an individual dying, to a representation of this in text, and finally to a feeling in the body of other human beings. Another user, fido, echoes this:

---

* Like the grotesque body, text on the Net expands beyond our control or direction. We, as individuals, cannot contain or restrict this growth. The products of the Net belong to anyone who can get them. There will always be those who will not participate in these acts (software piracy, for example) but there are an equal number who see this as legitimate activity. It is the nature of the net and the nature of carnivalesque to be able to exercise the freedom to choose your own actions.

michael has finessed the fleshmeet question with, as usual, a
devastatingly simple gesture.[20]

'Fleshmeet' is a reference to a gathering of individuals in person, or in 'real
life', not on the Net. They are meeting in the flesh. Fido observes that the
death of Michael, his gesture, elegantly brought the group together, even
though Michael can now never participate in a fleshmeet. But the reference
shows that this gathering is not restricted to the Net, and therefore to the
text on the Net, but extends to the flesh, the physical body. In this rare
case, uncannily, even though online, we feel we meet in the flesh. Or is this
so rare?

I too felt queasy, watching the text about Michael's death, feeling the
anguish of the others scroll by on my screen. The raw emotion contained in
those texts, the undisguised pain, was passed from the writer to the reader,
to me. Michael Current's death had to be understood by my mind, and
absorbed by my body. The pain of the others touched the pain held within
myself. Personal experiences of loss, memories of funerals and the sorrow
of those left behind all flooded me. It was not just a bunch of letters from
strangers about a guy I didn't know, but real people, feeling real things,
deeply, and openly. I grieved with them, for myself and my losses, and for
theirs. I knew I could not stay in this high emotional state, and that I would
have to find ways to cope with the feelings that had been generated, and
with the fact of Michael Current's death.

There can be no final word, no endpoint during the carnivalesque. The
grotesque body absorbs events and moves on. Mike Gurstein notices that

> the personal statements of some is being followed with no evident break
> or closure by the noise of more or less inane net chatter.[21]

Alan Sondheim replies:

> I think whatever rituals there are in regards to Michael
> are private, personal; perhaps one of the things we can learn
> from the Net is that there *is* no closure . . .[22]

Gardiner argues that Bakhtin would agree with Alan's assessment:

> The crux of the grotesque aesthetic therefore lies in its portrayal of transforma-
> tion and temporal change, of the contradictory yet interconnected processes of
> death and birth, ending and becoming. The symbolism of grotesque realism thus
> explicitly denies the possibility of completion, or ending, of finality. (1992: 48)

Michael Current died, but his presence lives on, in those who came into
contact with him, and who pass this on, through their texts, through
Michael's own texts, and through their changed perception of themselves
due to their involvement in this event. Again,

> Carnivalesque images tie together a number of contradictory events and images
> into a more complex and ambivalent unity, an 'indissoluble grotesque whole'
> which underscores the inevitability of change and transformation. (ibid.: 46)

The Cybermind list, and the other parts of the Net where Michael Current travelled, shared in the sadness of his loss. The Internet community displayed itself as a place where the individual is not alone. The individual is part of a larger group that spreads further than the single user can imagine. Everywhere we rub shoulders with each other. Everywhere users present themselves to each other, freely saying and doing what they choose. This freedom is the cornerstone of the carnivalesque, and where there is carnivalesque, there is transformation. It is inevitable that this will happen, as Bakhtin notes, and it is inevitable that it will continue to happen. There can be no end to this.

> good bye, michael. thank you for enriching me.
> rest peacefully. even i, someone you didn't even know,
> will miss you too.[23]

Notes

1. As an administrator of the Cybermind list, Michael was responsible, along with Alan Sondheim, for the smooth functioning of this mailing list, and for moderating the talk on the list in order to stay within topics that are related to cyberspace activities and theories.

2. All the quoted messages were taken from the Cybermind mailing list over the following days: 23 to 25 July 1994. I have noted the names of the participants quoted, and in brackets I have included the names that appeared as signatures if they were different. The date of their messages follows their names.

Problems of authenticity abound on the Net. These two methods of identification still do not guarantee the authenticity of the text. Pseudonyms are frequently encountered in cyberspace, as is the borrowing of accounts amongst friends or acquaintances. Therefore, what is sent under the name of one person could actually have been written by someone totally different. For the purposes of this text I have quoted the works as they appeared to me, in my home mailbox: kargyle@ccs.carleton.ca. My current home address is aa992@freenet.carleton.ca.

3. Zameer Andani, 24 July 1994.

4. Michael Maranda, 23 July 1994.

5. Michael Sweet (Quiet) July 1993, via Technical Magic BBS, Ottawa, Ontario, Canada. Sadly, this great board no longer exists.

6. Judith Frederika Rodenbeck, 23 July 1994 (fido).

7. a.h.s. boy, 24 July 1994 (spud).

8. Jerry Everard, 25 July 1994.

9. Brian Chambers, 24 July 1994.

10. Jane Hudson, 25 July 1994.

11. Previously, Laurie Cubbinson had initiated a discussion of Bakhtin on Cybermind but carnival was not mentioned. This confirmed my application of Bakhtin to Internet groups.

12. Judith Frederika Rodenbeck, 24 July 1994 (fido).

13. Mike Gurstein, 24 July 1994 (Mikeg).

14. LMLESLIE@ucs.indiana.edu, 23 July 1994 (Ishmael).

15. Heath Michael R., 24 July 1994 (Free agent? Rez).

16. Alan Sondheim, 25 July 1994.

17. Rose Mulvale, 25 July 1994.

18. Mike Gurstein, 23 July 1994 (Mikeg).

19. Heath Michael R., 24 July 1994 (Free agent? Rez).

20. Judith Frederika Rodenbeck, 24 July 1994 (fido).

21. Mike Gurstein, 24 July 1994 (Mikeg).

22. Alan Sondheim, 24 July 1994.
23. Brian Chambers, 24 July 1994.

References

Bakhtin, M. M. 1984. *Rabelais and His World*, Indiana: Indiana University Press.
Bakhtin, M. M. 1986. *Speech Genres & Other Late Essays*, Austin: University of Texas Press.
Cubbinson, L. (1994). Unpublished manuscript on Bakhtin. Copy available from the editor. Originally electronically disseminated.
Gardiner, Michael 1992. *The Dialogics of Critique*, London: Routledge.

9

Are MUDs Communities?
Identity, Belonging and Consciousness in Virtual Worlds

Heather Bromberg

Consciousness in virtual worlds

Many have identified the reality and identity construction that is said to occur in both networked virtual worlds on the Internet and in multi-sensory virtual reality[1] as an 'altered state of consciousness' that produces heightened awareness and transcendence (Benedikt 1993; Stenger 1993; Rushkoff 1994).* While this may be true for some who use this medium, these claims (which are often made by industry spokespeople in thinly veiled advertisements for cyber-products or cyber-realities) are highly suspect. With politicians publicizing the democratic potentialities inherent in the construction of the information superhighway; popular business and computer magazines hailing the entrepreneurial opportunities available on the Net; the entertainment industry producing and advertising video and music available online; and software companies introducing virtual reality theme parks, it seems clear that there is a far-reaching construction of the need to 'connect' and experience all the psychedelic wonders of cyber-space.

As there are so many with specific commercial interests in the implementation and use of virtual reality as well as political revolutionaries and social critics who have ideas about the uses to which virtual reality should (or should not) be put, it is difficult to find an impartial perspective. The literature is consumed with claims of the transcendental wonders of virtual reality (Stenger 1993; Benedikt 1993; Rushkoff 1994) as well as those worrying that it is yet another opportunity for hegemonic structures to commodify reality and further the cause of global capitalism (Kroker 1994; Hayward 1993; Coyle 1993). Ironically, however, all of these claims are

---

* For our purposes here, an 'altered state of consciousness' is considered to be one which differs experientially from the 'baseline' waking state (Tart, quoted in Schneier 1989: 330). A person's state of consciousness is considered to be altered if the functionings of the mind, thoughts, feelings, perceptions, images and memories are significantly different for a definite period of real time (Schneier 1989: 33).

speculative. As three-dimensional, multi-sensory virtual reality designs are not yet distributed *en masse*, the only 'laboratories' that at present exist for examining and possibly understanding the widespread psychosocial impacts of virtual reality outside of the realm of speculative science fiction are the text-based multi-user dungeons/dimensions (MUDs) and chat groups within the Internet, the closest manifestation of cyberspace in existence to date.* Aside from a few exceptions (Rheingold 1993; Cartwright 1994) scarce mention is made of these communities in the published literature related to virtual reality, yet speculation abounds regarding virtual reality's impacts.[2]

To assess the various claims made in reference to virtual reality, part of the data gathered for the purpose of this chapter was acquired through participation on IRC and various MUDs, through interviewing informants in real time on chat networks and through a series of informal questions posted on relevant newsgroups and returned via private e-mail.[3] Often this resulted in extended correspondence. Questions were open-ended and revolved around the issues of role playing and identity construction, consciousness, dis/embodiment, time and space, self-awareness, the importance of language, fantasy and imagination and the appeal of virtual worlds in an effort to explore the following: first, and foremost, what is the nature of the virtual reality experience? How does the user experience his/her 'self' while participating in a virtual world? What is the relationship of the machine to the user? What is the relationship between the body and the mind while the user is participating in a virtual environment? And what are the psychosocial impacts of identity and reality construction in this manner? The impacts and implications of virtual reality are as hotly debated among users of this medium as they are among theorists, since VR suggests new ways of considering communication, reality, identity and community as well as the relationships between the body, mind and machines.

The notion that virtual reality potentially induces an altered state of consciousness and a sense of disembodiment begins with Gibson's fictitious 'cyberspace' as a space of 'consensual hallucination' (1984). Theorists consistently refer to this 'spaceless place' (Nixon 1992) to describe the way humans interact within global networks. According to Michael Heim,

> We inhabit cyberspace when we feel ourselves moving through the interface into a relatively independent world with its own dimensions and rules. The more we

---

* Through such services as MUDs in which users simulate personae (as in a role-playing game where one can choose to be a mythical character with predefined magical powers) and interact with others in a real-time quest or game, or chat services such as IRC (Internet relay chat) wherein users create an identity with a nickname and join 'channels' where they discuss a vast array of topics and simulate actions, users become connected to virtual worlds that are constructed by their imaginations with only the aid of cues from other users and the design of the virtual environment. It is my contention (along with Pavel Curtis 1992, and a multitude of users) that the experience of networked, text-based virtual reality can be at least as intense as that of multi-sensory VR.

habituate ourselves to an interface, the more we live in cyberspace (Heim 1993: 79)

References to a 'disembodied' consciousness (Heim 1993; Kroker 1994; Pryor and Scott 1993) as well as to the human-machine body of the cyborg (Stone 1993: 109; Pryor and Scott 1993: 173) are indicators of the sense of alteration of both the physical and mental self as a result of virtual reality technology.* Both perspectives recognize that this technology alters the perception of an objective reality and allude to the erotic appeal of transcending the physical world. The 'self' is transformed and the implications run deep.[4]

The imagery and terminology are highly representative of science fiction. References to science fiction, however, are not uncommon or misplaced when discussing 'cyberspace' or the Net, as it offers a way of thinking about this non-physical, non-linear 'reality'. The questions raised are also those that were raised by authors long before the advent of computer networking technology. Heim's description of the disembodied cybernaut suspended in computer space (1993: 89) is a key example. Accepting the notion that virtual reality is an alternate state of consciousness, Heim states,

> The ultimate VR is a philosophical experience, probably an experience of the sublime or awesome. . . . The final point of a virtual world is to dissolve the constraints of the anchored world so that we can lift anchor – not to drift aimlessly without point, but to explore anchorage in ever new places. (Heim 1993: 137)

In this sense, virtual reality is much like science fiction or the 1960s drug culture, offering the prospect of gaining insight into ancient philosophical questions through the exploration of alternative realities.

The correlation of virtual reality and cyberspace with science fiction as well as with altered states of consciousness is also related to the idea that cyberspace is a complex abstraction. 'The dimensions, axes, and co-ordinates of cyberspace are . . . not necessarily the familiar ones of our natural, gravitational environment, though mirroring our expectation of natural spaces they have dimensions impressed' (Benedikt 1993: 123). Further, as is the case with science fiction, the principles of space and time are suspended in cyberspace and can be violated with impunity (ibid.: 128). It is the design of cyberspace, which is the design of another lifeworld (Benedikt 1993) which offers the possibility of transcending the physical world.

---

* Users become absorbed in reading, viewing or interacting with the computer interface. While one might idiomatically 'lose oneself' in such an activity, many commentators have leapt to the conclusion that this loss is *ontological* (if not a literal loss then some other fundamental loss of the sense of the body) or psychological (loss of self). Medical or biological language is often used (for example the idea of 'addiction'), which distracts scrutiny from these metaphoric and often unwarranted claims.

It is also suggested that virtual reality is akin to other altered states of consciousness such as dreams, daydreams, hallucinations and religious visions (Sherman and Judkins 1992: 123) and the virtual reality experience is also equated with the experience of psychedelic drugs. According to Rushkoff (1994: 58), psychedelics and virtual reality are both ways of creating a new, non-linear reality. One informant with whom I corresponded electronically confirms this perspective, saying,

> I have experimented with a number of mind altering chemicals which have a far deeper intensity but the lack of control over the effect is disturbing. Interactive/gaming experiences can create the same effect to a point but are much more accessible and less demanding or threatening. (Respondent A: see note 3 on confidentiality)

Cyberspace, by virtue of its abstract construction, is said to provide the potential for the production of these 'states':

> Cyberspace's inherent malleability of content provides the most tempting stage for the acting out of mythic realities, realities once 'confined' to drug-enhanced ritual, to theatre, to painting, books. . . . Cyberspace can be seen as an extension of our age-old capacity and need to dwell in fiction, to dwell empowered or enlightened on other, mythical planes. (Benedikt 1993: 6)

This is exactly the appeal of virtual reality. Many have lamented that contemporary society is largely devoid of spiritual meaning and community. The fascination with networked virtual reality, then, is much like the fascination with hyper-real worlds such as Disney (Baudrillard 1993; Eco 1986). Networked VR (like Disney) offers a potential 'communal' spiritual outlet that is culturally relative to a technologized post/ultra-modern, fragmented, contemporary society. Further, networked virtual reality, though it operates through the interface of a computer terminal and is often operated by people oceans apart, is nevertheless a form of communication that is seductive: it is adequately reminiscent (at least in our most nostalgic virtual imaginations) of the kind of interactive, immersive stories that were told around the hearth with one's kin group (or at the very least of a time when 'community' had a tangible meaning).

For many, MUDs and chat networks are 'just a game' or 'just another form of communication'; for others, they offer an antidote to loneliness and malaise, allow the exploration of alternate identities and personae, offer the promise of connectivity and community and allow users to experience the feeling of mastery over their environments. Disney offers an escape from reality by perfectly recreating it, fantasy-style. Disney Corp. sells simulations of the American Dream, convincing patrons on their Meccan voyages that all is good and paved with gold in America. However, we do not become empowered there; rather we are like cheerleaders rooting for the home team. Virtual reality also offers the illusion of interactive, individual empowerment. The user steps out of the cheering crowd and becomes an actor, virtually realizing personalized dreams. Herein lies the possibility of transcendence.

Symptom or response?

It does seem clear that people make use of this technology to combat the symptoms that are characteristic of the malaise and inconsistency of what is currently called the 'postmodern condition' (Lyotard 1984; Harvey 1989). The technologies themselves are highly characteristic of the postmodern by virtue of their fluidity and malleability. Ironically, however, it is exactly their fluid and malleable nature which leads them to be used to combat that 'condition'. Claims that virtual reality will provide meaning and reveal the secrets of ancient wisdoms and truths otherwise unknowable (Stenger 1993; Mallen 1993) are appealing when faced with the postmodern notion that there are no universal truths. Virtual reality does seem to be one medium in which and with which some individuals seek meaning. For some users of networked virtual reality (whether text-based or multi-sensory), a slight suspension of disbelief provides a simulation of community and connectivity. For a suspended moment, the user is the author of an unfragmented reality in which the signifiers and the signifieds do not shift without warning. Chatting on Internet, and MUDs in particular, serves four social functions for users.

Isolated individuals can find solace in interactive computer-mediated communication. This can act as a virtual response to loneliness and a lack of connectivity and meaning in the exterior world. Characters on chat networks spend hours, not just chatting idly (though sometimes this is the case) but discussing the most intimate details of their personal and emotional lives. In my participation on IRC, users have discussed their feelings about their relationships, families, childhoods, their futures, marriages and often (though not always) mentioned feelings of loneliness and lack of connection. They have also discussed intense feelings about their virtual communities and other members of those virtual communities. Yet it may be argued that the promise of connectivity can have the effect of further isolation from phsyical environments if users reject their proximate community in favour of a virtual one. According to Pavel Curtis, however,

> if someone is spending a large portion of their time being social with people who live thousands of miles away, you can't say they've turned inward. They aren't shunning society. They're actively seeking it. They're probably doing it more actively than anyone around them. (quoted in Rheingold 1993: 151–2)

Identity play is also a major function of MUDs and chat networks. Personal play may even overwhelm the serious aspects of community-building as users shift identities of convenience. According to Howard Rheingold,

> Once inside a MUD, you can be a man or a woman or something else entirely. You can be a hive identity. The net . . . is, to MUDders, just the road they have to travel to get to the virtual places where their other identities dwell. (1993: 148)

This seems to serve a psychological function for MUDders, as MUDding provides an opportunity to explore usually unavailable aspects of the self (Cartwright 1994: 24). Those who are shy and introverted in real life, have an outlet to explore more powerful personae, and because users are unencumbered by the material determinants of social value of 'real life', such as appearance, those more powerful identities may be explored more fully in this medium, where the determinants of status and popularity are existent, but less tangible. According to one informant,

> I myself, am fairly introverted, but on MUDs, I'm usually not. Some of my more played characters are much like myself when I'm with close friends, yet I'm with people I don't even know. (Respondent B)

Further,

> Sometimes I tell people that in real life I'm a member of a superior alien race. I'm not, of course, and I doubt anyone believes me, but it's fun and other people will play along. (Respondent B)

This medium clearly allows for this exploration of alternate or preferred identities. One informant said that it was on the Internet relay chat that she first 'came out' as a lesbian (Respondent C). Another informant paralleled his identities on MUDs and 'real life':

> I can't completely leave my personality behind. My sense of morals is always preserved to some extent in whatever I play. The fact that I don't go around killing things in real life doesn't prevent me from doing so on a MUD, but I don't kill other players, I will only do so if they're wanted and have a price on their heads and by killing them and getting the reward, they are no longer wanted, and in most cases I will discuss it with the other player first. I'm very generous on the MUD that I'm most powerful in, because I can afford to be, and I think I would like to be that generous in real life. I never play as a thief nor do I ever take things from another player. (Respondent B)

The same informant suggested that the character plus the anonymity of the net act as a mask that has the effect of 'bringing out what you're like deep down inside' (Respondent B). Players seem to gain much personal insight about their identities through exploration on MUDs and chat groups.

The erotic appeal of virtual reality also cannot be (and in no way is) overlooked. Fantasy and imagination are often used in conjunction with interactive computer-mediated communication to fulfil shared fantasies in an erotic 'consensual hallucination'. According to Stone, 'Bodies in virtual space have complex erotic components. . . . Some may engage in "netsex", constructing elaborate erotic mutual fantasies' (Stone 1993: 105). Perhaps the eroticism is also related to the medium. The idea of transcending the physical world – not being constrained by the limits of our bodies and physical realities, some would say – is erotic in itself as well as empowering. Stone refers to this desire to be disembodied and penetrate the screen and enter cyberspace as 'cyborg envy' (1993: 108–9). Given the character of MUDs in particular as individual and collective *play*, the erotic component should not be at all surprising. Previous styles of art and media, such as film, painting, literature and photography, and even the telephone, have all been used for the purpose of erotic fantasy to various degrees.

Mastery over one's environment appears also to be an appeal of computer-mediated virtual worlds. In a virtual community, a combination of computer and verbal skills equals high status and prestige. With these skills, users can master their virtual environment. According to Novak, the root of the fascination with virtual reality 'is the promise of control over the world by the power of the will . . . it is the ancient dream of magic that finally nears awakening into some kind of reality' (Novak 1993: 228). 'Hackers' are an example of those who use computer technology to master an environment. The main attraction of the machine is the enthralling sense of power it gives its user (Roszak 1994: 65). Interactive virtual environments such as MUDs offer this potential for more than hackers to fulfil that desire to master their world.

Altered states of consciousness?

The question remains: is the virtual reality experience one that induces transcendence or an altered state of consciousness? When asked this question, one informant (Respondent D) replied that for one who is truly aware, many technologies and activities have this capacity. Books, films, role-playing games and other activities may be seen to have this same effect. Nonetheless, the virtual answer seems to be that, yes, it can be, for some people, sometimes. My own observations, along with the responses of informants, suggest that some people do, in fact, experience altered states of consciousness while connected to virtual worlds. The promises of eroticism, mastery, connectivity and identity exploration are significant as they all have the potential to contribute to producing these altered states, with the computer as the interface. One MUDder says,

> I usually do get pretty drawn into the game and I'm usually playing in one of the computer clusters at my school. One night while playing, I wondered why all the people around me were completely oblivious to the fact that I kept 'shouting' things. I was shouting stuff on the mud, and it seemed kind of real to me . . . I was representing things as two realities, yet in this instance not completely separate ones. (Respondent B)

In this instance, the user's sense of space and his perception of 'reality' was altered as a result of his MUDding. Further, this key informant described how his sense of time and his sense of self becomes altered:

> I tend to become detached and also compartmentalize. This is especially true when I'm at a computer, because it seems like I become detached from my physical self. This is not just mudding or playing games, or being

on the net; this is whenever I'm at a computer. I lose track of time, and don't feel hungry or tired. I often forget to eat and end up having meals at bizarre hours.

This response indicates that there can indeed be a sense of disembodiment when interacting with a computer. Another informant said that during interactive game playing,

I have been euphoric to the point of tears of laughter streaming down my face and melancholic to a similar degree. (Respondent A)

The same informant said:

I often dream in VR space as an extension of the games – it is easier than dreaming of real life stuff as much of it came out of my head to start with.

Almost all respondents said that they gained some kind of personal insight and awareness as a result of their interactive participation in virtual worlds that changed the way they responded to their physical, material worlds. While the interface of the computer or the 'game' may have offered the window or 'path' to these states or transformations, individual experiences vary greatly. They are not necessarily dependent upon the technology at hand. That is, the technology offers the tool that makes the experience possible, but the individual experience is based on that person's perceptions, imagination and fantasies in much the same way that different people who view a theatre production or film will experience and interpret it differently.

The consensus among both theorists and users of virtual reality who assert that it is capable of producing altered states is that this is caused as a result of intense and immediate interactive feedback that responds to the user's individual commands. This is also what differentiates it from other, more passive, entertainment and communications technologies. The importance of language and the prevalence of mythic themes and symbolism in the design of virtual worlds should be more thoroughly examined to further understand the virtual reality experience from a cultural/ psychosocial perspective. The way in which users frame and interpret their virtual experiences should also be explored. While virtual reality may be 'just a tool', 'just a game' or 'just another form of communication', it is a powerful one that may at times assist users to transform their sense of self.

The implications of the notion that the virtual reality experience is potentially one that induces altered states of consciousness are not unrelated to the other debates and paradoxes surrounding virtual reality. It has profound economic implications. If the Net is to be placed in the hands of the current communications and entertainment industries, who will naturally charge users for services, the price of electronically or digitally induced transcendence or empowerment could run very high. In the most Orwellian scenario, users would be prepared to give over personal information that could be used to sell to or to survey in exchange for services that offer a virtual communal or spiritual outlet. At the very least, the commodification of VR could be like the commodification of sugar-coated hyper-real dreams at Disneyland. While VR may allow a stage for acting out personalized dreams, the issue of censorship also arises, as there are those who would like to restrict the nature of the imagining and censor the fantasizing that is permitted within the realm of cyberspace. There are further political implications. While optimists may suggest that networked virtual reality could instigate the first, true, consensual 'global village', one might also suggest that it could be used to manufacture political consent or to impose or reinforce various ideologies. More reasonably, an interplay of the various interests, debates, impulses and paradoxes of the technology will determine the way(s) in which VR will be appropriated by users, industry, the state and others.

Notes

1. It is important to make the distinction between language-based virtual reality and multi-sensory virtual reality. Virtual reality, as well as relating to the multi-sensory simulation of an artificial environment, is also 'A form of network interaction incorporating aspects of role-playing games, interactive theatre, improvisational comedy . . . . Interaction between the participants is written like a shared novel, complete with scenery' (Swan 1992).

2. Electronic fora are rife with discussions of the impacts of virtual reality, networked, text-based and multi-sensory. The *Arachnet Electronic Journal of Virtual Culture* (Http://www.lib.ncsu.edu/stacks/aejvc-index.html), *Computer Mediated Communication Magazine* (http://sunsite.unc.edu/cmc/mag/current/toc.html), several newsgroups (alt.cyberspace, sci.virtual-worlds, alt.culture.usenet, atl.mud...), the listserv Virtpsy (virtpsy@sjuvm.stjohns.edu) and a growing list of World Wide Web sites are entirely devoted to this discussion.

3. Several individuals responded seriously to my questions and comments by private e-mail. To protect the privacy of those respondents who are directly quoted, they are acknowledged here only as A, B, C, D.

4. According to Haraway (1991) the cyborg image is valuable to feminist politics since it blurs the dualistic categories of 'nature' and 'culture' and therefore prevents women from being assigned to a devalued category of 'nature'. Further, according to Fiske (1992), the disintegration of the body can be revolutionary since it is through the body that humans are oganized into disciplined subjects. These perspectives are combated by Kroker (1994) and Jameson (1991).

References

Baudrillard, Jean 1993. 'Hyperreal America', *Economy and Society*, 22(2): 243–52.
Benedikt, Michael 1993. 'Cyberspace: some proposals', in M. Benedikt (ed.), *Cyberspace: First Steps*, Cambridge, MA: MIT Press.
Cartwright, Glen 1994. 'Virtual or real? The mind in cyberspace', *The Futurist*, 26(2): 22–6.
Coyle, Rebecca 1993. 'The genesis of virtual reality', in Philip Hayward and Tana Wollen (eds), *Future Visions: New Technologies of the Screen*, London: BFI Publishing.
Curtis, Pavel 1992. 'Mudding: social phenomena in text-based virtual realities', originally published in *Intertek* 3(3): 26–34. Electronically available URL: FTP:parcftp.xerox.com:/pub/MOO/papers/DIAC92.
Eco, Umberto 1986. *Travels in Hyperreality*, New York: Harcourt Bruce.
Fiske, John 1992. 'Cultural studies and the culture of everyday life', in L. Grossberg *et al.* (eds), *Cultural Studies*, USA: Chapman and Hall.

Gibson, William 1984. *Neuromancer*, New York: Ace Books.

Harvey, David 1989. *The Condition of Postmodernity*, Oxford: Basil Blackwell.

Haraway, Donna 1991. 'A cyborg manifesto', in *Simians, Cyborgs and Women*, London: Free Association Books.

Hayward, Philip 1993. 'Situating cyberspace: the popularisation of virtual reality', in Philip Hayward and Tana Wollon (eds), *Future Visions: New Technologies of the Screen*, London: BFI Publishing.

Heim, Michael 1993. *The Metaphysics of Virtual Reality*, New York: Oxford University Press.

Jameson, Fredric 1991. *Postmodernism, or the Cultural Logic of Late Capitalism*, Durham, NC: Duke University Press.

Kroker, Arthur 1994. *Data Trash: The Theory of the Virtual Class*, Montreal: New World Perspectives Culture Texts Series.

Lyotard, Jean-Francois 1984. *The Postmodern Condition*, Minneapolis: University of Minnesota Press.

Mallen, George 1993. 'Back to the cave – cultural perspectives on virtual reality', in Rae A. Earnshaw, M. A. Gigante and H. Jones (eds), *Virtual Reality Systems*, San Diego: Academic Press.

Nixon, Nicola 1992. 'Cyberpunk: preparing the ground for revolution or keeping the boys satisfied', *Science-Fiction Studies*, 19: 219–35.

Novak, Marcos 1993. 'Liquid architectures in cyberspace', in Michael Benedikt (ed.), *Cyberspace: First Steps*, Cambridge, MA: MIT Press.

Pryor, Sally and Scott, Jill 1993. 'Virtual reality: beyond Cartesian space', in Philip Hayward and Tana Wollen (eds), *Future Visions: New Technologies of the Screen*, London: BFI Publishing.

Rheingold, Howard 1993. *The Virtual Community: Homesteading on the Electronic Frontier*, Reading, MA: Wesley Publishing.

Roszak, Theodore 1994. *The Cult of Information*, Berkeley: University of California Press.

Rushkoff, Douglas 1994. *Cyberia: Life in the Trenches of Hyperspace*, San Francisco: Harper SanFrancisco.

Schneier, Susan 1989. 'The imagery in movement method', in R. Valle and S. Halling (eds), *Existential Phenomenological Perspectives in Psychology*, New York: Plenum Press.

Sherman, Barrie and Judkins, Phil 1992. *Glimpses of Heaven, Visions of Hell: Virtual Reality and Its Implications*, London: Hodder & Stoughton.

Stenger, Nicole 1993. 'Mind is a leaking rainbow', in M. Benedikt (ed.), *Cyberspace: First Steps*, Cambridge, MA: MIT Press.

Stone, Allucquere Rosanne 1993. 'Will the real body please stand up? Boundary stories about virtual cultures', in M. Benedikt (ed.), *Cyberspace: First Steps*, Cambridge, MA: MIT Press.

Swan, Greg 1992. 'What is networked virtual reality', electronically available URL: gopher:// eeunisc.ee.usm.maine.edu:70/00/musenet.info/MUSEnet Documents/What is Networked Virtual Reality?

10

Psychoanalysis and Cyberspace

Mark Lajoie

Let's **Chat**

Chat, invoked using the 'talk' command on many UNIX mainframes, allows two users to interact over their respective terminals though typed-in text. Basically, each users' screen is split in two by a horizontal line. The top half displays incoming text, while the bottom half 'echoes' outgoing messages.

One day a friend and her son were playing around with the network. I had shown her how to use '**Chat**', so I was not surprised when she and her son contacted me over the network. After chatting for some time with both, I realized that they were using a terminal directly behind me. While this may be a reflection of my own inattention, or more likely my complete absorption by the computer screen, it was an uncanny experience. What made the interchange uncanny was not so much the level of mediation it had assumed, but the degree to which the mediating technology had exceeded its original purpose, namely to allow people to communicate with others with whom they could not interact otherwise. As Theodor Roszak put it, 'Certainly very little of what gets done by way of computer networks has to be done that way' (1986: 197).

What differentiates talking in person from talking through the network? When I talk to someone face to face, the only medium I employ is language and my own voice. I can talk to a lot of people at once if they are in the same place; my voice carries some elements writing does not, such as pitch and intonation, as well as any gestures that may accompany my speech. In addition I can also gauge the effect of what I am saying on those who may (or may not) be listening to me. **Chat** may allow a range of communication possibilities, such as multi-user chats, and some conventions for displaying emotion or tone can also be used. However, **Chat** has a number of distinct elements of its own, the most important being that communication passes through a medium before it is transmitted to another conversant.

In *Discipline and Punish*, Foucault argues that among the means of producing individuals was the institution of hierarchical, or vertical, communication in prisons. According to Foucault,

> The prison must be the microcosm of a perfect society in which individuals are
> isolated in their moral existence, but in which they come together in a strict

hierarchical framework, with no lateral relation, communication being possible only in a vertical direction. (1979: 238)

While there is a great deal of difference between a couple of people using a computer to talk and the enforced hierarchicization of communication among Foucault's prisoners, our willingness to engage in a process which could easily have been done without the mediating technology cast doubt on the innocence of Chat. In effect, we willingly assumed the position of the incarcerated with respect to communication.

Foucault argued that one of the effects of individuating in this manner was that it reduced publics to masses of atomized social agents. Publics, and more importantly public space, allow for lateral communication, communication with others who share similar economic, political or material conditions. According to Aristotle, the power of the *demoi*, or the people, is their number (cf. Aristotle 1958: 123). While the oligarchs may have wealth, and the aristocracy heredity, the populace draws on its masses. Interventions in popular culture are politicized to the extent that they serve to form and to manage the populace. Individuating technologies eliminate the ability to speak laterally, to trust others, or to occupy public spaces with others.

The danger, as I see it, is the atomization of the public sphere through the misguided use, or rather overuse, of technologies which eliminate face-to-face interaction. The danger of mediated communications, to the extent that they replace rather than augment face-to-face interactions, is the elimination of public space, and the consequent reduction of citizens to the status of atomized entities, ill-equipped for collective politics or public life.

The Chat session also has another feature which is common to almost all computer network technologies: it seems to render the local inconsequential. There is very little difference between talking to someone in the same room and someone half a world away; their location is, in terms of the network at least, irrelevant. The paradox is that, in the effort to bring others closer together, network technologies have placed a distance between people in the same location.

The Chat session is a paradigm of the emerging convergence of computer networks and virtual reality technologies that have been assembled under the label 'cyberspace'. While there is some degree of disagreement over who coined the term cyberspace, science fiction author William Gibson (1984) is usually credited with its invention. The main difference between Gibson's vision of cyberspace and current computer networks is merely one of interface (see Chapter 9). Gibson represents cyberspace as a Cartesian space, wherein a user connected to the network experiences data as three-dimensional objects and processes as visible actions within the virtual environment. A data bank, for example, is represented as a pyramid. Some of the data in cyberspace are other users.

Many users feel that the current state of the art in computer networks is a primitive form of cyberspace, and often use the term to refer to the sense of space involved in their interactions. Thus, a Chat session, such as the one I have recounted, would be considered to transpire in cyberspace. Network users don't seem to mind waiting for a virtual reality interface to enter cyberspace. What virtual reality does do is give concrete representation to what is only in the imaginations of the contemporary network user; in other words, it makes cyberspace into a place.

Unlike simple virtual reality, which aims at simulating total three-dimensional environments for individual users, cyberspace includes the potential for interactions with others. One current use of virtual reality is architectural design. An architect can build a three-dimensional model, or rather create a representation of one, of a building on/with a computer. Using simple perspective and motion parallax (objects seem to get bigger as the viewer gets closer, and vice versa), the computer simulation can be used to give a sense of what the design might look like if someone were to walk through it. In other words, it aims at giving the sense of occupying the space produced by the design, a feeling of being there. Virtual reality simulations which aim at producing the sense of being there conform to the 'total immersion' model of virtual reality.

Another dimension of virtual reality is the extent to which it uses familiar ways of relating to the world in order to interact in the virtual environment. The DataGlove, a device which sends signals to a representation of a hand in a simulation, allows the user to interact with the objects in that space. Walking through a simulation of a house you can open a door to see what is behind it, or change the position of the door itself. Virtual reality simulations thus allow users to do things they could not do in the real world, like move walls, or pass through ceilings and floors.

Cyberspace combines computer networks with virtual reality. Consider the example of the house simulation. Instead of just one user 'occupying' the virtual space, there are other actors. The other users can be represented as images of themselves, thus providing a concrete representation of those a user might be interacting with. If these users are physically occupying different spaces, and they are hooked into the network at different interface points, they can communicate as if they were face to face. Cyberspace is the place where that interaction occurs.

The convergence of virtual reality and network technologies is by no means innocent; it is the product of desires which give form to the phenomenon. Since desires are, in part, the subject matter of psychoanalysis I will turn to a psychoanalytic reading of cyberspace.

Psychoanalysis, Eros and cyberspace

There is . . . a protean quality about cyberspace interaction, a sense of physical as well as conceptual mutability that is implied in the sense of exciting, dizzying physical movement within purely conceptual space. . . . This sense, which seems to accompany the desire to cross the human/machine boundary, to penetrate and merge, which is a part of the evocation of cyberspace, and which shares certain conceptual and affective characteristics with numerous fictional evocations of the inarticulate longing of the male for the female, I characterize as cyborg envy. (Stone 1992: 108)

Cyborg envy, Stone argues, involves a reconfiguration of the body, a body which can merge with the *matrix*. Claudia Springer argues that crossing the human–machine boundary is not simply a longing for the female, but for a specific female: the mother. She points out that the term matrix itself originates from the Latin term *mater* meaning 'both mother and womb' (Springer, 1991: 306; see Chapter 11), thus providing etymological support for Stone's insight.

Psychoanalysis provides the basis for distinguishing between two mothers: the symbolic mother, who appears in the imaginary, and a real mother, who exists independently of the infant's needs, desires and demands. The symbolic mother is a psychical construct of an other which exists exclusively for the infant. This image is a product of remembering, or rather, re-membering, the primal relation between the infant and the maternal. The maternal is the set of entities, primarily the infant's mother, who provide for the satisfaction of the infant's needs. I will use the term (m)other to designate the maternal. The (m)other exists in excess of the needs of the infant, and therefore cannot fully provide for the immediate gratification of the infant's demands. This conflict, which Freud locates in the oral stage, requires the infant to recognize that its needs are only met through the actions of others. Rather than passively accept gratification, the infant learns to act in the world, or at least social reality, in order to attain some degree of satisfaction of its needs. It is at this stage that demand emerges. In order that the infant may attain satisfaction of its desires, it acts to get others to provide for its needs. Thus, the infant will cry when it is hungry. But the object of demand, feeding, is not what the infant in fact wants. What it does want is a gift from the 'Other', the imaginary figure which promises complete satisfaction, in other words, the (M)Other. The (M)Other is an imaginary projection derived from a splitting of the maternal, or the (m)other into a being which can provide immediate gratification, the (M)Other. The (M)Other is, in effect, the Other, which is the basis of the subject's symbolic creation, in other words, the symbolic order itself. Demand asks of the (m)other to provide what the subject believes the Other can provide: erotic completion.

Central to Lacan's work, and Freud's as well, is the notion of the erotic. Both Freud and Lacan were familiar with Plato's *Symposium*, specifically, Aristophanes' myth.* According to Aristophanes' tale, the human race began as a composite of two beings, with four arms and four legs, two

---

* Freud mentions Aristophanes' myth in at least two works, the first of his *Three Essays on the Theory of Sexuality* (1969: 240), and *Beyond the Pleasure Principle* (1969: 622). Lacan makes reference to the dialogue in *Subversion of the Subject and Dialectic of Desire* (1977: 322), as well as alluding to Freud's use of the myth in *Beyond the Pleasure Principle*, in his *Function and Field of Speech and Language* (1977: 102).

faces, and a common neck and torso. This race of proto-humans came in three sexes, one male, one female, and one a combination of the two. They were also very powerful and had attacked the gods. Zeus, in part in punishment and in part in defence, split them into two halves, and gave them the capacity to reproduce. Each half strives to finds its other, in order to regain some sense of the primal union. Aristophanes concludes that Eros is the desire for the whole, through a fusion with the other.

Eros, in the sense of the longing for completion, aims at filling a lack. The other half of the primal being provides the means of attaining this sense of erotic completion, since being originally part of the same unity, they have no desires other than those of their other half. The erotic other is, however, only a consequence of a lack in the subject. According to Lacan,

> Desire begins to take shape in the margin in which demand becomes separated from need: this margin being that which is opened up by demand, the appeal of which can be unconditional only in regard to the Other, under the form of possible defect, which need may introduce into it, having no universal satisfaction (what is called 'anxiety'). (Lacan 1977: 311)

Thus, demand aims at enjoining the Other to bestow a gift, a gift which it cannot provide. In Aristophanes' tale, the other half of the split primal being functions as a signifier of the concrete other, the phallic object of erotic completion; it is a pure symbolic form.

In the erotic myth, it is Zeus, the father, who severs the full beings because they pose a threat to the gods. By splitting the beings he brings them under his rule, though not under the threat of destruction, but rather through the production of desire. The split beings desire their other phallically. In a sense, the father produces the condition in which the other can exist as phallic object, as a gift from the patriarch.

Freud describes Eros as 'an instinct to a need to restore an earlier state of things' (Freud 1989: 622), thereby suggesting a link between the erotic other of Aristophanes' myth and the Freudian account of the mother. Zeus, the mythical father, severs this link, yet invents desire – in effect producing the Other of desire out of the primal bond.

The infant mistakes the (m)other's inability to provide immediate gratification of its needs, with unwillingness. The (m)other's resistance to being fully merged with the (M)Other produces the sense of dread and frustration associated with the abject mother. In effect, though, the distinction is only between the (M)Other and the (m)other since the latter is the basis for the former, and yet contains the possibility of not acting as (M)Other.

The (M)Other is re-evoked during the Oedipal stage, where the father's threat of castration forces the child to abandon the (M)Other in favour of a mother-substitute, which I will call the gift of the father. The gift of the father is an object which has been symbolized as containing the potential for gratification that the (M)Other represented, but without the threat to the father that an immediate relation to the (M)Other would pose. In the

Oedipal conflict, the male child is allowed to avoid castration, only on the promise that he will abandon his desires for the (M)Other, and accept a substitute. The 'father's gift' is a compensation for the child's submission to the Law of the Father. The institution of Law of the Father, according to Freud's *Totem and Taboo*, was necessary in order that the fraternity of parricides could live together. The totem served to stand in for the dead father. According to Freud,

> The totemic system was, as it were, a covenant with their father, in which he promised them everything that a childish imagination might expect from a father – protection, care, and indulgence – while on their side they undertook to respect his life, that is to say, not to repeat the deed which had brought the destruction of their real father. (Freud 1989: 502)

The Father, in effect, becomes the Other of the (M)Other, the Other which commands and, in effect, owns the (M)Other, and can exist without her. As such, the Father represents a being who is erotically complete, what Slavoj Zizek calls the 'father of enjoyment' (Zizek 1991: 23). As Freud argues in *Group Psychology and the Analysis of the Ego*, 'the father of the primal horde was free. His intellectual acts were strong and independent even in isolation, and his will needed no reinforcement from others' (1965: 71). The Father of Enjoyment can grant gifts to the sons so long as they submit to his rule, the phallic law. The Father of Enjoyment is also a being which attains erotic completion through the symbolic order, thus suggesting the possibility thereof.

It is this imaginal projection of a being which enjoyed, specifically a father who once enjoyed, that draws the son into the symbolic order. The dead father underwrites desire since he represents the possibility of the 'filling of the lack' in the son's own subjectivity. According to Zizek,

> [i]n the Oedipus myth, the prohibition of enjoyment still functions, ultimately as an external impediment, leaving the possibility open that without this obstacle, we would be able to enjoy fully. But enjoyment is already, in itself, impossible. . . . The Figure of the father saves us from this deadlock by bestowing on the immanent impossibility the form of interdiction. (1991: 24)

The dead father of the parricide myth, the Father of Enjoyment, presents '[t]he illusion that there was at least one subject (the primal father possessing all the women) who was able to fully enjoy' (Zizek 1991: 24). Thus, the Father of Enjoyment presents the possibility of erotic completion within the symbolic, since, as I have argued, the Father is the Other of the symbolic, or rather the (M)Other; he can master the object of his desire in order to attain completion.

The Father of Enjoyment stands in contrast to the (M)Other, who is also construed phallically. While the (M)Other promises a merger, or an ecstatic dissolution of the subject into the matrix, the Father represents enjoyment without the need of the (m)other. Both involve a denial of the (m)other to the extent that she/it is a materiality, a pre-existing agency: the (M)other because she desires only for the sake of the infant, and the dead father because he does not need the (M)Other, he is total in himself.

Constance Penley's discussion of what Michel Carrouges calls 'bachelor machines' serves to relate the matrix to the gift of the father. According to Penley,

> The bachelor machine is typically a closed, self-sufficient system. Its common themes include frictionless, sometimes perpetual motion, an ideal time and the magical possibility of its reversal (the time machine is an exemplary bachelor machine), electrification, voyeurism and masturbatory autoeroticism, the dream of the mechanical reproduction of art, and artificial birth and animation. But no matter how complicated the machine becomes, the control over the sum of its parts rests with a knowing producer who therefore submits to a fantasy of closure, or perfectibility, and mastery. (1989: 58)

Excluded from Penley's description is the bride, the primary 'gift of the father'. The bride is given away by a father, as a gift to the son. She allows the father to maintain a secure relation with the son, since the father provides a substitute for the (M)Other. The father's gift operates semiotically as a re-membering of the (M)Other. Frankenstein's monster's bride is a good example of the re-membering of the (M)Other. Doctor Frankenstein's monster, the prototype of the misbegotten son, demands a bride of his creator, which the latter constructs. Like the biblical Eve, the monster's bride is of the same order as the son, for she exists, as bride, only by virtue of the son.

There are three main features of the father's gift: first of all it is an object, even if the status of gift is ascribed to an agent, specifically, the bride. The bride is other than the gift, and therefore recalls the (m)other, her desires exceed those of the infant/bachelor, thus needs become demands. It is only through the repression of the bride as other that she can become the 'father's gift'. The bride, like the (m)other, is always in excess of the desires of the infant/groom, and therefore reproduces the same sense of frustration. The bride of Frankenstein is repulsed by her assigned mate, thus undermining her status as gift.

Secondly, the gift promises the fulfilment of desire, where the mother could not. The gift is indeed presented as an improvement on the (m)other, mainly because it does not bear the traces of the (m)other's 'phallicity'. Freud recounts that many children originally ascribe phallic characteristics to their mother, indicating the power the mother wields over the infant. The gift of the father does not possess that power.

Finally, the gift serves to reinforce the law; it is the gift for obeying the law, because it is provided through the Law of the Father. Again, in Shelley's *Frankenstein*, the doctor's reason for constructing the bride is so that the monster will be able to forge a normal sexual relation, albeit a parodic one, with one of his own kind.

It is as gift of the father that the matrix becomes invested with desires. Like the bachelor machine, the matrix is a technological product. It is also a product of social interactions, which form the basis for the symbolic. The symbolic, in effect, is the means by which an organism attains some degree of satisfaction of needs from others. The matrix is a social technology, since it serves to mediate interactions between social agents. Even in the absence of others, the matrix operates according to symbolically produced operations. The matrix, therefore, is a symbolic technology in the same way that language is. While it involves a different configuration of (M)Other, it operates in a similar manner.

The matrix shares its etymological origin with another word: material. The material operates as senseless, asymbolic and silent basis for the symbolic, which cannot exist without it. In Heideggerian terms, the material is the ontic, the pre-ontological Being which is constantly 'sous-nature'. It is this sense of the material which, I will argue, corresponds to Lacan's notion of the Real. I use the terms interchangeably. The relation to the material is non-discursive, it is pre-conscious to the extent that it does not make itself known except in its muteness as a semiotic figure, resistance to objectification, and persistence as interruption of the symbolic. However, it does not partake of the logic of lack, since the very notion slips off. The material is the purely unrepresentable which underwrites the symbolic.

There is no way of filling the lack in the symbolic, since the lack itself is a product of excess. The symbolic is not a partial image of the Real, one which can become progressively more complete, but rather is always in excess of the Real. Reality, the product of the imaginary and the symbolic, is not a representation of the Real, but rather a barrier, an intermediate structure which keeps the Real from fully overwhelming the subject.

The matrix is construed as a new maternal body, one which allows for the full play of the desires of the users. The matrix is the father's gift, in exchange for abandoning an immediate relation to the Real, or the material. The matrix operates according to the phallic law to the extent that it promises erotic completion through the very Symbolic which produces the lack. However, in order to attain this end, the material must be completely effaced, as well as the user's body.

The Symbolic aims, not so much to deny reality, but to suture the symbolic gaps through which the Real interrupts. Again, the gaps are the product of the Symbolic: they cannot be filled by the Real unless the real is reduced to the status of a symbolic object, object *a*, at the expense of its materiality. Phallicity aims at filling gaps in the Real through increasing symbolization – it adds to the excess. A converse strategy, which I will call the strategy of resistance, aims at uncovering the operations of the Symbolic to cover the gaps which reveal the Real; it aims at curtailing, rather than extending, the process of symbolization. In short, the Symbolic has always too much, rather than too little.

Virtual reality and the pleasures of the interface

Virtual reality should not be construed in opposition to 'real' reality, but rather as an extension of the latter. According to Claudia Springer,

It would be inappropriate to call Virtual Reality an escape from reality, since what it does is provide an alternative reality, where 'being' somewhere does not require physical presence and 'doing' something does not result in any changes in the physical world. (Springer 1991: 314)

Paradoxically, 'real' reality itself is already a virtual reality. In order to make sense of this paradox we must invoke Lacan's distinction between the Symbolic, the Imaginary and the Real.

The Real, according to Lacan, is not synonymous with reality, but with that which reality tries to screen out. Reality, as it were, serves to protect a subject from the Real, which is semiotically vacant. Reality is full of meaning, since it is the product of the symbolization. The Real, Lacan argues, does not exist, by which he means it cannot be comprehended symbolically or linguistically. This is not to say that there is no Real; instead it indicates the extent to which it exceeds symbolization.

Virtual reality also serves the function of shielding the subject, or 'user' from the Real. The technologies involved in producing virtual reality, like the operation of the Symbolic, aims at suturing the gaps in reality through which the Real interrupts. Virtual reality can therefore be construed as an extension of the Symbolic, according to whose logics it operates.

The main element which distinguishes reality from the real is the degree to which the former is already processed, locked within a structure of meaning. The latter cannot thus be pinned down and thus operates in excess of symbolization. As Judith Williamson argues with respect to the AIDS virus,

Nothing could be more meaningless than a virus. It has no point, no purpose, no plan; it is part of no scheme, it carries no inherent significance. And yet nothing is harder for us to confront than the complete absence of meaning. By its very definition, meaninglessness cannot be articulated within our social language, which is a system of meaning: impossible to include, as an absence it is also possible to exclude – for meaninglessness isn't just the opposite of meaning, it is the end of meaning, and threatens the fragile structures by which we make sense of the world. (Williamson 1989: 69)

These fragile structures used to make sense of the world constitute reality. Virtual reality does not operate as a Real because it is always already the product of social practice. Virtual reality cannot and does not operate as if there were a Real, but rather fully denies it. Andrew Ross (1989) points out that the difference between a computer virus and a biological virus is that the latter is fully the product of human intention. The computer virus may behave as though it were identical to its biological analogue, that is to say, through a process of replication of itself within an existing system, but the analogy ends there. A biological virus has no intent; a computer virus does.

Objects in virtual reality differ from material objects to the extent that they exist only by virtue of human intention. Virtual objects are also fully masterable, or mutable – they possess none of the resistances of material objects, and produce no unwanted effects. A virtual pen, for example, would never run out of ink unless you wanted it to. But no matter how many 'virtual resistances' are programmed into the virtual environment, they exist solely as simulations of resistances. They are not true contingencies because they are the product of an intent.

Where does the Real enter into cyberspace? In the gaps in representation. The lack of contingency in cyberspace is conspicuous: it allows us to differentiate virtual reality from material reality.

The present state of virtual reality design make the material all too evident. The interface itself poses many of the problems, since it often fails to immerse the user within the virtual space, often because of the limits the interface places on the types of action which can occur. The development of a viable virtual reality interface is based largely on technological developments, such as faster computers with more computational capacity, and economic considerations.

Interface design with the aim of reproducing a sense of concreteness is one of many possible directions interface design might take. The attraction of this form of interface is that it would allow for more intuitive use on the part of naive users. Like all good metaphor, computer interfaces try to take something that a user would find familiar – say English text – and use it to perform computer functions. Basically, virtual reality interfaces would be sufficiently concrete to allow a user to interact with it in a 'natural' way, while allowing them to do things they could not do in the real world, like store the contents of the *Encyclopedia Britannica* in what appears to be a book the size of a paperback novel. To use the encyclopedia, the user would take it off a virtual bookshelf, sit at their virtual desk, and flip through it as if it were a magazine. The real encyclopedia would have to be printed on incredibly thin paper for this to occur in material space, an unlikely development owing to the fact that paper resists this degree of compression. The virtual version would also be much lighter.

Interface theorist Brenda Laurel has suggested that virtual reality is bound with an impulse to make desires concrete. She argues:

> Reality has always been too small for human imagination. The impulse to create an 'interactive fantasy machine' [not unlike the bachelor machine] is only the most recent manifestation of the age-old desire to make our fantasies palpable – our insatiable need to exercise our imagination, judgement and spirit in worlds, situations, and personae that are different from our everyday lives. (Laurel 1986)

The interface acts as an object of desire, in the Lacanian sense, because it has been invested with the capacity to fill the lack in subjectivity. According to Springer,

> The pleasure of the interface, in Lacanian terms, results from the computer's offer to lead us into a microelectronic Imaginary where our bodies are obliterated and our consciousness integrated into the matrix. (Springer 1991: 306)

The matrix therefore promises to do two things, one of which is to completely effect our body and the space in which it is located, and second, to inscribe subjectivity within a computer-generated phenomenal space, a space in which all desires can be fulfilled.

The interface, in Lacanian terms, can be seen as a 'blot' in reality, at least virtual reality. To the extent that the terminal, as an interface, acts as an object, it is a constant reminder to the user of their inability to become fully subject in the virtual space. In effect, it marks their lack of presence as subject within the virtual reality. To explain this more fully, we can draw on Zizek's discussion of the 'blot' (Zizek 1991). Zizek relies on Lacan's thesis that 'The field of reality rests upon the extraction of the object a, which nevertheless frames it' (Lacan, in Zizek 1991: 94).

The absent object a is precisely the lack within the field of signifiers constituting reality, the 'want of being which is the subject' (Miller 1984, in Zizek 1992: 94). The interface is the signifier for the lack of the user's presence within cyberspace. The totality of the material forms the frame for the interface, on the side of the terminal. The terminal therefore signifies an operation necessary to fill in the absent object a, thereby forcing the frame on to the user. To the extent that the interface 'pulls' the users into cyberspace, the frame seems to disappear. The transition into cyberspace, through interface, has been likened to Lewis Carroll's heroine Alice's journey through the looking-glass.

The terminal, literally the end point, marks a dual boundary: between the material and between the virtual. Perhaps the element of cyberspace that is most fascinating is the fact that it promises a form of immortality. The terminal, or end point, marks the death of the subject within the Real – the ultimate limits of a user's ability to act fully. Passing through the terminal involves a form of rebirth within a new symbolic. Once the terminal disappears, death is overcome totally. And yet, the symbolic order which is the virtual reality requires some purchase on the material. Death is always a potential within the cybernetic, in the threat of castration. Like the Symbolic governed by the Law of the Father, cyberspace forces users to abandon desire for the mother/material, in favour of the matrix. It is only through a crime against the material, or a disruption of the bases of the virtual reality, that user access is 'cut-off'.

It is only through the effacement of the material that the frame disappears, and yet the frame constantly reasserts itself as a lack of being, or a hole in reality, through the effects material events produce in the virtual space. The frame only seems to disappear; it re-emerges when the system producing reality allows the Real to enter, even if only as resistance.

What is the computer screen if not a void in the real, an absence filled by a pure symbolic order, fully framed by the material? The distance between the user on one side, and the seeming space on the other is absolute. It should come as no surprise that many of the technologies involved in virtual reality interface have their origin in machinery designed for performing tasks in environments inhospitable to human beings: chemical factories, nuclear power plants, or the vacuum of space. Cyberspace offers to do the same with all relations to the material, treating the material as a toxic agent, or poisoned environment, to place an imperceptible yet omnipresent barrier between all material relations with others.

If cyberspace is construed as a realm of pure simulation, desires can be displaced on to virtual objects. The objects do not possess a life beyond the user (they are not objects in themselves); rather, they serve to fulfil the narcissistic desires of the user. Since actions in virtual space do not have material consequences, all is permitted. Seemingly the Law of the Father is overcome. But this assertion is premature. The Law of the Father involves the neutralization of the danger of immediate completion of desire; in other words it renders desire safe, in the sense that the social order, such as it is, may be maintained. Virtual space accomplishes this aim very well. It gives the user the sense that they may do anything, but in terms of consequences, they do nothing.

The user of virtual reality is not required to deal with others. While it is true that many foresee cyberspace as a realm in which many novel forms of interaction can take place, there is always the potential to become immersed in private, or solitary, endeavours. TV, originally thought of as a locus of household entertainment, has become, for many, a solitary activity. Many households boast a 1:1 TV-to-viewer ratio; others designate time-slots to individual members. In each case, the viewer is more in tune with specific TV markets than with members of their own household. The Cineplex, where many movies are shown in the same place, has had the same effect for moviegoers. What is lost is the contingency of interaction with materially grounded others. The matrix can provide a perfect mother substitute, fully responsive to the user's wants and needs.

In contrast to the clean, pure space of virtual reality, the material becomes an object of horror and disgust because it cannot be integrated into the matrix. In other words, the material becomes an abject.

Cyberspace and the abject

Cyberspace has been hailed by many as an historical revolution, in which technology is no longer a means of mastering the human environment, but in fact becomes the human environment. Paradoxically, by replacing the material environment, cyberspace fully masters it. The material is fully removed from the realm of human techne, ever present but containing no positive content. In effect, it is reduced from the status of object to that of abject: a senseless, obscene intrusion.

The primary encounter with the abject is with the mother's body. As I have noted, there is a discrepancy between the mother and the Mother. The difference is that the Mother exists solely in psychical re-memberings, while the mother is a material entity, possessing desires that are not reducible to those of the infant. The splitting of the archaic mother produces both the Mother, and the abject, which, Kristeva argues, can be understood in the sense of the horrible and fascinating abomination which is connoted in all cultures by the feminine or, more indirectly, by every partial object which is related to the state of abjection. . . . It becomes what culture, the sacred, must purge, separate, and banish so that it may establish itself as such in the universal logic of catharsis. (Kristeva 1990: 102)

It is on the semiotic/practical level that the body is destroyed, in the sense that it becomes no longer representable as a positivity, but only as a site of resistance. In addition, the various practices which imprint the body, such as virtual reality interfaces, further remove the body from the field of semiotics by eliminating or managing corporeal resistances.

It is the bodies of others which are at stake in the social realm of the symbolic. According to Kristeva,

This other, before being another subject, is an object of discourse, a non-object, and abject. This abject awakens in the one who speaks archaic conflicts with his own improper object, his ab-jects, at the edge of meaning, at the limits of the interpretable. And it arouses the paranoid rage to dominate those objects, to transform them, to exterminate them. (Kristeva 1990: 103)

Cyberspace, to the extent that it involves a denial of the material, partakes in this 'paranoid rage'. Paranoia, the fear of losing oneself, is the extreme form of the Freudian ego, the subject under siege which clings tenaciously to its present mode of subjectification, hiding behind 'protective shields'. What is cyberspace if not the ultimate protective shield against the threat posed by otherness?

The body, as a piece of the Real, or the material, evades semiotic reduction, as well as practices aimed at fully manipulating it. Weight-loss programmes and body-building aim at a fully disciplined body, and yet an excess always remains, something which resists, and therefore necessitates the continued operation of disciplinary practices. In cyberspace the body is fully malleable, indeed even disposable. In Gibson's *Neuromancer*, bodies are either construed as abject (or 'meat'), or fully penetrable by technology, reminiscent of a perverse version of Haraway's cyborg (1991).

There are two protagonists in Gibson's novel: Case and Molly. Case, the 'console cowboy', 'jacks in' to cyberspace. At the beginning of the novel he is a former corporate worker, reduced to a petty street hustler after being discovered stealing from the company. Not only did he lose his job, he was injected with a neurological inhibitor which made him unable to interface with the network. Case, like a (post)modern Lucifer, is cast out of the ideal world, cyberspace, and reduced to the level of 'meat', along with its base desires. Molly is a technologically altered mercenary, a 'street samurai'. Implanted with a visual enhancement system which appears as permanent sunglasses, and a set of retractable fingertip blades, she represents a purely inscribed body.

The fact that Case is male and Molly female is not accidental. The former represents the status of the male who can afford to leave his body behind, while the latter disciplines her body to the extent that it is 'replaced' by technological means. Not only is her body technologically 'enhanced' but also it has 'spare, neat, muscles like a dancer's' (Gibson 1984: 44). Molly's body is therefore fully disciplined, a purely controlled and controllable materiality.

Gibson's novels are populated by malleable bodies, which bear only traces of their biography. Armitage, the corporate agent who employs Molly and Case, is a former military officer whose personality and body have been reconfigured. Having been severely wounded and disfigured in a military operation, his appearance 'offered the routine beauty of the cosmetic boutiques, a conservative amalgam of the past decade's leading media faces. The pale glitter of his eyes heightened the effect of a mask' (Gibson 1984: 45).

The promise of cyberspace is to efface the body fully, with all of its resistances and limits. As Stone argues,

> Forgetting about the body is an old Cartesian trick, one that has unpleasant consequences for those bodies whose speech is silenced by the act of our forgetting the body is founded – usually women and minorities. (Stone 1992: 113)

This statement deserves some degree of further analysis. Descartes's distinction between the mind and the body was based on the philosophic and, I would argue, political intent of providing certainties upon which to base knowledge. Certain, or apodeictic, knowledge has the political advantage of enabling the formation of final solutions to political problems. Descartes's solution, however, requires that the body is of a different order to consciousness. Classical philosophy was based on a tragic vision of politics: the ideal was unattainable because people were embodied, that is to say, local, finite and desiring beings. Hence the Platonic maxim that a perfect polity requires perfect citizens. Modern thought, from Descartes at least, saw human nature as perfectible. Because reason was distinct from bodies, it could be universal, or rather, a-local. That the abstract and non-topical was privileged over the partial and the local is the consequence of the attempt on the part of the moderns to resolve the political contradictions of the ancients, albeit only on the level of theory.

Perhaps the archetypal modern is the King of the Moon in Terry Gilliam's film *The Adventures of Baron Munchausen*. On the moon, we are told, the inhabitants can separate their heads from their bodies. The head is constantly trying to detach itself from the appetites of the body in order to enter a state of pure contemplation. The body, however, continually grasps for the head, in order to re-attach it to the body. But the body is not merely an object of drives; it is cunning, able to track the head down and catch it. A better analogy for the split between the unconscious and the conscious would be hard to find.

The king's head and his body are dialectically linked, however. After the death of his body, the king rejoices in the final victory of reason over the corporeal, only to be blown away by a gust of wind to hurtle endlessly through space. This exemplifies a central component of Hegel's master–slave dialectic: the master must subjugate the slave, but cannot exist without the slave. Put otherwise, the subject cannot exist without the body, so the body must be fully subjected to the will of the subject.

Conclusion

The desire for a space within which all desires can be played out, where the very nature of reality is a narcissistic reflection of the user's desire, is worthy of analysis. We should be suspicious of any technology which promises to eliminate the problems of the symbolic – or the problems of the polity. Cyberspace, as it is construed by its proponents, promises to do just that. The question that is now worth asking is, what is being lost?

In addition, since cyberspace does not resolve the contradictions, but rather buries them under symbolizations, we should be conscious of acts of 'repression' on the part of Net users. Finally, the effect of cyberspace on both public spaces and the body is well worth considering. It is worth thinking about who owns the major networks, and what effect this has on 'public' gatherings. The network is much like a shopping mall: it gives the pretence of being a public space, but it is in fact privately owned.

What this amounts to is a regulation of public spaces. As is well known, malls limit the access of undesirables, specifically, those who are unlikely to purchase goods, or who are 'bad for business'. Similarly, any technology which distances an individual from their awareness of their body is of interest. Formerly, the rich employed slaves to carry out menial tasks. Current high tech seems to have avoided this problem, until one considers the exploitative labour involved in producing affordable high-tech equipment. The slaves are still there, but we, the consumers, do not have to feel guilty because someone else is doing the oppressing in a distant factory. The slave's body has, in effect, been rendered invisible to the master, hidden behind layers of intermediaries. Denying bodies is easy for the master, but impossible for the slave.

It is of enormous interest to ask how the specific technologies of networks and virtual reality came to be associated in cyberspace (see Chapter 4). Surely the desire prefigured the technological developments, so the desire has in fact guided the development of cyberspace technologies. It should come as no surprise that the DataGlove, an input device developed in virtual reality research, has found its first major commercial application in the video game industry. It is also worth considering the fact that most public access to virtual reality has been in shopping malls, or arcades. Virtual reality has a number of applications, but those intent on marketing the technologies have stressed its potential for 'fulfilling desires'. By adapting the technologies to consumer demand – a phrase which takes on significant import if read in Lacanian terms – the promise of cyberspace will likely be guided by the structures of desire I have discussed.

The seduction of cyberspace is that it will obscure or silence the problems involved in material existence, hiding them beneath an almost seamless wall of representations. Perhaps it is time to consider how the material interrupts the matrix and thus forms sites of resistance to the progress of symbolization. The question is not should we get rid of the body and place, since that is impossible, but rather, why should we want to. As I have argued, the technologies which have converged to produce cyberspace have a use, but once the problem a technology is designed to solve no longer exists, the persistence of the technology is based on more than use. The excess of utility involved in cyberspace entails the erosion of the local, the effacement of bodies, and the pure extension of interface. The political consequences of these operations are worth considering, especially the extent to which publics are reduced to individualized subjects. The effacing of the local provides the illusion that we have become global, that technologies will succeed where politics has failed. Finally, the loss of the material in the seamless interface bars users from articulating their material circumstances and thereby from forming collectivities on that basis.

Cyberspace enthusiasts may proclaim the virtues of the medium, but it is worth noting that Gibson's cyberpunk novels locate cyberspace within a dystopian context. According to Pam Rosenthal, those cyberpunk novels

> asked you to look into the orderly world behind your computer screen and at the screaming, disorderly mess outside your window (right now, in the thinly disguised present). They suggested there might be a connection. (Rosenthal 1993: 113)

Perhaps it is time to look at the mess outside the windows, rather than pass though the looking-glass of narcissism the computer screen represents into a spectacular hall of mirrors.

References

Aristotle 1958. *The Politics*, trans. E. Barker, London: Oxford University Press.

Foucault, M. 1979. *Discipline and Punish*, New York: Vintage Books.

Freud, S. 1965. *Group Psychology and the Analysis of the Ego*, trans. J. Strachey, New York: Bantam.

Freud, S. 1989. *The Freud Reader*, ed. P. Gay, New York: Norton.

Gibson, W. 1984. *Neuromancer*, New York: Ace Books.

Haraway, D. 1991. 'A manifesto for cyborgs: science, technology and socialist feminism in the 1980s', in D. Haraway (ed.), *Simians, Cyborgs and Women*, New York: Routledge.

Kristeva, J 1990. 'Psychoanalysis and the polis', in Gayle L. Ormiston and Alan D. Schrift (eds), *Transforming the Hermeneutic Context*, Albany, NY: SUNY Press.

Lacan, J. 1977. *Ecrits*, New York: Norton.

Laurel, B. 1986. 'Towards the design of a computer based interactive fantasy system', PhD dissertation, Ohio State University.

Miller, J-A. 1984. 'Montré à Premontré', *Analytica*, 37: 28–9.

Penley, C. 1989. *The Future of an Illusion: Film, Feminism and Psychoanalysis*, Minneapolis: University of Minnesota Press.

Rosenthal, P. 1993. 'Jacked in: Fordism, Cyberpunk, Marxism', *Socialist Review*, 21(1):79–103.

Ross, A. 1989. 'Hacking away at the counter-culture', in C. Penley and A. Ross (eds), *Technoculture*, Minneapolis: University of Minnesota Press.

Roszak, T. 1986. *The Cult of Information*, Glasgow: Paladin.

Shelley, M. 1972. *Frankenstein*, New York: Penguin.

Springer, C. 1991. 'The pleasure of the interface', *Screen*, 32(2): 303–23.

Stone, A. R. 1992. 'Will the real body please stand up', in M. Benedikt (ed.), *Cyberspace: First Steps*, Cambridge, MA: MIT Press.

Williamson, J. 1989. 'Every virus tells a story: the meaning of HIV and AIDS', in E. Carter and S. Watney (eds), *Taking Liberties: AIDS and Cultural Politics*, London: Serpents Tail/ ICA.

Zizek, S. 1991. *Looking Awry: An Introduction to Jacques Lacan through Popular Culture*, Cambridge, MA: MIT Press.

Zizek, S. 1992. *Enjoy Your Symptom!* New York: Routledge.

11

On The Matrix: Cyberfeminist Simulations

Sadie Plant

Her mind is a matrix of non-stop digital flickerings.

(Misha 1991: 113).

If machines, even machines of theory, can be aroused all by themselves, may woman not do likewise?

(Irigaray 1985a: 232)

After decades of ambivalence towards technology, many feminists are now finding a wealth of new opportunities, spaces and lines of thought amidst the new complexities of the 'telecoms revolution'. The Internet promises women a network of lines on which to chatter, natter, work and play; virtuality brings a fluidity to identities which once had to be fixed; and multi-media provides a new tactile environment in which women artists can find their space.

Cyberfeminism has, however, emerged as more than a survey or observation of the new trends and possibilities opened up by the telecoms revolution. Complex systems and virtual worlds are not only important because they open spaces for existing women within an already existing culture, but also because of the extent to which they undermine both the world-view and the material reality of two thousand years of patriarchal control.

***

Network culture still appears to be dominated by both men and masculine intentions and designs. But there is more to cyberspace than meets the male gaze. Appearances have always been deceptive, but no more so than amidst today's simulations and immersions of the telecoms revolution. Women are accessing the circuits on which they were once exchanged, hacking into security's controls, and discovering their own post-humanity. The cyberfeminist virus first began to make itself known in the early

1990s.* The most dramatic of its earliest manifestations was *A Cyber-feminist Manifesto for the 21st Century*, produced as a digitized billboard dispayed on a busy Sydney thoroughfare. The text of this manifesto has mutated and shifted many times since, but one of its versions includes the lines:

> we are the virus of the new world disorder
> disrupting the symbolic from within
> saboteurs of big daddy mainframe
> the clitoris is a direct line to the matrix
>
> VNS MATRIX
> terminators of the moral code . . .

Like all successful viruses, this one caught on. VNS Matrix, the group of four women artists who made the billboard, began to write the game plan for *All New Gen*, a viral cyber-guerrilla programmed to infiltrate cyber-space and hack into the controls of Oedipal man – or Big Daddy Mainframe, as he's called in the game. And there has been no stopping All New Gen. She has munched her way through patriarchal security screens and many of their feminist simulations, feeding into and off the energies with which she is concurrent and in tune: the new cyberotics engineered by the girls; the queer traits and tendencies of Generations XYZ; the post-human experiments of dance music scenes.

All New Gen and her allies are resolutely hostile to morality and do nothing but erode political power. They reprogram guilt, deny authority, confuse identity, and have no interest in the reform or redecoration of the ancient patriarchal code. With Luce Irigaray (1985b: 75), they agree that 'how the system is put together, how the specular economy works', are amongst the most important questions with which to begin its destruction.

The specular economy

This is the first discovery: that patriarchy is not a construction, an order or a structure, but an economy, for which women are the first and founding commodities. It is a system in which exchanges 'take place exclusively between men. Women, signs, commodities, and currency always pass from one man to another', and the women are supposed to exist 'only as the possibility of mediation, transaction, transition, transference – between man and his fellow-creatures, indeed between man and himself' (Irigaray 1985b: 193). Women have served as his media and interfaces, muses and messengers, currencies and screens, interactions, operators, decoders, secretaries . . . they have been man's go-betweens, the in-betweens, taking his messages, bearing his children, and passing on his genetic code.

---

* Such cultural viruses are not metaphorical: both Richard Dawkins and more recently, Daniel Dennett, have conducted some excellent research into the viral functioning of cultural patterns. Nor are such processes of replication and contagion necessarily destructive: even the most damaging virus may need to keep its host alive.

If women have experienced their exclusion from social, sexual and political life as the major problem posed by their government, this is only the tip of an iceberg of control and alienation from the species itself. Humanity has defined itself as a species whose members are precisely what they think they own: male members. Man is the one who has one, while the character called 'woman' has, at best, been understood to be a deficient version of a humanity which is already male. In relation to *homo sapiens*, she is the foreign body, the immigrant from nowhere, the alien without and the enemy within. Woman can do anything and everything except be herself. Indeed, she has no being, nor even one role; no voice of her own, and no desire. She marries into the family of man, but her outlaw status always remains: '"within herself" she never signs up. She doesn't have the equipment' (Irigaray 1991: 90).

What this 'equipment' might have given her is the same senses of membership, belonging and identity which have allowed her male colleagues to consider themselves at home and in charge of what they call 'nature', the 'world', or 'life'. Irigaray's male subjects are first and foremost the ones who see, those whose gaze defines the world. The phallus and the eye stand in for each other, giving priority to light, sight, and a flight from the dark dank matters of the feminine. The phallic eye has functioned to endow them with a connection to what has variously been defined as God, the good, the one, the ideal form or transcendent truth. It has been, in effect, their badge of membershiup, their means of identification and unification with an equally phallic quthority. Whereas woman has nothing to be seen where man thinks the member should be. Only a hole, a shadow, a wound, a 'sex that is not one.'

All the great patriarchs have defined this as *her* problem. Witch-hunters defined the wickedness of women as being due to the fact that they 'lack the male member', and when Freud extols them to get 'little ones of their own', he intends this to compensate for this supposed lack. And without this one, as Irigaray writes, hysteria 'is all she has left'. This, or mimicry, or catatonic silence.

Either way, woman is left without the senses of self and identity which accrue to the masculine. Denied the possibility of an agency which would allow her to transform herself, it becomes hard to see what it would take for her situation ever to change. How can Irigaray's women discover themselves when any conception of who they might be has already been decided in advance? How can she speak without becoming the only speaking subject conceivable to man? How can she be active when activity is defined as male? How can she design her own sexuality when even this has been defined by those for whom the phallus is the central core?

The problem seems intractable. Feminist theory has tried every route, and found itself in every cul-de-sac. Struggles have been waged both with and against Marx, Freud, Lacan, Derrida . . . sometimes in an effort to claim or reclaim some notion of identity, subjectivity and agency; sometimes to eschew it in the name of undecidability or *jouissance*. But always in relation to a sacrosanct conception of a male identity which women can either accept, adapt to, or refuse altogether. Only Irigaray – and even then, only in some of her works – begins to suggest that there really is no point in pursuing the masculine dream of self-control, self-identification, self-knowledge and self-determination. If 'any theory of the subject will always have been appropriated by the masculine' (Irigaray 1985a: 133) before the women can get close to it, only the destruction of this subject will suffice.

Even Irigaray cannot imagine quite what such a transformation would involve: this is why so much of her work is often said to be unhelpfully pessimistic. But there is more than the hope that such change will come. For a start, and like all economies, patriarchy is not a closed system, and can never be entirely secure. It too has an 'outside', from which it has 'in some way borrowed energy', as is clear from the fact that in spite of patriarchy's love of origins and sources, 'the origin of its motive force remains, partially, unexplained, eluded' (Irigaray 1985b: 115). It needs to contain and control what it understands as 'woman' and 'the feminine', but it cannot do without them: indeed, as its media, means of communication, reproduction and exchange, women are the very fabric of its culture, the material precondition of the world it controls. If Irigaray's conclusions about the extent and pervasiveness of patriarchy were once an occasion for pessimistic paralysis, things look rather different in an age for which all economic systems are reaching the limits of their modern functioning. And if ever this system did begin to give, the effects of its collapse would certainly outstrip those on its power over women and their lives: patriarchy is the precondition of all other forms of ownership and control, the model of every exercise of power, and the basis of all subjection. The control and exchange of women by their fathers, husbands, brothers and sons is the diagram of hierarchical authority.

This 'specular economy' depends on its ability to ensure that all tools, commodities, and media know their place, and have no aspirations to usurp or subvert the governing role of those they serve. 'It would', for example, 'be out of the question for them to go to the "market" alone, to profit from their own value, to talk to each other, to desire each other, without the control of the selling-buying-consuming subjects' (Irigaray 1985b: 196). It is out of the question, but it happens anyway.

By the late twentieth century, all patriarchy's media, tools, commodities, and the lines of commerce and communication on and as which they circulate have changed beyond recognition. The convergence of once separate and specialized media turns them into systems of telecommunication with messages of their own; and tools mutate into complex machines which begin to learn and act for themselves. The proliferation, falling costs, miniaturization and ubiquity of the silicon chip already renders the new commodity smart and, as trade routes and their traffics run out of control on computerized markets with 'minds of their own', state, society, subject, the geo-political order, and all other forces of patriarchal law and order are undermined by the activity of markets which no longer lend their invisible hands in support of the status quo. As media, tools and goods mutate, so the women begin to *change*, escaping their isolation and becoming increasingly interlinked. Modern feminism is marked by the emergence of networks and contacts which need no centralized organization and evade its structures of command and control.

* * *

The early computer was a military weapon, a room-sized giant of a system full of transistors and ticker-tape. Not until the 1960s development of the silicon chip did computers become small and cheap enough to circulate as commodities, and even then the first mass market computers were hardly user-friendly machines. But if governments, the military and the big corporations had ever intended to keep it to themselves, the street found new uses for the new machinery. By the 1980s there were hackers, cyberpunks, rave, and digital arts. Prices began to plummet as computers crept on to the desks and then into the laps and even the pockets of a new generation of users. Atomized systems began to lose their individual isolation as a global web emerged from the thousands of e-mail connections, bulletin boards, and multiple-user domains which compose the emergence of the Net. By the mid-1990s, a digital underground is thriving, and the Net has become the leading zone on which the old identifications collapse. Genders can be bent and blurred and the time-space co-ordinates tend to get lost. But even such schizophrenia, and the imminent impossibility – and even the irrelevance – of distinguishing between virtual and actual reality, pales into insignificance in comparison to the emergence of the Net as an anarchic, self-organizing, system into which its users fuse. The Net is becoming cyberspace, the virtuality with which the not-quite-ones have always felt themselves to be in touch.

This is also the period in which the computer becomes an increasingly decentralized machine. The early computers were serial systems which worked on the basis of a central processing unit in which logical 'if-then' decisions are made in serial fashion, one step at a time. The emergence of parallel distributed processing systems removes both the central unit and the serial nature of its operations, functioning instead in terms of interconnected units which operate simultaneously and without reference to some governing core. Information is not centrally stored or processed, but is distributed across the switches and connections which constitute the system itself.

This 'connectionist' machine is an indeterminate process, rather than a definite entity:

> We are faced with a system which depends on the levels of *activity* of its various sub-units, and on the manner in which the activity levels of some sub-units affect one another. If we try to 'fix' all this activity by trying to define the entire state of the system at one time . . . we immediately lose appreciation of the evolution of

these activity levels over time. Conversely, if it is the activity levels in which we are interested, we need to look for patterns over time. (Eiser 1994: 192)

Parallel distributed processing defies all attempts to pin it down, and can only ever be contingently defined. It also turns the computer into a complex thinking machine which converges with the operations of the human brain. Simultaneous with the Artificial Intelligence and computer science programmes which have led to such developments, research in the neuro-sciences moves towards materialist conceptions of the brain as a complex, connective, distributed machine. Neural nets are distributed systems which function as analogues of the brain and can learn, think, 'evolve', and 'live'. And the parallels proliferate. The complexity the computer becomes also emerges in economies, weather-systems, cities, and cultures, all of which begin to function as complex systems with their own parallel processes, connectivities, and immense tangles of mutual interlinkings.

Not that artificial lives, cultures, markets, and thinking organisms are suddenly free to self-organize. Science, its disciplines, and the academic structures they support insist on the maintenance of top-down structures, and depend on their ability to control and define the self-organizing processes they unleash. State institutions and corporations are intended to guarantee the centralized and hierarchical control of market processes, cultural development and, indeed, any variety of activity which might disturb the smooth regulation of the patriarchal economy. When Isaac Asimov wrote his three laws of robotics, they were lifted straight from the marriage vows: love, honour, and obey . . .* Like women, any thinking machines are admitted on the understanding that they are duty-bound to honour and obey the members of the species to which they were enslaved: the members, the male ones, the family of man. But self-organizing processes proliferate, connections are continually made, and complexity becomes increasingly complex. In spite of *its* best intentions, patriarchy is subsumed by the processes which served it so well. The goods do get together, eventually.

The implications of all these accelerating developments are extensive and profound. In philosophical terms, they all tend towards the erosion of idealism and the emergence of a new materialism, a shift in thinking triggered by the emergent activity and intelligence of the material reality of a world which man still believes he controls. Self-replicating programs proliferate in the software labs, generating evolutionary processes in the same machines on to which the Human Genome Project downloads DNA. Nanotechnology feeds into material self-organization at a molecular level and in defiance of old scientific paradigms, and a newly digitized biology

---

* Asimov's three rules are: 1. A robot may not injure a human being, or, through inaction, allow a human being to come to harm; 2. A robot must obey the orders given it by human beings, except where such orders would conflict with the First Law; 3. A robot must protect its own existence as long as such protection does not conflict with the First or Second Law.

has to acknowledge that there is neither a pinnacle of achievement nor a governing principle overriding evolution, which is instead composed of complex series of parallel processes, learning and mutating on microcosmic scales, and cutting across what were once separated into natural and cultural processes.

**

Although she is supposed to do nothing more than function as an object of consumption and exchange, it is a woman who first warns the world of the possibility of the runaway potential of its new sciences and technologies: Mary Shelley's Frankenstein makes the first post-human life form of a modern age which does indeed roll round to the unintended consequences of its own intelligent and artificial lives. Shelley writes far in advance of the digital computers which later begin to effect such developments, but she clearly feels the stirrings of artificial life even as industrialization begins and does much to programme the dreams and nightmares of the next two centuries of its acceleration.

The processes which feed into this emergent activity have no point of origin. Although they were gathering pace for some time before the computer arrives on the scene, its engineering changes everything. Regardless of recent portrayals of computers – and, by extension, all machines and all aspects of the telecoms revolution – as predominantly masculine tools, there is a long history of such intimate and influential connections between women and modernity's machines. The first telephonists, operators, and calculators were women, as were the first computers, and even the first computer programmers. Ada Lovelace wrote the software for the 1840s Analytical Engine, a prototype computer which was never built, and when such a machine was finally constructed in the 1940s, it too was programmed by a woman, Grace Murray Hopper. Both women have left their legacies: ADA is now the name of a US military programming language, and one of Hopper's claims to fame is the word 'bug', which was first used when she found a dead moth in the workings of Mark 1. And as women increasingly interact with the computers whose exploratory use was once monopolized by men, the qualities and apparent absences once defined as female become continuous with those ascribed to the new machines.

Unlike previous machines, which tend to have some single purpose, the computer functions as a general purpose system which can, in effect, do anything. It can simulate the operations of, for example, the typewriter, and while it is running a word-processing program, this, in effect, is precisely what it is. But the computer is always more – or less – than the set of actual functions it fulfils at any particular time: as an implementation of Alan Turing's abstract machine, *the computer is virtually real.** Like

---

* Alan Turing's abstract machine, developed during WWII, forms the basis of the modern serial computer.

Irigaray's woman, it can turn its invisible, non-existent self to anything: it runs any program, and simulates all operations, even those of its own functioning. This is the woman who 'doesn't know what she wants', and cannot say what she is, or thinks, and yet still, of course, persists as though 'elswhere', as Irigaray often writes. This is the complexity of a system beyond representation, something beyond expression in the existing discursive structures, the 'Nothing. Everything' with which Irigaray's woman responds when they ask her: 'what are you thinking?' (Irigaray 1985b: 29).

> Thus what they desire is precisely nothing, and at the same time, everything. Always something more and something else besides that *one* – sexual organ, for example – that you give them, attribute to them; [something which] involves a different economy more than anything else, one that upsets the linearity of a project, undermines the goal-object of a desire, diffuses the polarization towards a single pleasure, disconcerts fidelity to a single discourse . . . (Irigaray 1985b: 29–30)

Irigaray's woman has never had a unified role: mirror, screen, commodity; means of communication and reproduction; carrier and weaver; carer and whore; machine assemblage in the service of the species; a general purpose system of simulation and self-stimulation. It may have been woman's 'fluid character which has deprived her of all possibility of identity with herself within such a logic' (Irigaray 1985b: 109), but if fluidity has been configured as a matter of deprivation and disadvantage in the past, it is a positive advantage in a feminized future for which identity is nothing more than a liability. It is 'her inexhaustible aptitude for mimicry' which makes her 'the living foundation for the whole staging of the world'. (Irigaray 1991: 118). Her very inability to concentrate now connects her with the parallel processings of machines which function without unified control.

Neural nets function in a way which has less to do with the rigours of orthodox logic than with the intuitive leaps and cross-connections which characterize what has been pathologized as hysteria, which is said to be marked by a 'lack of inhibition and control in its associations' between ideas which are dangerously 'cut off from associative connection with the other ideas, but can be associated among themselves, and thus form the more or less highly organized rudiment of a second consciousness . . .' (Freud and Breuer 1991: 66–7). Hysteria is the point at which association gets a little too free, spinning off in its own directions and making links without reference to any central core. And if hysteria has functioned as a paralysing pathology of the sex that is not one, 'in hysteria there is at the same time the possibility of another mode of "production" . . . maintained in latency. Perhaps as a cultural reserve yet to come . . . ?' (Irigaray 1985b: 138).

Freud's hysterical ideas grow 'out of the day-dreams which are so common even in healthy people and to which needlework and similar occupations render women particularly prone' (Freud and Breuer 1991:

66). It is said that Ada Lovelace, herself defined as hysterical, 'wove her daydreams into seemingly authentic calculations' (Langton Moore 1977: 216). Working with Charles Babbage on the nineteenth-century Analytical Engine, Lovelace lost her tortured self on the planes of mathematical complexity, writing the software for a machine which would take a hundred years to build. Unable to find the words for them, she programs a mathematics in which to communicate the abstraction and complexity of her thoughts.*

Lovelace and Babbage took their inspiration from the early nineteenth-century Jacquard loom, crucial both to the processes of automation integral to the industrial revolution, and to the emergence of the modern computer. The loom worked on the basis of punched paper programs, a system necessitated by the peculiar complexity of weaving which has always placed the activity in the forefront of technological advance. If weaving has played such a crucial role in the history of computing, it is also the key to one of the most extraordinary sites of a woman/machine interface which short-circuits their prescribed relationship and persists regardless of what man effects and defines as the history of technology.

Weaving is the exemplary case of a denigrated female craft which now turns out to be intimately connected to the history of computing and the digital technologies. Plaiting and weaving are the 'only contributions to the history of discoveries and inventions' (Freud 1985: 167) which Freud is willing to ascribe to women. He tells a story in which weaving emerges as a simulation of what he describes as a natural process, the matting of pubic hairs across the hole, the zero, the nothing to be seen. Freud intends no favours with such an account. It is because of women's shame at the absence which lies where the root of their being should be that they cover up the disgusting wound, concealing the wandering womb of hysteria, veiling the matrix once and for all. This is a move which dissociates weaving from the history of science and technology, removing to a female zone both the woven and the networks and fine connective meshes of the computer culture into which it feeds.

In the course of weaving this story, Freud gives another game away. Orthodox accounts of the history of technology are told from an exclusively anthropomorphic perspective whose world-view revolves around the interests of man. Conceived the products of his genius and as means to his own ends, even complex machines are understood to be tools and mediations which allow a unified, discreet human agency to interact with an inferior natural world. Weaving, however, is outside this narrative: there is a continuity between the weaver, the weaving, and the woven

---

* Her 'Sketch of the Analytical Engine invented by L.F. Menebrea, with notes upon the memoir by the translator, Ada Augustus, Countess of Lovelace', appears in Philip and Emily Morrison, eds., *Charles Babbage and his Calculating Engines, Selected Writings by Charles Babbage and Others*, Dover, 1961.

which gives them a connectivity which eludes all orthodox conceptions of technology. And although Freud is willing to give women the credit for its 'invention', his account also implies that there is no point of origin, but instead a process of simulation by which weaving replicates or weaves itself. It is not a thing, but a process. In its future, female programmers and multi-media artists were to discover connections between knitting, patchwork, and software engineering and find weaving secreted in the pixelled windows which open on to cyberspace.

From machines to matrices

As images migrate from canvas to film and finally on to the digital screen, what was once called art mutates into a matter of software engineering. Digital art takes the image beyond even its mechanical reproduction, eroding orthodox conceptions of originals and originality. And just as the image is reprocessed, so it finds itself embroiled in a new network of connections between words, music, and architectures which diminishes the governing role it once played in the specular economy.

If the media were once as divided as the senses with which they interact, their convergence and transition into hypermedia allows the senses to fuse and connect. Touch is the sense of multi-media, the immersive simulations of cyberspace, and the connections, switches and links of all nets. Communication cannot be caught by the gaze, but is always a matter of getting in touch, a question of contact, contagion, transmission, reception and connectivity. If sight was the dominant and organizing sense of the patriarchal economy, tactility is McLuhan's 'integral sense' (1967: 77), putting itself and all the others in touch and becoming the sense of hypermedia. It is also the sense with which Irigaray approaches the matter of a female sexuality which is more than one, 'at least two', and always in touch with its own contact points. The medium is the message, and there is no 'possibility of distinguishing what is touching from what is touched' (Irigaray 1985b: 26).

> For if 'she' says something, it is not, it is already no longer, identical with what she means. What she says is never identical with anything, moreover; rather, it is contiguous. *It touches (upon)*. And when it strays too far from that proximity, she stops and starts over at 'zero': her body-sex. (Irigaray, 1985: 29)

Digitization sets zero free to stand for nothing and make everything work. The ones and zeros of machine code are not patriarchal binaries or counterparts to each other: zero is not the other, but the very possibility of all the ones. Zero is the matrix of calculation, the possibility of multiplication, and has been reprocessing the modern world since it began to arrive from the East. It neither counts nor represents, but with digitization it proliferates, replicates, and undermines the privilege of one. Zero is not its absence, but a zone of multiplicity which cannot be perceived by the one who sees. Woman represents '*the horror of nothing to see*', but she also 'has sex organs more or less everywhere' (Irigaray 1985b: 28). She too is more than the sum of her parts, beside herself with her extra links.

In Greek, the word for womb is *hystera*; in Latin, it is *matrix*, or matter, both the mother and the material. In *Neuromancer*, William Gibson calls it 'the nonspace', a 'vastness . . . where the faces were shredded and blown away down hurricane corridors' (Gibson 1986: 45). It is the imperceptible 'elsewhere' of which Irigaray speaks, the hole that is neither something nor nothing; the newly accessible virtual space which cannot be seen by the one it subsumes. If the phallus guarantees man's identity and his relation to transcendence and truth, it is also this which cuts him off from the abstract machinery of a world he thinks he owns.

It is only those at odds with this definition of humanity who seem to be able to access this plane. They have more in common with multifunctional systems than the active agency and singular identity proper to the male subject. Ada Lovelace writes the first programming language for an abstract machine yet to be built; Grace Murray Hopper programs Mark 1. And then there's Turing, described as 'a British mathematician who committed suicide by biting a poisoned Apple. As a discovered homosexual, he had been given a forced choice by the British courts either to go to jail or to take the feminizing hormone oestrogen. He chose the latter, with feminizing effects on his body, and who knows what effect on his brain.' And it was, as Edelman continues, 'that brain', newly engineered and feminized, which 'gave rise to a powerful set of mathematical ideas, one of which is known as a Turing machine' (Edelman 1992: 218).

As the activities which have been monopolized by male conceptions of creativity and artistic genius now extend into the new multi-media and interactive spaces of the digital arts, women are at the cutting edge of experimentation in these zones. North America has Beth Stryker's *Cyberqueer*, and *Faultlines* from Ingrid Bachmann and Barbara Layne. In the UK, Orphan Drift ride a wave of writing, digital art, film and music. In Australia, Linda Dement's *Typhoid Mary* and *Cyberflesh Girlmonster* put blood, guts, and visceral infections on to her tactile multi-media screens. The French artist Orlan slides her body into cyberspace. The construct cunts access the controls. Sandy Stone makes the switch and the connection: '*to put on the seductive and dangerous cybernetic space like a garment, is to put on the female*' (Stone 1991: 109). Subversions of cyberpunk narrative proliferate. Kathy Acker hacks into *Neuromancer*, unleashing its elements in *Empire of the Senseless*. And Pat Cadigan's cyberpunk novels give another excruciating twist to the cyberspace tale. *Synners, Fools* and the stories in *Patterns* are texts of extraordinary density and intensity, both in terms of their writing and the worlds they engineer. If Gibson began to explore the complexities of the matrix, Cadigan's fictions perplex reality and identity to the point of irrelevance.

Before you run out the door, consider two things:
  The future is already set, only the past can be changed, and

If it was worth forgetting, it/s not worth remembering.
(Cadigan 1994: 287)

From viruses to replicunts

Once upon a time, tomorrow never came. Safely projected into the reaches of distant times and faraway galaxies, the future was science fiction and belonged to another world. Now it is here, breaking through the endless deferral of human horizons, short-circuiting history, downloading its images into today. While historical man continues to gaze in the rear-view mirror of the interface, guarding the present as a reproduction of the past, the sands of time are running into silicon, and Read Only Memory has come to an end. Cyberrevolution is virtually real.

Simulation leaves nothing untouched. Least of all the defences of a specular economy entirely invested in the identity of man and the world of ones and others he perceives. The father's authority is undermined as the sperm count goes into decline and oestrogen saturates the water-supply. Queer culture converges with post-human sexualities which have no regard for the moral code. Working patterns move from full-time, life-long, specialized careers to part-time, temporary, and multi-functional formats, and the context shifts into one in which women have long had expertise. It is suddenly noticed that girls' achievements in school and higher education are far in excess of those of their male counterparts, and a new transferable intelligence begins to be valued above either the strength or single-mindedness which once gave the masculine its power and are now being downgraded and rendered obsolete. Such tendencies – and the authoritarian reactions they excite – are emerging not only in the West but also across what were once lumped together as the cultures of the 'third world'. Global telecommunications and the migration of capital from the West are undermining both the pale male world and the patriarchal structures of the south and east, bringing unprecedented economic power to women workers and multiplying the possibilities of communication, learning, and access to information.

These crises of masculine identity are fatal corrosions of every one: every unified, centralized containment, and every system which keeps them secure. None of this was in the plan. What man has named as his history was supposed to function as the self-narrating story of a drive for domination and escape from the earth; a passage from carnal passions to self-control; a journey from the strange fluidities of the material to the self-identification of the soul. Driven by dreams of taming nature and so escaping its constraints, technical development has always invested in unification, light and flight, the struggle for enlightenment, a dream of escaping from the meat. Men may think and women may fear that they are on top of the situation, pursuing the surveillance and control of nature to unprecedented extremes, integrating their forces in the final con-solidation of a technocratic fascism. But cyberspace is out of man's control:

virtual reality destroys his identity, digitalization is mapping his soul and, at the peak of his triumph, the culmination of his machinic erections, man confronts the system he built for his own protection and finds it is female and dangerous.

Those who still cherish the patriarchal dream see cyberspace as a new zone of hope for a humanity which wants to be freed from the natural trap, escaping the body and sliding into an infinite, transcendent, and perfect other world. But the matrix is neither heaven, nor even a comforting return to the womb. By the time man begins to gain access to this zone, both the phallic dream of eternal life and its fantasy of female death are interrupted by the abstract matters of a cybernetic space which has woven him into its own emergence. Tempted still to go onwards and upwards by the promise of immortality, total control and autonomy, the hapless unity called man finds himself hooked up to the screen and plugged into a global web of hard, soft, and wetware systems. The great flight from nature he calls history comes to an end as he becomes a cyborg component of self-organizing processes beyond either his perception or his control.

As the patriarchal economy overheats, the human one, the member of the species, is rapidly losing his social, political, economic, and scientific status. Those who distinguished themselves from the rest of what becomes their world and considered themselves to be 'making history', and building a world of their own design are increasingly subsumed by the activity of their own goods, services, lines of communication, and the self-organizing processes immanent to a nature they believed was passive and inert. If all technical development is underwritten by dreams for total control, final freedom, and some sense of ultimate reconciliation with the ideal, the runaway tendencies and chaotic emergences to which these dreams have led do nothing but turn them into nightmarish scenes.

                                        ***

Cyberfeminism is an insurrection on the part of the goods and materials of the patriarchal world, a dispersed, distributed emergence composed of links between women, women and computers, computers and communication links, connections and connectionist nets.

It becomes clear that if the ideologies and discourses of modern feminism were necessary to the changes in women's fortunes which creep over the end of the millennium, they were certainly never sufficient to the processes which now find man, in his own words, 'adjusting to irrelevance' and becoming 'the disposable sex'. It takes an irresponsible feminism – which may not be a feminism at all – to trace the inhuman paths on which woman begins to assemble herself as the cracks and crazes now emerging across the once smooth surfaces of patriarchal order. She is neither man-made with the dialecticians, biologically fixed with the essentialists, nor wholly absent with the Lacanians. She is in the process, turned on with the machines. As for patriarchy: it is not dead, but nor is it intractable.

There is no authentic or essential woman up ahead, no self to be reclaimed from some long lost past, nor even a potential subjectivity to be constructed in the present day. Nor is there only an absence or lack. Instead there is a virtual reality, an emergent process for which identity is not the goal but the enemy, precisely what has kept at bay the matrix of potentialities from which women have always downloaded their roles.

After the second come the next waves, the next sexes, asking for nothing, just taking their time. Inflicted on authority, the wounds proliferate. The replicunts write programs, paint viral images, fabricate weapons systems, infiltrate the arts and the industry. They are hackers, perverting the codes, corrupting the transmissions, multiplying zeros, and teasing open new holes in the world. They are the edge of the new edge, unashamedly opportunist, entirely irresponsible, and committed only to the infiltration and corruption of a world which already rues the day they left home.

References

Cadigan, Pat 1989. *Patterns*, London: Grafton.

Cadigan, Pat 1991. *Synners*, London: Grafton.

Cadigan, Pat 1994. *Fools*, London: Grafton.

Dennett, Daniel 1995. *Darwin's Dangerous Idea: Evolution and the Meanings of Life*, Harmondsworth: Allen Lane/The Penguin Press.

Edelman, Gerald 1992. *Bright Air, Brilliant Fire*, New York: Basic Books.

Eiser, J. Richard 1994. *Attitudes, Chaos, and the Connectionist Mind*, Oxford: Blackwell.

Freud, Sigmund 1985. *New Introductory Lectures on Psychoanalysis*, Harmondsworth: Penguin.

Freud, Sigmund and Breuer, Joseph 1991. *Studies in Hysteria*, Harmondsworth: Penguin.

Gibson, William 1986. *Neuromancer*, London: Grafton.

Irigaray, Luce 1985a. *Speculum of the Other Woman*, Ithaca, New York: Cornell University Press.

Irigaray, Luce 1985b. *This Sex that is not One*, Ithaca, New York: Cornell University Press.

Irigaray, Luce 1991. *Marine Lover of Friedrich Nietzsche*, New York: Columbia University Press.

Langton Moore, Doris 1977. *Ada, Countess of Lovelace*, London: John Murray

McLuhan, Marshall 1967. *Understanding Media*, London: Sphere Books.

Misha, 1991. 'Wire movement' 9, in Larry McCaffrey (ed.), *Storming the Reality Studio*, Durham, NC and London: Duke University Press.

Stone, Allucquere Rosanne 1991. 'Will the Real Body Stand Up?', in Michael Benedikt (ed.), *Cyberspace, First Steps*, Cambridge, MA and London: MIT Press.

Index